W9-BKL-625

The Internet Business Book

The Internet Business Book

Jill H. Ellsworth, Ph.D.
Matthew V. Ellsworth

JOHN WILEY & SONS, INC.

New York • Chichester • Brisbane • Toronto • Singapore

Publisher: Katherine Schowalter
Editor: Tim Ryan
Managing Editor: Mark Hayden
Editorial Production & Design: SunCliff Graphic Productions

Designations used by companies to distinguish their products are often claimed as trademarks. In all instances where John Wiley & Sons, Inc. is aware of a claim, the product names appear in Initial Capital or all CAPITAL letters. Readers, however, should contact the appropriate companies for more complete information regarding trademarks and registration.

This text is printed on acid-free paper.

Copyright © 1994 by Jill Ellsworth and Matthew Ellsworth

All rights reserved. Published simultaneously in Canada.

This publication is designed to provide accurate and authoritative information in regard to the subject matter covered. It is sold with the understanding that the publisher is not engaged in rendering legal, accounting, or other professional service. If legal advice or other expert assistance is required, the services of a competent professional person should be sought.

Reproduction or translation of any part of this work beyond that permitted by section 107 or 108 of the 1976 United States Copyright Act without the permission of the copyright owner is unlawful. Requests for permission or further information should be addressed to the Permission Department, John Wiley & Sons, Inc.

Library of Congress Cataloging-in-Publication Data

Ellsworth, Jill, 1949–
    The Internet Business Book / Jill Ellsworth and Matthew Ellsworth
       p.   cm
    Includes bibliographical references and index.
    ISBN 0-471-05809-2 (pbk. : acid-free paper)
    1. Business enterprises—Communication systems. 2. Internet (Computer network). 3. Information networks. 4. Communication, International   I. Title.
HD30.335.E44   1994
650 ′ .0285—dc20   94-17865
                                                               CIP

Printed in the United States of America

10 9 8 7 6

Dedicated to the memory of
John V. Ellsworth and Doris E. Ellsworth

Contents

Section V   Professional and Business Resources on the Internet   261

CHAPTER 13   Online Resources, Databases, and Libraries of General Interest   263

Acknowledgments

We would like to offer special thanks to Tim Ryan for his excellent ongoing assistance in this project and for his continued enthusiasm for a book light on jargon and heavy on information.

Among the other helpful people at John Wiley & Sons we particularly appreciate the insights and efforts of Bob Ipsen.

Introduction

News about the Internet is everywhere, and it seems to be everything to everybody. It's a global computer network! It's a new form of business! The Information Superhighway! The National Information Infrastructure! The blare of television, newspapers, radio, and magazines makes it difficult to separate the hype from the reality. But that's exactly what this book can do for you. Here you'll get clear answers to these questions:

- What is the Internet, and who is using it?
- How do I get access to the Internet?
- What opportunites are there for my business on the Internet?
- How do I actually use the Internet for business?

The call to action here is not a false alarm or a passing fad. This is not CBs or baby vegetables or 8-track tapes. As the telephone system before it, the Internet is becoming a major, multibillion-dollar, integral part of international business. A recent NBC report stated: "Connecting people in new ways has become a major business in this country." The Internet has doubled in size in the last nine months and has been predicted to have 100 million people online by 1998.

The Internet is a new medium, which means you must develop new strategies to utilize it. Unlike the broadcast and print media, the Internet is an interactive, two-way communication system. It crosses time zones and country borders in such a seamless way that discussions and information exchanges may go on without the participants necessarily being aware that they may be in different countries. And unlike the telephone system, which is also interactive, the Internet allows information to be stored, searched, and retrieved worldwide, with ease. Also, discussions can take place in open, multi-person configurations unlike anything that is available via the normal telephone system.

In the past the Internet was primarily for research, government, and education institutions. Now the Internet is open to individuals and businesses, as long as they abide by *acceptable use policies*. These acceptable use policies are extremely important—businesses have severely damaged their reputations literally overnight, because they didn't understand the Internet's rules and guidelines. This book will show you how to do business on the Internet safely and successfully.

In a recent speech about the National Information Infrastructure, Vice President Al Gore spoke of the changes that increased networking will bring to businesses: "The impact on America's businesses will not be limited just to those who are in the information business, either. Virtually every business will find it possible to use these new tools to become more competitive. And by taking the lead in quickly employing these new information technologies, America's businesses will gain enormous advantages in the worldwide marketplace. And that is important because if America is to prosper, we must be able to manufacture goods within our borders and sell them not just in Tennessee but Tokyo—not just in Los Angeles but Latin America."

In other words, if the Internet is where business is happening, then that is where businesses must be. Being on the Internet now makes a company stand out as a sophisticated, up-to-date company. With the current growth of businesses on the Internet, it may not be too long before *not* being on the Internet will be considered a sign of a hopelessly outdated company. The Internet tools and resources described in this book can open wide the door to the Internet for both you and your business, or your non-profit organizations.

HOW TO USE THIS BOOK

The Internet is said to have a steep learning curve, due to user-hostile, or at least not user-friendly, software, but that is rapidly changing for the better. And this book will allow you to take each of Internet tools, one at a time, to learn and practice the necessary skills in a logical order.

To some people the Internet looks like nothing more than a large e-mail system—because that is the only Internet tool they have learned. Getting an account with an Internet access provider (as described in Chapter 2) and practicing each Internet tool as it is presented, will be by far the best way to learn about the *real* nature of the Internet.

This book is divided into five main parts:

Part I.   The Internet: What It Is, and How to Get Connected

After explaining what the Internet is in Chapter 1, we immediately deal, in Chapter 2, with how to gain access to the Internet. Within a day or two of reading this chapter you should have an account with an Internet access provider; you then can learn to navigate the Internet as you read this book.

Part II.   Creating a Business Presence on the Internet

Chapters 3, 4, and 5 reveal why it is important to create a business presence on the Internet; Chapter 4 details which techniques are acceptable and which are unacceptable; and Chapter 5 outlines some techniques businesses are using to do this. Experienced Internet users will find this part plus Chapter 11 valuable for doing business on the Internet.

Part III.   Internet Tools and Resources

Chapters 6–10 deal with powerful Internet software and tools, and with general resources needed by anyone using the Internet. Just using the tools mentioned in Chapter 10 will put you way ahead of the average Internet user.

Part IV.   Doing Business on the Internet

Chapters 11 and 12 discuss how these Internet tools and resources might be brought together for your specific business, and gives details on specific Internet companies and resources that are useful for putting your business on the Internet.

Part V.   Resources on the Internet

Here, Internet resources, categorized by their value to various professions and business functions, are listed and discussed. The Epilogue discusses the future of the Internet. The three appendices are designed for those new to any kind of online computing. You'll find information on hardware and software requirements and sources, uploading and downloading files, and UNIX commands needed for the Internet.

From time to time, in this book we will mention that certain aspects of the Internet and its software can safely be ignored. Just as we operate, and derive great value from, cars, computers, and TV sets that most of us do not fully understand; so the Internet, too, can be used successfully without completely understanding all of its technical aspects. But, just as the TV would be of rather limited value without learning about the volume control and channel changer, the Internet will not yield much without certain basic tools being understood. So the bottom line is, just try using each Internet tool according to the instructions given, and expect understanding and insights to continue coming for a long time.

A system like the Internet, which has doubled in size in the last nine months, is obviously going through a lot of changes. Sites where resources are stored and ways of using the Internet tools are changing. If a resource is not where it is currently shown in this book, use one of the Internet search tools (such as discussed in Chapter 10) to relocate the information. This book is a starting point—to really benefit from the Internet you will need to stay with it, learning more about it and keeping up with it as it changes and grows.

CONVENTIONS

In parts of this book, I'll show you exactly what commands you need to enter on your computer to navigate the Internet. The commands that you are to type in are given in **boldface**. Some commands require that you use two keys at once—for instance, Ctrl-K means "Hold down the Ctrl key and press K." For your convenience, e-mail addresses are also in **boldface** so that you can easily pick them out of the text.

AND NOW? . . .

Chapter 1 describes what the Internet is, how large it is, who is in charge, and what people do when they get there.

Bon voyage!

The Internet: What It Is, and How to Get Started

What Is the Internet?

What is the Internet? There are more opinions on that than there are people on the Internet. There is no real "location," no exact idea of how large it is, and no agreement on who is actually on the Internet. That's okay, though, because the Internet works, and works well. Here's some background that will help you develop your own working definition of what the Internet is.

WHERE THE INTERNET CAME FROM

Understanding the history of the Internet is vital to understanding what is happening today on the Internet. Rules, customs, and many layers of technical protocols were designed with the goals and objectives of the sponsors and inhabitants of the original networks. While the Internet is changing very rapidly now, it is still strongly a product of this history.

What is known today as the Internet has its roots in a network set up by the U.S. Department of Defense in the early 1970s. This network (ARPAnet), established by the Advanced Research Projects Agency (ARPA), connected various military and research sites and was itself a research project in how to build reliable networks. The methods they developed included a "protocol" allowing dissimilar computer systems to communicate, and a method that routed data through multiple communications paths using groups of data with their own destination addresses built in (packets). These methods were so successful that many other networks adopted these standards, known today as TCP/IP.

Beginning in the late 1980s the National Science Foundation (NSF), a federal agency, started expanding its own NSFNET in steps, using the technology developed by ARPAnet, and a high-speed backbone network.

3

NSFNET Backbone Service 1993

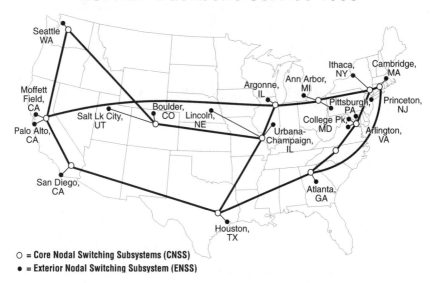

O = Core Nodal Switching Subsystems (CNSS)
● = Exterior Nodal Switching Subsystem (ENSS)

Figure 1.1 The Internet Backbone.

This was done at first to allow campuses and research centers to use NSF's supercomputers, but increasingly the connections were used for e-mail and for transferring data and information files between sites. With this growth, of what came to be called the Internet, and the subsequent upgrading of the system, came broader understandings of the goals of the Internet and the groups that should have access to it.

Other networks communicating among themselves and through the Internet have, in the last two years, brought a large commercial presence to the Internet and much easier access for individuals who are not part of a government or educational institution.

The Internet backbone provides very high-speed links. It is funded by the National Science Foundation (NSF) and is currently managed by Advanced Network System (ANS). See Figure 1.1 for a basic diagram of the Internet's backbone network.

THE INTERNET TODAY

Because the Internet is made up of over 25,000 networks that can transfer data via many routes, it is nearly impossible to pin down any exact numbers concerning its size. A *Wall Street Journal* article estimated that there are 20

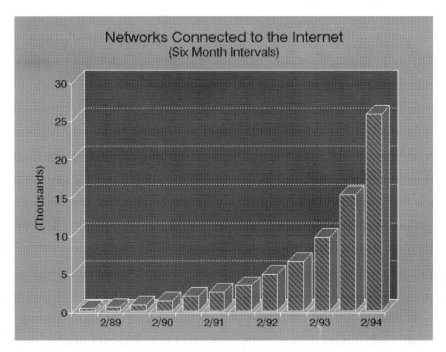

Figure 1.2 Statistics from Merit Network Information Center (nic.merit.edu).

million people on the Internet. Here are some highlights of the Internet's growth and size (Figure 1.2 shows this information graphically.):

- Growth is close to 10 percent per *month*!
- There are currently more than 2,200,000 host computer systems connected to the Internet.
- There are estimates that 30,000,000 people worldwide have e-mail access to the Internet.
- Use of one Internet file search and retrieving tool is currently growing at 1,000 percent annually.
- Dr. Vinton Cerf, one of the developers of the Internet's data transfer protocols, testified to the U.S. House of Representatives that "there is reason to expect that the user population will exceed 100 million by 1998."

The news media has discovered the Internet as well. Two years ago, U.S. newspapers carried about three articles about the Internet per month; last year, there were approximately 70 per month; now there are over 300 per month.

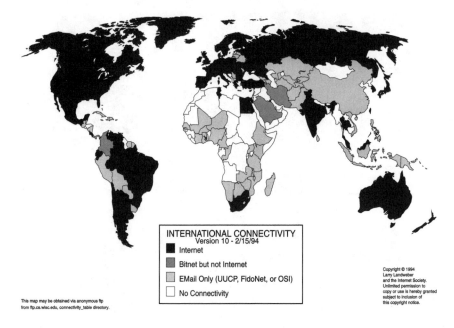

INTERNATIONAL CONNECTIVITY
Version 10 - 2/15/94
■ Internet
■ Bitnet but not Internet
■ EMail Only (UUCP, FidoNet, or OSI)
□ No Connectivity

This map may be obtained via anonymous ftp
from ftp.cs.wisc.edu, connectivity_table directory.

Copyright © 1994
Larry Landweber
and the Internet Society.
Unlimited permission to
copy or use is hereby granted
subject to inclusion of
this copyright notice.

Figure 1.3   World map showing countries with Internet access.

Who Is Part of the Internet?

In the broadest sense, individuals, organizations, companies, governments, colleges, schools, and ad hoc groups are part of the Internet. In a more limited definition, approximately 25,000 networks are part of the Internet.

An individual does not "sign up for an Internet account." Instead, an individual gets an account on an organization's host computer that is connected in some way to the Internet. This may be a for-profit or a not-for-profit organization. The individual's connection to this organization's computer could be via one of the host computer's hard-wired terminals or via phone lines (using a modem and a personal computer). Chapter 2 explains the details of getting access to the Internet.

Networks in countries around the world are continuing to join the Internet—often first with e-mail connections and then later with full access to Internet services. Countries with at least some Internet access are shown in Figure 1.3, and host distribution is shown in Figure 1.4.

The majority of networks that make up the Internet are from the English-speaking world, and while all languages can be, and are, used, even sites in non-English-speaking countries often provide services and

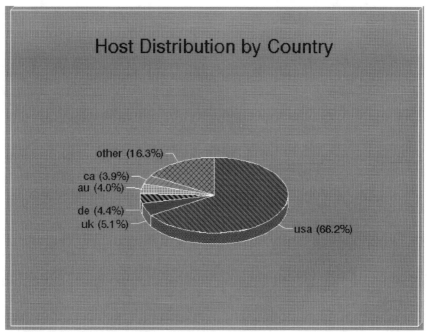

Statistics from Merit Network Information Center (nic.merit.edu), USA = United States, UK = United Kingdom, DE = Germany, AU = Australia, CA = Canada, OTHER = 66 other countries

Figure 1.4   Internet Networks by Country.

resources in English. Many services in Europe, for example, will have their opening menus in English, and then give other language options.

As you can see in Table 1.1, the last few years have seen a dramatic increase in the number of countries obtaining their initial connection to the Internet. Even Antarctica has Internet networks.

Table 1.1   Internet-Connected Networks by Country

CODE	COUNTRY	NETWORKS CONNECTED	INITIAL CONNECTION
aq	Antarctica	2	2/94
ar	Argentina	3	10/90
au	Australia	731	5/89
at	Austria	181	6/90
be	Belgium	117	5/90

(continues)

Table 1.1   (Continued)

CODE	COUNTRY	NETWORKS CONNECTED	INITIAL CONNECTION
br	Brazil	113	6/90
bg	Bulgaria	10	4/93
cm	Cameroon	1	12/92
ca	Canada	1,002	7/88
cl	Chile	39	4/90
cr	Costa Rica	2	1/93
hr	Croatia	6	11/91
cy	Cyprus	19	12/92
cz	Czech Republic	268	11/91
dk	Denmark	49	11/88
ec	Ecuador	85	7/92
eg	Egypt	7	11/93
ee	Estonia	33	7/92
fj	Fiji	1	6/93
fi	Finland	315	11/88
fr	France	1,105	7/88
de	Germany	1,220	9/89
gh	Ghana	1	5/93
gr	Greece	36	7/90
gu	Guam	2	10/93
hk	Hong Kong	47	9/91
hu	Hungary	84	11/91
is	Iceland	26	11/88
in	India	5	11/90
id	Indonesia	32	7/93
ie	Ireland	136	7/90
il	Israel	128	8/89
it	Italy	393	8/89
jp	Japan	1,087	8/89
kz	Kazakhstan	1	11/93
ke	Kenya	1	11/93
kr	Korea, South	167	4/90
kw	Kuwait	4	12/92
lv	Latvia	1	11/92
lb	Lebanon	4	10/93
li	Liechtenstein	2	6/93
lu	Luxembourg	26	4/92

Table 1.1   (Continued)

CODE	COUNTRY	NETWORKS CONNECTED	INITIAL CONNECTION
my	Malaysia	5	11/92
mx	Mexico	58	2/89
nl	Netherlands	246	1/89
nz	New Zealand	188	4/89
ni	Nicaragua	1	2/94
no	Norway	164	11/88
pe	Peru	1	11/93
pl	Poland	102	11/91
pt	Portugal	68	10/91
pr	Puerto Rico	4	10/89
ro	Romania	13	4/93
ru	Russian Federation	188	6/93
sg	Singapore	42	5/91
sk	Slovakia	25	3/92
si	Slovenia	25	2/92
za	South Africa	140	12/91
es	Spain	192	7/90
se	Sweden	177	11/88
ch	Switzerland	252	3/90
tw	Taiwan	166	12/91
th	Thailand	28	7/92
tn	Tunisia	9	5/91
tr	Turkey	66	1/93
ua	Ukraine	20	8/93
ae	United Arab Emirates	2	11/93
gb	United Kingdom	1,242	4/89
us	United States	14,782	7/88
ve	Venezuela	7	2/92
vi	Virgin Islands	1	3/93

TOTALS: 71 countries 25,706 networks
Statistics from Merit Network Information Center (nic.merit.edu)

Within the United States, the number of networks per state generally follows state population numbers. Rural areas, while having dial-up access to the Internet, have much higher communications charges. Table 1.2 shows how many networks each state has hooked up to the Internet.

Table 1.2   NSFNET Networks by U.S. State (as of March 1, 1994)

Code	U.S. State	Connected Networks
AL	Alabama	157
AK	Alaska	7
AZ	Arizona	94
AR	Arkansas	32
CA	California	3,107
CO	Colorado	597
CT	Connecticut	148
DE	Delaware	12
FL	Florida	314
GA	Georgia	216
HI	Hawaii	53
ID	Idaho	36
IL	Illinois	294
IN	Indiana	201
IA	Iowa	83
KS	Kansas	39
KY	Kentucky	38
LA	Louisiana	74
ME	Maine	43
MD	Maryland	570
MA	Massachusetts	825
MI	Michigan	435
MN	Minnesota	376
MS	Mississippi	63
MO	Missouri	129
MT	Montana	12
NE	Nebraska	74
NV	Nevada	8
NH	New Hampshire	86
NJ	New Jersey	318
NM	New Mexico	116
NY	New York	1,110
NC	North Carolina	259
ND	North Dakota	4
OH	Ohio	889
OK	Oklahoma	54
OR	Oregon	315
PA	Pennsylvania	368

Table 1.2   (Continued)

Code	U.S. State	Connected Networks
RI	Rhode Island	40
SC	South Carolina	135
SD	South Dakota	41
TN	Tennessee	164
TX	Texas	852
UT	Utah	72
VT	Vermont	16
VA	Virginia	982
WA	Washington	386
DC	Washington D.C.	287
WV	West Virginia	17
WI	Wisconsin	99
WY	Wyoming	18
AA	Military—Asia	9
AE	Military—Europe	77
AP	Military—Pacific	21
AX	Military—Unspecified	8
XX	(Unknown)	2

Total US Nets: 14,782
Statistics from Merit Network Information Center (nic.merit.edu)

Who Is In Charge?

Who's in charge? Nobody, and at least 25,000 groups.

Nobody is in charge, because no one individual, network, or organization owns the entire network, nor any absolutely necessary part of the network. Certainly the backbone links provided by NSF are very important, and NSF therefore has great influence on net activities, but networks often use links that bypass the NSF. One could say equally well that since there are 25,000 networks connected, there are at least 25,000 groups in charge; or that since the networks are made up of organizations that own their own host computers, more than two million groups are in charge, or. . . .

The important point is that the Internet is a voluntary, cooperative undertaking. The networks have agreed on common communications protocols, addressing methods, and rules. Several groups such as the Internet Society, Internet Engineering Task Force, the Internet Assigned

Number Authority, the Federal Networking Council, Network Information Centers, and the Internet Architecture Board provide an organized means for deriving these rules and protocols. To be part of the Internet, the business person should be aware of the nature of this Internet "organization" and of the resulting acceptable use policies for different networks. Chapter 4 discusses acceptable and unacceptable uses of the Internet.

WHAT DO YOU DO WHEN YOU GET THERE?

Okay, when you get there, what can you do? Here are a few ideas:

- Search for, retrieve, and read literally millions of files stored on computers throughout the world.
- Exchange e-mail with any of tens of millions people with e-mail accounts (by some estimates there are 30 million people worldwide with e-mail access to the Internet).
- Search for and retrieve shareware, freeware, and commercial software.
- Search databases of organizations, individuals, and government sources for files on thousands of topics.
- Join subject-oriented discussion groups (more than 9,000 different topics).
- Send and receive program data files such as spreadsheets, CAD files, and desktop publishing files.
- Send and receive pictures and sound files.
- Set up temporary or permanent discussion/work groups.
- Browse through resources of public and private information services.
- Search library catalogs at many public, university, and research libraries.
- Search for, and order online, magazine articles.
- Browse and search "catalogs" of goods and services, and purchase many of the items via the Internet (some of the catalogs even have pictures).
- Communicate in real time, via the keyboard, with others connected to the Internet.
- Set up a site with information about your company and its products.
- Conduct test marketing.
- Distribute electronic publications.
- Sell products and services.

These activities can be combined to provide a business presence on the Internet with marketing, sales, research, and customer support components.

Now that you've seen a brief sketch of the nature of this mammoth Internet, you can use the rest of this book to learn what specifically you can do on the Internet and how to get it done. The Internet offers your business an incredible variety of marketing and research opportunities.

WHERE FROM HERE . . .

Since the best way to learn to swim is to actually get into the water, the next chapter provides directions to this Internet ocean, and information on how to obtain access to the Internet. Getting an account with an Internet access provider and trying things out as you go through this book will make what is being discussed much more understandable, and you'll get to see the power of the Internet yourself.

CHAPTER 2

How to Get Access to the Internet

Gaining access to the Internet is getting easier and easier. The cost is going down and the number of choices is rising. Your connection to the Internet can be as simple as purchasing an account from a commercial bulletin board system (BBS) like CompuServe, or as complex as dedicating a portion of one of your company's computers to becoming an Internet node (an actual "permanent" part of the Internet itself). Many businesses fear that connecting to the Internet will be too expensive. Because of the range of Internet access available, this is absolutely not the case—anyone can connect for a reasonable price. You can even get started for as little as $5.00 a month!

And, connecting to the Internet is not difficult. In the last four years, many companies called "service providers" have begun to offer dial-up, SLIP, and other Internet connection services. For a fee, these service providers will give you access to the Internet; all you need is a computer, a modem, and a phone line.

Get Access Now

You can spend a lot of time researching the best way to get access to the Internet, but the most important thing is to get access now! You don't have to make any long-term commitments with an access provider. If you don't like the provider's service or your needs change, you can cancel your service at any time. Sign up now and start learning.

You will need an account in order to use the Internet—be it on your corporate system, through commercial dial-up services, or a shell account. Business users in large corporations and high-tech industries may find that their companies are already on the Internet through their engineering or research departments, so you may already have access and not know it. Contact your network system administrator or MIS department for help in getting an account.

Whether you access the Internet from your company's network or from your own stand-alone PC, you will need some equipment. For stand-alone PC use (often called *dial-up* use), you will need a computer, a modem, a telephone line, and some type of communications software. For LAN use you will need a personal computer, a LAN connection, and some kind of communications software.

You can use a variety of communications packages: Procomm, Crosstalk, White Knight, and so on. Check the software's specifications to make sure it can emulate a VT 100 terminal that will provide an adequate interface for text-based Internet information. Many times such software is included with your modem purchase. (See Appendix 1 for information on communications software and hooking up a modem.)

This chapter cannot cover every Internet service provider—there are just too many, and the number of providers is growing rapidly. It will, however, show where lists of these providers can be found, profile several services, and provide information for deciding on the type of services that could be useful to your business.

Throughout the rest of this chapter, you will find advice on deciding exactly how to connect with the Internet. To do this, you'll be guided through the following steps:

1. Define which Internet services are available and the types of connections they require.

2. Choose which Internet services you need and which connections you can afford.

3. Choose a service provider and get an Internet account—this may involve registering with a dial-up service like Delphi or CompuServe, hiring a service provider, or using your company's computers to become a node on the Internet itself.

ACCESS TO INTERNET TOOLS

Before you make a firm decision about the kinds of services you need, you might want to look at other chapters for full descriptions of these tools. Chapters 5 and 12 may be especially helpful to you. There are three basic tools: e-mail, Telnet, and FTP.

E-mail

E-mail is the basic service that you will get no matter how you hook up to the Internet. E-mail lets you exchange text messages with anyone else who has an Internet account. If you are just looking for e-mail connectivity, you are in luck! You have many choices, most of them fairly inexpensive and very easy to sign up for. Commercial BBSs like CompuServe, Prodigy, and America Online may meet your needs while also providing user-friendly software and services. You may even be able to find a local BBS that offers Internet access.

Telnet

With Telnet, you can connect to an enormous number of remote computers on the Internet and interactively search them for text, files, software, and other information. To do this, you (or the Internet service provider you sign up with) must have software like Gopher, Veronica, WWW, WAIS, or archie. Having Telnet will be important to you for doing marketing research, and for setting up things like an interactive store on the Internet.

FTP

The Internet File Transfer Protocol (FTP) enables you to obtain software (spreadsheet files, word processing files, graphics, etc.) from other computers on the Internet, as well as to send software. If this is important to your business, make sure that your Internet service provider offers FTP.

THE FOUR LEVELS OF INTERNET CONNECTIONS

There are four main levels of Internet access. Each type of access has its own cost and its own equipment requirements, and gives you different Internet services. Some of these types of access are very expensive, so you should consider your connection method at the same time you are deciding what type of Internet services you want.

Business users in large corporations may find that their companies are already on the Internet through their engineering or research departments, and many high-tech industries are already connected, so you may already have access and not know it. Potential users should contact their system operator for help in getting an account.

Gateway

Gateway access is provided through local BBS services, FidoNet, and many commercial providers such as America Online or CompuServe. It involves simple e-mail or other minimal access through a gateway to the Internet, and is usually not appropriate for business users.

Note that most of the commercial providers and BBS services are not *on* the Internet—they are simply gateways for Internet e-mail. This has three significant drawbacks: (1) Mail is not delivered as quickly. (2) Some BBSs limit the size of your e-mail messages. Watch for message size limitations and extra charges associated with message traffic volume, size, and file storage. America Online, for example, limits your incoming messages to a maximum of 8KB for PC users and 27KB for Mac users, with an outgoing e-mail message limit of 32KB. (3) In addition, many of the commercial BBS services still offer a limited amount of real Internet access—no FTP, no Telnet, no Gopher, and so on. This may change in the future.

For personal Internet access, many community organizations have created Freenet, and some computer user groups are also beginning to make the Internet available to their members. For individual use, many organizations provide Internet access—for example, academic institutions provide accounts for current students, community members, or alumni. Remember, however, businesses should consider the acceptable use limitations of these services before deciding to use them for commercial purposes. (See Chapter 4.)

You don't need high-powered computers for this type of connection: Any PC, a modem (9,600 baud or higher recommended), a phone line, and communications software will do. If you want to run Windows-based communications software, however, you should have at least a 386 PC.

Dial-Up or Shell Accounts

These Internet connections provide e-mail, FTP, Telnet, and most of the other Internet services. Shell accounts are often called UNIX shell accounts, although this can be a misnomer, since some of the providers actually run VAX mainframes. These kinds of accounts are excellent for small to medium-sized businesses, and for some functions of larger businesses.

With a dial-up or shell account, your computer is not on the Internet; rather, you are using a host that is on the Internet. Many dial-up access providers also allow businesses to arrange a corporate FTP and Gopher area on the host machine for promoting the subscriber's business.

The hourly usage rates usually range from $1 to $4 depending upon the service, and $5 to $40 per month for the account. Most services have moderate usage plans such as 20/20, where you pay $20 a month for the first 20 hours, and then $1 or less per additional hour. Some services provide just e-mail for a fee, and will provide Telnet and FTP for an additional charge. Additional services such as larger amounts of disk storage, Gopher, or anonymous FTP services featuring your business, will add costs.

Equipment needs are very modest for this kind of access—I know many users who run an old 8086 or 286 to support their connections. This option will take care of most of the needs of small and medium-sized businesses, or businesses that are not computer intensive.

SLIP/PPP

SLIP (Serial Line Internet Protocol), or PPP (Point-to-Point Protocol), lands somewhere between dial-up and dedicated lines in features and cost. SLIP provides the opportunity to run Internet software on your own computer just using standard phone lines—you can run the client software for Gopher, and so on. SLIP also allows for direct FTP and use of the Mosaic user interface software. SLIP is thus a dial-up service using normal phone lines and special software. This is appropriate for small or medium-sized businesses. It can be attached to a company's local area network (LAN), allowing for multiple users.

SLIP is an excellent solution for many business users. The up-front equipment costs are a bit higher than for dial-up, requiring a 486 PC or a Macintosh Quadra, and a higher-speed modem—9,600 baud minimum, 14,400 or 28,000 recommended. In addition, the monthly charge is in the neighborhood of $180 to $250 per month plus installation charges, and can be higher in certain regions. The telephone charges are modest, requiring only a normal phone line. This option is best for businesses that have greater needs for traffic and connectivity than simple dial-up, without going "whole hog" into a dedicated line.

Dedicated Lines and Registering as an Internet Node

With a dedicated line, your computer becomes an Internet node, that is, a "permanent" part of the Internet. Dedicated lines give you full, high-speed, Internet connectivity, and all the rights reserved for computers that are a full node of the Internet. While SLIP can be configured as a node, dedicated T3 connections are the Rolls-Royce of nodes.

Dedicated leased lines are used by large institutions or corporations and offer complete access to all Internet facilities as a node, with an almost unlimited number of users. Such lines are frequently referred to as 56KB (see Table 2.1), T1, or T3. (Just in case you are wondering, there are T2 lines, but they are rare.) These configurations are expensive to set up and to keep running. Dedicated lines are the most powerful and flexible Internet connections.

The up-front costs of a high-speed dedicated line are considerably more than for any other connection. It normally requires fairly sophisticated minicomputers and large disk arrays, a router costing $10,000 to $15,000. Also needed are the costly installation and maintenance of the dedicated leased line. The charges for a leased line may range from $750 per month for a 56KB line to $2000–$4000 per month or more for a T3. Installations often require considerable personnel time; in addition, in some areas, these higher-capacity lines are very expensive to install, or are not even available.

Many businesses are interested in having their company names as a node name, such as **oakridge.com**. Becoming a true node can happen two ways: through a full dedicated line connection, and through certain full-time SLIP connections. In addition, though, many dial-up service providers are allowing companies to have domain names through the use of mailboxes or aliasing. This means that a provider furnishes a service, allowing you to look as if you are **oakridge.com** without actually being a node. The World Software Tool & Die (**world.std.com**) described later in this chapter, is one such company.

An organization wanting to start a new Internet node contacts the Inter-Networking Information Center (InterNIC) for a domain name. NSF has given InterNIC the contract to assign and keep track of all domain names in the United States. These names are assigned on a first-come, first-served basis. The domain name is then registered for use by one organization.

Phone Lines

The type of connection you choose will also depend on the type of telephone wiring you have. Connection types range from simple dial-up modem connections using ordinary multiple-use telephone lines, through dedicated leased high-capacity data lines (see Table 2.1).

Table 2.1   Internet Connections and Phone Line Types

Connection	Type of Line Required	Speed	Features
Gateway, Dial-up, SLIP/PPP	Regular voice line	0–28.8KB	No extra costs
Node	Leased line	56KB	Dedicated data link
Node	T1	1.54MB	Dedicated data link for heavy user
Node	T3	45MB	Major network or corporate

In addition—as they say, "coming soon"—there is another type of service called Integrated Services Digital Network (ISDN). This is a *digital* service using the same twisted pair line technology as the current analog lines. ISDN is slowly becoming available in some areas, so it may be worth contacting your local telephone company (telco) to discuss options.

DECIDING WHAT INTERNET SERVICES AND CONNECTIONS YOU NEED

Internet Service Providers are fast-growing Internet businesses, expanding and changing constantly. Now, many of the mid-level networks also provide individual and business access to the Internet. Here is a closer look at the three major methods of Internet access of interest to business users:

For business use, you will first want to consider the types of resources that your business intends to utilize and the services that your business will be providing on the Internet. Next, it is important to research access providers in order to decide which provider can best meet your business needs. What do you want and need to do? Use e-mail, read Usenet, Telnet, find files using FTP, create a virtual storefront? Does your business want its own node, or would a pseudo-node provided by someone else work just as well?

You do not have to know how all of these connections and hardware work to get started. Chapters 4 and 5 will help you in making these decisions, too.

Issues to Consider When Choosing the Type and Level of Service

Does the access provider have any restrictions regarding use by businesses?

❑ Yes   ❑ No

Ask Internet access providers if they have any of their own restrictions concerning business activities. Also check to see if they have limitations on message size, disk storage size, and so on, that would restrict normal business activities. It may seem obvious, but if the service will not take business accounts, you should look elsewhere.

Type of use (check all that apply—all of these options are discussed fully in later chapters):

❑ E-mail
❑ Telnet

❏ FTP

❏ Usenet

❏ WWW

❏ Mosaic or Lynx

❏ Business Gopher area

❏ Business FTP area

❏ Multiple users

❏ Company node

If you have only checked e-mail, any type of connection will probably be sufficient; you can use a gateway connection like the ones offered by CompuServe, Delphi, and AOL. If you have checked 2–7 boxes, a good dial-in shell or other account will likely be appropriate, although you might consider a SLIP connection. In addition, you might look into one of the providers like **netcom.com** or **world.std.com** that offer a variety of business-related services. If you have checked 8–10 boxes, you ought to seriously consider a full-time SLIP connection, or possibly a 56KB line.

What kind of computer system do you currently have or will you be using?

❏ DOS

❏ Windows

❏ Macintosh

❏ OS/2

❏ Workstation

❏ UNIX

❏ Minicomputer

❏ Mainframe

❏ Other

Will your major computer system support the connection you wish to install? If you checked just DOS, Windows, OS/2, or Macintosh, you can support all dial-in services and most SLIP connections, but not full connectivity. Workstations and UNIX boxes can easily support SLIP, as well as some leased-line connectivity.

Will you be using a LAN?

❏ Yes   ❏ No

If you are not using a LAN, you will lose some of the advantages of SLIP and a leased line, such as multiple user accounts.

What speed modem do you have or will you be purchasing?

- ❑ 2,400 baud or slower
- ❑ 9,600 baud
- ❑ 14,400 or 28,000 baud

With a 2,400 or slower modem, you will be able to support all dial-in connections, but they will be frustratingly slow for uploading and downloading information. A 9,600 baud modem or faster can support SLIP. A leased line requires an even faster modem. At today's prices, there is no reason not to buy at least a 9,600 baud modem. Even 14,400 baud modems can be purchased for $125. If you have a slower modem, upgrade—it's the best money you'll ever spend.

Do they offer all the Internet services you require?

- ❑ Yes   ❑ No

Are there any major restrictions to use of these services?

Some service providers (such as America Online) limit the size of e-mail messages that you can send and receive. Many charge different rates for use during standard business hours.

Do they have any policies against doing business online (see Chapter 4)?

- ❑ Yes   ❑ No

How important are reliability and availability?

- ❑ Low
- ❑ Medium
- ❑ High
- ❑ Very high

If reliability is important, you should choose a provider with experience and multiple lines. Noisy lines or breakdowns can cause a loss of productivity; users who depend on their e-mail for conducting business, telecommuting, or while traveling will want to make sure that the service is always available, and does not have a lot of down time.

Ease of Use

How easy is the service to use? Many of the dial-up services provide no "front end," and simply present you with a $ or % prompt. How important is a user-friendly interface or easily available help?

Speed

Some systems are faster than others, so you may want to use some of the services on a trial basis to see if they have substantial delays in responding to you or transferring e-mail. Be sure to ask service providers what speed modems they use.

Long Distance Charges

In urban areas there are many services available through local calls, whereas smaller cities and rural areas must depend on long distance for their service. Make sure that a service provider gives you a local number to call when you want to connect with them. Otherwise, you'll be paying a long distance charge in addition to the service provider's hourly rate.

Price: The Bottom Line

Once you have put together a service plan, you will, of course, want to price the various providers' plans and services. There are many differences among them, and you may wish to take bids as well.

COMMERCIAL INTERNET PROVIDERS

There are many choices to make among the service providers. The following three examples show some of the range of services currently available.

Delphi

Delphi is a major provider of on-line services and Internet access. It focuses its services on the individual dial-up user, providing a menu-driven interface and optional PC-based user interface software. It provides all of the major Internet tools, including e-mail, Telnet, FTP, and Internet Relay Chat (IRC). It also provides access to search tools such as Gopher, Hytelnet, WAIS, and WWW. Delphi provides Usenet news, and an array of conferences, reference resources, and databases (much like some of the commercial BBS services).

While Delphi provides a full line of Internet tools, it provides only dial-up access—there are no SLIP or PPP connections available. In addition, Delphi states that the "use of DELPHI for advertising or promotion of a commercial product or service without the express, written consent of Delphi is prohibited," and its policies limit your ability to create your own mailing lists.

A service like this is best used by individuals, or for research and communication, rather than for creating a business presence on the

Internet. For Delphi Internet information, contact **walthowe@delphi.com**, or 800/544-4005 (voice).

NETCOM

NETCOM is a full-service Internet connection provider, focusing on business and high-demand individual users. Since it began in 1988, its clients have included large defense contractors, chip manufacturers, oil companies, large computer manufacturers, investment companies, and small businesses of all kinds. NETCOM provides reliable service 24 hours each day, 7 days each week, 365 days each year.

NETCOM charges flat fees, without connect time charges. The network is owned, operated, and maintained by NETCOM, so there are no commercial use restrictions.

NETCOM allows you to have your own permanent IP address so that Internet users can, for example, transfer files or Telnet to or from your site. Connections to NETCOM can be made by any computer workstation or server with a standard voice telephone line, high-speed V.32bis or V.42bis modem, and PPP or SLIP communications software.

NETCOM also provides Internet domain registration services for your node, as well as a Class C IP address, and routes Internet traffic (e.g., electronic mail) to your site.

A service like NETCOM is appropriate for the more demanding business user who wants to establish connections via SLIP or a leased line. For more information, send e-mail to **info@netcom.com**, or call (voice) 408/554-8649.

The World Software Tool & Die

In business since 1989, The World provides dial-up access to the Internet. It offers the full range of Internet services that include electronic mail, Usenet, Telnet, FTP, Internet Relay Chat, Gopher, WAIS, WWW, Clarinet news service, a text archive, and other services. Using ordinary terminal emulation software, customers of The World have access to a UNIX-based computer that supports all the software and utilities for Internet access. In addition, The World provides access to the Internet mailing lists, and customers can opt to create and manage their own lists.

The World provides reliable service through multiple high-speed (T1) links to the Internet. The World supports modems with v.32bis, v.32, v.42bis, v.42, and MNP5 protocols.

Since businesses are the fastest growing segment of the Internet community, The World offers several special services for corporate customers. Its corporate mailbox service, for example, allows your business to register an Internet domain name and receive e-mail addressed to your own custom Internet address. FTP and Gopher archive areas can be created to allow the distribution of information about your business and products. In addition, they offer special rates for business customers with multiple accounts, and on-site Internet training.

A service like this is appropriate for small and medium-sized businesses that are in the process of going on the net and wish to create a business presence on the Internet. Contact The World at **office@world. std.com**, or 617/739-0202 (voice).

Some Other Providers

Table 2.2 gives a short list of contacts for a few of the other commercial Internet providers.

If you are interested in high-speed leased lines, you may want to contact your local telco, or SprintLink at 703/904-2680.

Internet access providers can be dialed directly by your modem, but if the provider does not happen to be in your city, there will, of course, be long distance telephone charges. To save on long distance charges, you may be able to use one of several telephone networks that provide a local phone number in many cities. (Not all providers are connected to these services.) Your modem calls this local phone number and then, in response to a prompt such as "Host Name," you type in the name of your Internet service. These network services are almost always cheaper to use than regular long distance, but not all areas of the country are served by such telephone networks. Each of the companies in Table 2.3 provides local call services in many cities for accessing some of the dial-up Internet access providers.

The best documents and resources concerning Internet providers are on the Internet itself. This presents the new user with a chicken-or-egg

Table 2.2   Internet Providers

Provider	E-mail address	Voice
AlterNet	**alternet-info@uunet.uu.net**	800/4UUNET3
ANS CO+RE	**info@ans.net**	914/789-5300
BIX	**bix@genvid.com**	800/695-4775
Digital Express	**info@digex.com**	301/220-2020
DMConnection	**info@dmc.com**	508/568-1618
MSEN	**info@msen.com**	313/998-4562
PANIX	**info@panix.com**	212/877-4854
PSI	**info@psi.com**	703/620-6651

Table 2.3 Service Providers That Offer Long Distance Options

Network	Voice Information
TYMNET	800/937-2862
CompuServe Packet Network	800/848-8199
PSINet	800/827-7482
	all-info@psi.com (e-mail)

problem for selecting the right provider. A good approach to handling this is to select one of the providers listed in this chapter, with the understanding that it may be a temporary account while you learn about the Internet. The NixPub List of publicly accessible UNIX sites lists a large number of sites that provide some form of Internet access. That document is available by FTP at **vfl.paramax.com** in the pub/pubnet subdirectory as **nixpub.long**. Another document called PDIAL (Public Dialup Internet Access List) is available by e-mail from **info-deli-server@netcom.com** with a subject send pdial, or available by way of FTP at **rtfm.mit.edu**. (Don't worry if some of this does not mean very much at this stage. You can get more information on e-mail in Chapter 6, and on FTP in Chapter 9.)

WHERE TO FIND MORE INFORMATION

There are several other chapters that will be useful in helping you make your decision about an Internet service provider.

- To learn more about why businesses are using the Internet, continue on to Chapter 3.

- To gain an understanding of the acceptable and unacceptable uses of the Internet, read Chapter 4.

- Chapter 5 discusses specific techniques for creating a business presence on the Internet, including global communication, corporate logistics, and virtual storefronts. This should help further in choosing the type of connection to the Internet you will need.

Once you get connected to the Internet, you may want to learn more about the basic Internet tools such as e-mail, Telnet, FTP, and the searching tools such as Gopher, archie, and Veronica. Chapters 6–10 will explain how to use these tools.

Creating a Business Presence on the Internet

CHAPTER 3

Why Businesses Are Using the Internet

Businesses are the fastest growing segment of the Internet, for many reasons: You can gather information, communicate, and actually transact business on the Internet. Some businesses are creating a corporate presence on the Internet, including virtual storefronts. There are both visible and invisible business users of the Internet. Many businesses use the Internet for transacting business, but their work is largely not seen by the average Internet user. Corporations are using e-mail for communication, and FTP for file and data transfers.

The largest invisible users of the Internet are financial and medical institutions. These industries have very high data traffic rates on the network. Most of these large companies have established "fire walls" to separate their own local data traffic from the rest of the Internet.

The most visible businesses on the Internet have a multifaceted corporate presence on the Internet. They are visible in product announcements, on lists, on Usenet, on Gophers, FTP, and more, and you will see their messages in *.plan* files and in signature files.

REASONS THAT BUSINESSES ARE USING THE INTERNET

Businesses use the Internet for almost as many reasons as there are businesses. The Internet is used by businesses for:

- Communication (internal and external)
- Corporate logistics
- Leveling the playing field—globalization

- Gaining and maintaining competitive advantage
- Cost containment
- Collaboration and development
- Information retrieval and utilization
- Marketing and sales
- Transmission of data
- Creating a corporate presence

Let's have a closer look at some of these reasons.

Communication (Internal and External)

E-mail is a low-cost method for maintaining local, regional, national, and international communication. Messages can be exchanged in minutes as opposed to days or even months using regular mail. E-mail is a shared information utility and said to be one of the most important productivity packages going. Often, the first and most frequent business use of Internet connectivity involves internal and external communications. Use of the Internet lets a business be in touch with branches and work teams at many locations, and permits high-speed access to vendors and customers. This can even create a virtual community in which people who might normally never meet or even communicate, find themselves in conversation about substantive matters. Corporate culture is being affected by e-mail—some people become more communicative because they prefer sending e-mail to talking on the phone. (See Chapter 4 for some more information on CMC and corporate culture.)

Businesses use the Internet to keep departments, work groups, and individuals in close contact. Just think—an end to busy signals and playing phone tag with your colleagues when you use e-mail. Listservs software (discussed in Chapter 7) allows work groups to communicate in an open manner similar to virtual meetings, and can serve as an ad hoc tool for Total Quality Management (TQM) or process reengineering projects. This can help team members keep in touch and involved even while they are traveling. Listserv can also assist group members in obtaining the most up-to-date versions of collaborative work, and provide current versions and comments to all members simultaneously.

It is not uncommon today for telephone conferences to occur, but not without considerable investment of time and effort in scheduling, planning, and discussion about who should and should not be included. Use of e-mailing lists can greatly facilitate such group conferencing, since the members can participate at various times and from various locations.

Electronic mail messages can be read and posted at convenient times and places.

Improving communication with colleagues, government agencies, the academic community, researchers, and even competitors, can help improve the industry in general. The culture of the Internet is such that genuine exchanges on industry-wide questions and improvement are increasingly common.

E-mail is the primary way that people on the Internet communicate with each other, so using e-mail is a good way to exchange information with your customers. Many people use the Internet daily because they prefer communicating by e-mail (rather than over the phone or by postal mail). Because these people prefer using e-mail, you are more likely to receive a quick but thoughtful reply if you send your message by e-mail.

Corporate Logistics

When communicating via e-mail, listservs, and electronic conferences, not all participants have to be in the same place at the same time to conduct business. Actual "real-time" communication is also possible, however, through the use of Talk, MOOs, and Internet Relay Chat (IRC). In fact, online, real-time meetings are possible among individuals in Siberia, Singapore, and Saskatchewan. Distance/time barriers are lessened by using the Internet for communication.

Logistical concerns that can dominate production planning can be eased by better contact through the Internet. The Internet is the "any-where/anytime" network, so exchanges with markets in Europe and Asia (across time zones) can be facilitated by the use of e-mail and conferencing.

It is increasingly common for companies to support telecommuting employees (even tailors are complaining because business people do not need as many suits anymore), and some corporations have employees in such far-flung places that they never come in to work. Work teams can be formed online, allowing these telecommuters to become part of the team. This can also be accomplished when employees are out of town or temporarily off-site.

In some cases, businesses have created a virtual company composed of individuals who work at a distance from one another. They may meet face-to-face only occasionally.

Globalization and Leveling a Playing Field

Using the Internet, many organizations are able to bring a global edge to a provincial business. With the Internet, you are much less aware of national boundaries and distance. Individuals from Taiwan converse with others in Toronto, Moscow, and Okemos, Michigan, easily. This opportunity for rapid communications can increase a businesse's visibility from local to global overnight.

Because access to the Internet has gotten cheaper, even tiny "cottage industries" can compete in the larger marketplace. Isolated businesses can compete at a much higher level. There are books being sold from Nova Scotia, mutual funds being managed from a ranch in Utah, and a software company that flourishes in the foothills of Appalachia.

For many companies, the use of the Internet creates a level playing field. Very small businesses can create an image on the network to compete with large businesses. It makes the pursuit of customers, vendors, and resources possible worldwide—allowing competition in a world market.

Gaining and Maintaining Competitive Advantage

Increasingly, businesses are taking a look at their own organizations, structures, and processes in an effort to become more competitive. The Internet is a wonderful tool for engaging in these activities. Many companies are using e-mail and group conferencing to engage in business process reengineering projects. Maintaining good communication and the exchange of data and documents is critical in undertaking the reengineering of business processes.

In addition, many companies use the Internet in the search for "best practices." As businesses try to become more competitive, many want to find existing practices that can help them improve their activities. In some cases, businesses are using the communications abilities of the Internet to engage in a Total Quality Management plan. Some companies use the Internet to maintain corporate process control across all company locations (or even continents).

What are other businesses doing? What kinds of information are available? The Internet mailing lists are terrific sources for keeping track of industry and government standards; in addition, various government databases also maintain regulatory and standards information.

Competitive advantage can be increased due to access to state-of-the art information on products, material, new ideas and even the status quo in a given industry. Many corporations use the Internet to engage in what some call "techno watch"—keeping a finger on the pulse of emerging and new technologies, and the market response to those technologies, both anecdotal and in terms of financial performance and the stock market.

Many People Prefer E-mail

You will find that many people prefer being contacted via e-mail. It can be a more informal or private exchange, or simply more convenient. In addition, some users appreciate that you are Internet-literate and have chosen that kind of approach to them. I often find that my contacts are much more responsive to an e-mail message than to a telephone or voice-mail message.

The public information and discussion groups available on the Internet provide insight and feedback that is hard to get in any other manner. Here, workers at all levels of industry, researchers, and the public exchange information on marketing, research, technological developments, internal processes such as accounting and personnel, and external activities such as purchasing and public relations. These discussion groups are useful both for the information presented in them and for the pointers they provide to important sites, contacts, and databases. Having the most up-to-date information about your markets and the state-of-the-art in your industry allows you to keep or increase your competitive edge.

In some cases, the Internet is a tool for solving problems by accessing information, documents, and experts. Many companies cannot afford in-house experts on every process or activity, and use the Internet to locate and network with experts, through the mailing lists or through e-mail.

Cost Containment

Many business are using the Internet to contain long distance telephone and mailing costs. Recent studies have shown that businesses can save thousands of dollars using e-mail, in lieu of some long distance phone calls and postal deliveries.

With first-class letters costing 29¢ each (soon to be higher), a mailing of 1,000 pieces to customers would cost $290 for postage alone, whereas the same information sent by e-mail would cost 2 to 3 cents each—and the messages would arrive in seconds as opposed to days or (weeks). Overnight mail (which typically costs at $8–$12 for each delivery) can't compete with e-mail for speed or cost.

Long distance telephone charges, particularly international long distance charges, are reduced by use of e-mail. In addition, FAX gateways allow further savings on those long distance charges.

Collaboration and Development

It is increasingly common for companies to form partnerships and collaborative development efforts—even IBM and Apple have done so. The development team and project participants often use the Internet to keep in touch, and to exchange data, programs, and working papers from far-flung locations. The Internet also allows several small businesses to band together much more easily for product development.

Formerly, companies tended to maintain separate projects, or would create a new division or production unit to handle a specific problem. Now, many companies are temporarily pooling resources to put out a new product or service, and are using the Internet to do this through e-mail, group conferencing, and exchange of spreadsheets, documents, drawings, pictures, and sound files. Such groups allow those in marketing, research, engineering, and accounting to keep track of and provide input on a project through every step of its development. This ongoing discussion helps to keep projects on track by insuring that the needs of sales, marketing, accounting, and so on, are included as integral parts of a plan. Such groups also tend to develop enthusiasm and a creative atmosphere.

Information Retrieval and Utilization

The coin of the realm for the Internet is information. Rich in resources, the Internet provides software, communications connections worldwide, and files of text, data, graphs, and images (from this world, and from out of this world via the orbiting Hubble telescope). The Internet provides access to databases, books, manuals, training information, experts in various fields, even sound and video clips.

And much of that information is free. In the movie *The Graduate* the young man played by Dustin Hoffman is told that the secret to his future success is "plastics." Today, the secret to success is "information." With roughly 2.5 million machines connected to the Internet, with databases, Usenet, Gopher servers, FTP archives, and conferences, the amount of information available is staggering.

Scientific and research data is available in large quantities. There are electronic newsletters, searchable databases, online experts—in some cases causing information overload. Some have compared using the Internet to drinking from a fire hose.

Some businesses find that the Internet is useful in helping employees learn new tasks and processes. There are many simulations, manuals, training aids, and tools available for software running on a variety of platforms, from UNIX tutorials to Windows tips and hints. There are also large quantities of instructional materials available online regarding the use of the Internet itself.

Marketing and Sales

As businesses use the Internet more, and Internet users become more accustomed to marketing activities, Internet marketing is becoming much more popular. Marketing on the Internet involves both research and active outflow of information.

Marketing research is common on the Internet, where attitudes are tested, conversations actively pursued, and opinions solicited from many groups. (I sent a message to NBC just the other day to participate in a customer poll—**nightly@nbc.com.**) Marketing plans are increasingly counting on Internet access for success.

One of the prime business uses of the Internet is in the area of customer support. Customers can reach a company on their own schedules—day or night—and obtain information from conferences, FTP, e-mail, and Gopher. The customer support information only has to be transferred to an archive once, and yet it may be accessed by thousands of customers and potential customers—a very labor-efficient and cost-effective way of distributing information. In addition, a business with a presence on the Internet is perceived as modern, advanced, and sophisticated.

Unsolicited Advertising

Never send unsolicited e-mail advertisements to people on the Internet. This is absolutely the surest way to damage your reputation. There are plenty of stories about recipients of unsolicited advertising who have boycotted a company and even had them thrown off the Internet.

In these days of a highly competitive global marketplace, the company that can reach and satisfy customers will have an advantage—and the Internet can help in maintaining relationships with customers. The Internet is also a fast and efficient way of networking with vendors and suppliers. With its global reach, the Internet can assist businesses in locating new suppliers and keeping in better touch with them to aid, for example, in zero inventory planning. A business might locate and coordinate with suppliers in Ecuador, Egypt, and Estonia; and the Internet system in some countries is often more stable than telephone service, which is often less than reliable and convenient.

Maintaining up-to-date postings of your company's product information and prices also allow your vendors to have continuous access to the information that is needed in order to promote and sell your products. Small suppliers find that that they can compete with larger industries by being easily available via the Internet.

In a business atmosphere promoting the concept of "getting closer to the customer," the Internet is becoming increasingly important. Internet-assisted sales, where customers are sought and served online through Gophers and a variety of virtual storefronts, are also becoming more popular. Customers are thus sought before the sale and supported after the sale.

Customer and product support and technical assistance by way of the Internet is time-efficient. Many companies provide e-mail assistance, including both individual and automated replies to e-mail questions and requests for information. Technical sheets, specifications, and support are offered through Gophers and FTP. Relationships with vendors and outlets are maintained via the Internet.

In some cases, companies are doing actual product sales transactions on the Internet. In addition, if the product is amenable to Internet delivery, as with software and information, the actual product is delivered via the Internet. Some companies are *arranging* product delivery through the Internet, where companies can create and support actual distribution channels.

Transmission of Data

Many companies have been using the Internet for the transmission of data. The major financial and medical institutions in the world use the Internet extensively for exchanging information and files. Publishers are using the Internet to receive manuscripts, and transmit files for printing over the Internet. Books are written and edited collaboratively using the Internet.

The Internet protocols allow for the exchange of both ASCII and binary information. Binary information includes executable programs (software), program data files (word processing files, spreadsheets, databases, etc.), graphics (pictures, maps, digitized images, CAD/CAM files, etc.) and sound files. The network's backbone can send the equivalent of a 20-volume set of an encyclopedia in just seconds.

Research and scientific organizations and educational institutions, the original inhabitants of the Internet, are using the Internet to transmit large quantities of data as well, but corporate users now transfer the largest portion of data.

Corporate Presence on the Internet

By creating a corporate presence on the Internet, businesses can participate in all the benefits of online marketing, publicity, and sales. They can
use such tools as Gopher, FTP Telnet, e-mail, and Usenet to build a
virtual storefront, create catalogs that can be browsed online, announce
products, take orders, and get customer feedback. Chapter 5 focuses
entirely on techniques and tools for creating this corporate presence on
the Internet.

GROWTH OF THE COMMERCIAL DOMAINS

It is said that the Internet as a whole is growing at the rate of 10 percent
per month, and that the largest and fastest growing segment of the
Internet is business. According to statistics gathered by the National
Science Foundation (NSF), commercial addressees now comprise 51 percent of network registrations—and this does not include companies that
are registered under some research- or education-related functions. The
graph in Figure 3.1 shows the distribution of network registrations. These

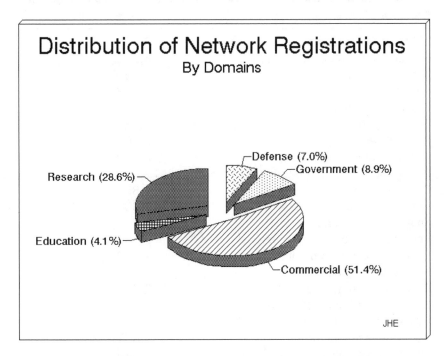

Figure 3.1 The Distribution of Internet Domain Registrations.

are network registration counts only, not counts of individual users. Substantial growth in the commercial domains is expected to continue.

"Power users" of the Internet include some of the major computer corporations, health care industries, pharmaceutical companies, banks and financial services, and high-technology manufacturers. Based on figures from the *Internet Letter* (Levin 1993) and the NSF, the top 20 companies on the Internet according to the number of externally reachable hosts are in Table 3.1.

Major financial institutions such as J. P. Morgan, Lehman Brothers, Paine Webber, and the Federal Reserve Board are all using the Internet for data transmission and research. According to the NSF, they are retrieving ten times as much data as they are sending out. This suggests that they are using the Internet in support of their financial research. Figure 3.2 shows the use by financial institutions. Medical institutions such as Massachusetts General, Health and Welfare Canada, and Rush Presbyterian also have a 10:1 ratio, and are major Internet users (see Figure 3.3).

Table 3.1 Top 20 Companies on the Internet

Company	Hosts
LSI Logic Corporation	6,670
Bell Communications Research	6,208
Xerox Corporation	4,769
Cadence Design Systems	3,593
Sterling Software	3,555
Dell Computer	3,539
Pyramid Technology	3,162
Portal Communications	2,950
Performance Systems International (PSI)	2,939
Cisco Systems	2,852
Honeywell Incorporated	2,600
Amgen Incorporated	2,477
Science Applications International	2,356
Cray Research Incorporated	2,333
Motorola Manufacturing	2,229
Rockwell International	2,211
Bristol-Myers Squibb Pharmaceuticals	1,989
Schlumber-Doll Research	1,729
Harris Semiconductor	1,555
MDCME Unigraphics	1,420

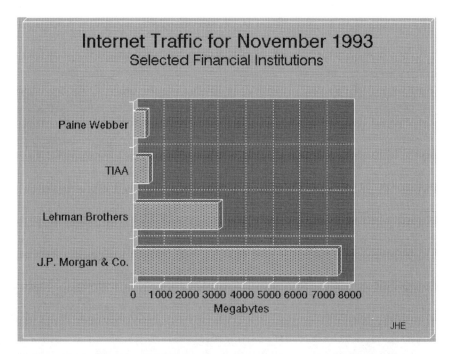

Figure 3.2 The Use of the Internet by Financial Institutions.

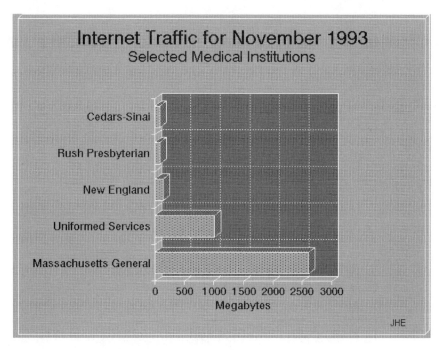

Figure 3.3 The Use of the Internet by Medical Institutions.

Another indicator of commercial use and interest in the Internet is found in the number of Internet-related trademark applications. Currently there are more than 60 trademarks using the word "Internet," and several others are pending with the U.S. Patent and Trademark Office.

There are other indicators of the growth of the business sector on the Internet. To illustrate, there are a growing number of paper-based and electronic publications about the Internet—for example, *The Internet Business Journal* (Strangelove), *Internet World* (Meckler), *The Internet Letter* (Net Week), *The Internet Demystifyer and Monthly Gazette* (Oak Ridge Research), *The Internet Business Report* (CMP), *Bits and Bytes Online* (Machado), and *E-D-U-P-A-G-E* (Educom). Some of these new publications are specifically about doing business on the Internet.

The magazine industry provides an indicator of business growth on the Internet. In the last six months of 1993, more than 100 magazines have started to offer some kind of online services to complement their paper-based magazines, and more are going online at the rate of 2–3 per week (Carmody, 1993). Most provide a table of contents and the full text of one of the major articles or reviews from current and back issues. In addition, some are adding value by providing online dialogs and events with editors, columnists, and experts.

EXAMPLES OF HOW COMPANIES ARE USING THE INTERNET

The Internet is not just used by large corporations! Many individuals, nonprofits, and small businesses use the Internet thorough the access service providers mentioned in Chapter 2. The ways in which businesses use the Internet are as varied as the businesses themselves. Some just use it for communication or the transfer of data. Others do market research and go so far as to create a virtual storefront. Here are some examples.

Quick Sampler

Following are some current business residents of the Internet with a brief description of how they are using the Internet.

- *WORDNET* is a foreign language translation, typesetting, and printing company with more than 1,000 translators. They use the Internet as well as other e-mail networks. For further information, see their Gopher entry at **gopher.std.com** or e-mail them at **wordnet@world .std.com**.

- *Take Two Photocraft* is a retail digital retouching and restoration service for damaged photos. It handles color and black-and-white scanning, as well as all file formats in Adobe Printshop, with a variety of input and output options. Contact them at **taketwo@world.std.com**.

- *The Dallas Art Museum* is using the Internet to gain members and advertise its exhibits and events. A collection of its art is available via the University of North Texas (**gopher.unt.edu**)—you can download the image files to your own computer and view them in full color. (I have both a Georgia O'Keefe and an Edward Hopper.)

- *Winn Dixie* supermarkets in Atlanta are offering computerized ordering of groceries online.

- *The Ford Motor Company* is offering the "Electronic Car Showroom," where it promotes its Lincoln line of cars. Information is provided about leasing, sales, and road test results through the Electronic Newsstand, which puts more than 80 magazines and newsletters on the network—Gopher to **internet.com**. "Have you driven a Ford lately" . . . on the Internet? But you cannot purchase the cars online—yet!

- *Tadpole Computers* keeps its offices in Cambridge, England, Austin, Texas, San Jose, California, Dallas, New York, and Paris, France in good communication using the Internet.

- *Lufthansa Airlines* uses a Gopher site provided by the Internet Company (**internet.com**) to market special flights, prices, and travel packages. In addition, "Lufthansa's destination of the month" offers in-depth information about a selected destination.

- *John Wiley & Sons* uses the Internet to communicate with its authors and to stay current with the computer industry. It also writes and edits books collaboratively over the Internet, cutting down on the turnaround time needed, and getting information into print faster. The Computer Science Division of *Addison-Wesley Publishers* conducts almost all of its manuscript preparation using the Internet for correspondence with authors. *PTR Prentice Hall* has a Gopher offering books for sale, and includes author, title, and ISBN searches, as well as tables of contents, and domestic and international order forms.

- *The Houston Chronicle, The Village Voice, The New York Times, The Economist*, and the *National Broadcasting Company* (better known as NBC) regularly query readers/viewers for interests and feedback using the Internet.

- *Schnieder National* of Green Bay, Wisconsin, one of the nation's largest trucking firms, uses the Internet to manage logistics and scheduling and even to alert driver of adverse road and weather conditions. *Newsweek* (1994) says that Schnieder may be an information system masquerading as a trucking line. By keeping its equipment and drivers busy, Schnieder doubled its revenue from 1989 to 1993.

- Even the *IRS* is using the Internet for data exchange, and is testing electronic submission of returns, though not via the Internet—yet.

A Few In-Depth Examples

The number of businesses with a visible presence on the Internet is growing very quickly. The following examples will show you how some large, medium, and very small businesses are using the Internet with their companies.

Flowers Online

Flowers Online is using the Gopher provided by Telerama (an Internet services provider) to advertise its products. You can buy fruit baskets and flowers for many occasions while online with Gopher. Here is what the main Gopher menu looks like:

```
          Internet Gopher Information Client 1.2VMS p10
          Order Flowers On Line


     1. Branch Information Services - Ordering Flowers.
     2. Happy Birthday or all occasion - BFL001 - $35 <Picture>
     3. All occasion - BFL006 - $35 <Picture>
     4. Classic Dozen Red Roses - BFL033 - $49 to $99 <Picture>
     5. New Baby Bouquet - BFL008 - $30 <Picture>
     6. Large Fruit Basket - BFL016 - $65 <Picture>
     7. Flower Order Form.
```

Notice that under numbers 2 through 6 you can actually download a picture (.GIF) of the item. The fruit basket and classic red roses look splendid! Flowers Online has an order form that you fill out, which asks you to identify the product item code, your e-mail address and phone number, the recipient's name, address, country, and phone number, the note for the card, and payment information via credit card. You then e-mail the form to **branch-info@branch.com**.

The company has been in business since 1947, and is using this marketing and delivery tool to gain a new niche for its products.

Greenville Tool and Die

Greenville Tool and Die makes automotive sheet metal stamping dies in Michigan. The dies are used by some of the large automobile companies. As with many manufacturing companies, its manufacturing and stocking processes have become heavily computerized. It uses the Internet to keep its computerized design and manufacturing (CAD/CAM) software up to date and running smoothly. Because of tight time lines, it must keep its software up and running at all times. It serves as a beta test site for software from a variety of sources. (Beta software is almost ready for release, but needs a bit more testing.)

Greenville Tool and Die formerly used the telephone for technical support and postal mail for software patches and updates. Now it uses the Internet for both. In addition, it uses the Internet to locate high-tech information, and to download public domain software. It also uses the Internet for internal and external (global) connectivity.

McCrerey Farm

McCrerey Farm in rural Pennsylvania sells handicrafts, dolls, natural fibers, and crafts supplies using the Gopher at Telerama. It has an online catalog, and its opening Gopher screen looks like this:

```
        Internet Gopher Information Client 1.2VMS p10
     McCrerey Farm: handcrafts & natural products

     1. About McCrerey Farm.
     2. Dolls and Santas.
     3. Handcrafted Traditionals and Gifts.
     4. Kits.
     5. Natural Fibers & Crafter's Supplies.
     6. Order Form.
     7. Ordering Information.
     8. The Legend of the McCrerey Angels.
```

When you choose "About McCrerey Farm," you find a letter to potential customers, outlining its products and services. It describes its products which have an emphasis on local natural products and crafts that are environmentally friendly, and include educational materials regarding the care and use of the items for sale. On the Gopher it also offers some local legends.

It providea a postal address and phone number for orders in addition to its online e-mail ordering address: **kristen@telerama.pgh.pa.us**.

MarketBase

MarketBase is a company that offers an Online Catalog of products and services for other businesses. Product purchasers have free access, while product advertisers pay a small monthly fee for placing their goods in the online catalog.

MarketBase provides a virtual storefront for vendors that allows consumers to access the information any time of the day or night. Using Gopher, potential purchasers are given menus and the ability to search for items. The company also provides access by way of Telnet, FTP, and dial-up modems. To register your product with MarketBase, send an e-mail message to **register@mb.com** requesting a product registration form; for more general information, send e-mail to **info@mb.com**.

MSEN

MSEN offers a wide range of services in information resources and networking, and provides a marketplace for others, sponsoring the Online Career Center and the Internet Business Pages. It is also an Internet service provider with shell accounts, Telnet, FTP, Usenet news, Reuters and UPI news, Gopher, IRC, and its own BBS with a forum for new Internet users.

Other services include Usenet news, WAIS, UUCP access, and full Internet access including dial-up and leased line services. MSEN's Gopher menu looks like this:

```
            MSEN Inc.

--> 1.  About The Msen Gopher.
    2.  Msen Open House:  6pm Friday, February 25, 1994.
    3.  About Msen/
    4.  What's New in the Msen Gopher/
    5.  Msen News Services/
    6.  Msen _Internet Review_/
    7.  Internet Business Pages/
    8.  Msen MarketPlace/
    9.  Netsurfing -- Interesting things to play with/
   10.  Selected internet resources/
   11.  FTP sites - search for software on the Internet/
   12.  Other Gopher and Information Servers/
   13.  Ann Arbor / Detroit Weather.
   14.  Ann Arbor Civic Information/
   15.  The Online Career Center/
```

The menu shows some of its services: News Service, Internet Review, the Internet Business pages, the Msen MarketPlace, and the Online Career Center, and local weather and civic information for Ann Arbor, Michigan, where MSEN is located.

The Online Career Center was formed by a group of 40 U.S. corporations, and is designed to help job seekers and employers to match job-related interests and skills. Job seekers may post their resumes and use the service for free, while the companies listing jobs have to pay a small fee for file maintenance. Currently there are more than 8,000 jobs listed. (Send mail to **occ-info@mail.msen.com** for information on The Online Career Center.)

```
The Online Career Center

    1.  Questions and Comments to: occ@mail.msen.com.
    2.  About Online Career Center/
    3.  Company Sponsors and Profiles/
    4.  Employment Events/
    5.  Career Assistance/
    6.  Help Wanted-USA (Information)/
    7.  Contract Recruiters/Employment Services available/
    8.  * Search Jobs */
    9.  * Search Resumes */
    10. * Search Jobs - Education */
    11. Help Files: Keyword Search/Enter Resume/Print/
    12. How To Enter A Resume.
    13. Online Career Center Liability Policy.
```

MSEN also has created a virtual yellow pages service called the Internet Business Pages. It is a free service in which a company can list its services and products. This is the Internet Business Pages Gopher entry from the MSEN main menu:

```
Internet Business Pages

    1. What are the Internet Business Pages?.
    2. Internet Business Pages Registration Form.
    3. Internet Business Pages - INDEX.
    4. Where Do I Get IBP Clients?.
    5. Search The Internet Business Pages <CSO>
```

You can obtain the IBP Registration Form via electronic mail from **ibp-info@msen.com**. Put "send form" in the Subject line or the text of the letter. For general information, send mail to **info@mail.msen.com** for a price list and service list, and to **Reuters-info@mail.msen.com** for Reuters information.

Nova Scotia Technical Network—Cybermall

The Nova Scotia Technical Network's (NSTN) Cybermall features Roswell's Bookstore, a vendor of software and peripherals, FitzGerald Webber consulting service, and the Virtual Record Store:

```
NSTN's Cybermall
```

```
1. DirectWARE The Electronic Superstore of Software and
     Peripherals/
2. FitzGerald Webber Marketing/
3. Roswell Electronic Computer Bookstore/
4. Virtual Record Store/
```

Choosing item 3 will connect you with Roswell's Gopher menu (shown below), where you can browse the "shelves," search by author, title, or ISBN, and look at its recent news releases. Roswell's is a real bookstore located in Halifax, Nova Scotia, carrying over 7,000 computer-related titles, and providing this virtual bookstore on the Internet.

```
Roswell Electronic Computer Bookstore
```

```
1. About Roswell Electronic Computer Bookstore.
2. Browse the Bookstore/
3. How To Order.
4. Internet Special Of The Month.
5. New Releases/
6. Search the bookstore by partial author, title, or ISBN. <?>
```

You can order online, through the mail, and by telephone. Roswell can be reached by e-mail at **roswell@fox.nstn.ns.ca**.

Choosing item 2 will connect you with FitzGerald Webber marketing. It provides services to Canadian businesses and offers the Desktop Lawyer software for use in setting up a business in Canada. It also provides information about some products under development such as The Home Office, The Consulting Package, Franchising, Real Estate Law, and Family Law.

```
FitzGerald Webber Marketing
```

```
1. About FitzGerald Webber Marketing.
2. About Desktop Lawyer/
3. New Businesses in Nova Scotia (mailing lists)/
4. Pricing, Ordering and Shipping information.
```

Choosing item 4 will connect you with the Virtual Record Store, where you can search two categories, Alternative and New Age, by artist, or the whole store (40,000 CDs) by title or product code. It can be reached at **vrs@nstn.ns.ca**.

The Schlumberger Corporation

Schlumberger is a company that provides oil field services and high-technology measurement devices to customers worldwide. This is a far-flung corporation with service locations ranging from Oklahoma to Japan and Siberia, and includes drilling platforms and a fleet of ships. All of its products and services are related to petroleum.

A highly distributed conglomerate with more than 2,000 locations, it has a need for very high-quality, rapid communication. It uses the Internet for e-mail, and for data transfer via FTP. The Internet is an important tool for information sharing and minimizing the vast time zone and location differences. It even maintains Gophers with pictures of employees so that it can communicate effectively, and verify identities.

It also uses the Internet to disseminate information to customers, and uses sophisticated security measures to protect proprietary information. It is engaged in collaborative projects with academics and other corporations, and trades information via e-mail, Gopher, and FTP. In addition, it is able to share software on the Internet.

Alain Pinel Realtors

Alain Pinel Realtors in San Jose, California, use a dial-up Internet service to transfer data regarding mortgages, escrow accounts, and title searches using the Internet. Agents can set up an escrow account and send the information to a title company to speed up transactions.

They also use the Internet to connect all offices and agents together. All 250 agents have an Internet address on their business cards, and they find that customers are increasingly using the Internet to make contact with the offices.

The World Software Tool & Die

The World Software Tool & Die is an Internet service provider—the first dial-up service in the United States. It provides marketing and sales opportunities for other businesses through its Gopher and its Shops on the World. In addition, it has joint projects with *Middlesex News* (an online version of a traditional newspaper) and the *Online Book Initiative*. It has an extensive Gopher:

```
            The World (Public Access UNIX)


    1.   Information About The World Public Access UNIX/
    2.   The World's ClariNews UPI/Reuters newswire index/
    3.   OBI The Online Book Initiative/
    4.   Internet and Usenet Phone Books/
```

```
 5.   Shops on The World/
 6.   Commercial Services via the Internet/
 7.   Book Sellers/
 8.   Bulletin Boards via the Internet/
 9.   Business Opportunities/
10.   Consultants/
11.   FTP/
12.   Government Information/
13.   Internet Information and Resources/
14.   Libraries/
15.   Membership and Professional Associations/
16.   News and Weather/
17.   Non-Profit Organizations/
18.   Other Gopher and Information Servers/
19.   Periodicals, Magazines, and Journals/
20.   Usenet Newsgroup and Mailing List Archives/
21.   University of Minnesota Gopher Server/
```

Found under item 19, the *Middlesex News* is a traditional newspaper serving the Boston area that formed a partnership with Software Tool & Die to create an electronic information service. You can read the paper's next day headlines, browse a calendar of events, and read movie and restaurant reviews. Its gopher menu shows some of its services and information:

```
                    Middlesex News

-->1. About this service
   2. About Middlesex News
   3. Tomorrow in the News (updated Mon-Fri around 6 p.m.
   4. Calendar/
   5. Movie Review/
   6. Restaurant reviews/
   7. Columns/
   8. Museums and nightclubs
   9. Government/
```

The World Software Tool & Die is a one-stop shopping place for businesses wanting to create a corporate presence on the Internet. It has created a new business for itself, and is assisting other businesses in increasing its visibility on the Internet. The Shops on The World provide a virtual storefront for subscribing businesses.

MOVING ON FROM HERE

As you can see, businesses are using the Internet in a variety of ways, and the development of the Internet system and its software will bring thousands of additional ways to use the Internet. But to maintain a good business image and access to the Internet, all businesses will need to be aware of the rules and customs of the Internet. Therefore, in the next chapter, the unique nature of the Internet will be discussed. Then, in Chapter 5, specific practical techniques for creating a business presence on the Internet will be explained in detail.

CHAPTER 4

Acceptable and Unacceptable Uses of the Internet

ACCEPTABLE USE AND ADVERTISING

There are two strong controls on the nature of advertising on the Internet: the formally written "acceptable use policies," and the informal concept of "giving back to the Internet." Understanding and following these concepts will help in building a positive image of your business on the Internet.

Acceptable Use Policies

There are about 25,000 networks connected to the Internet, and most of these have their own acceptable use policies (AUP). These are rules that must be abided by to maintain access to that network. The Internet users are expected to abide by the AUPs not only on the networkthrough which they enter the Internet, but on all of the networks through which their communications pass. In theory, this would be quite a task, since most users of the Internet aren't sure through which networks their messages are passing. In practice, there are two things that make this fairly easy to accomplish:

- Most of the AUPs are quite similar, and therefore, reading a few will give you an idea of what the most common rules are.
- Much of the Internet traffic flows through the NSF backbone system and therefore must comply with NSF's AUP, which is a rather conservative set of rules. By following the NSF's AUP you can feel relatively safe that you are complying with the other networks' AUPs.

THE NSFNET BACKBONE SERVICES ACCEPTABLE USE POLICY—1992

GENERAL PRINCIPLE:

(1) NSFNET Backbone services are provided to support open research and education in and between US research and instructional institutions, plus research arms of for-profit firms when engaged in open scholarly communication and research. Use for other purposes is not acceptable.

SPECIFICALLY ACCEPTABLE USES:

(2) Communication with foreign researchers and educators in connection with research or instruction, as long as any network that the foreign user employs for such communication provides reciprocal access to US researchers and educators.

(3) Communication and exchange for professional development, to maintain currency, or to debate issues in a field or sub-field of knowledge.

(4) Use for disciplinary-society, university-association, government-advisory, or standards activities related to the user's research and instructional activities.

Above is the current National Science Foundation's (NSF) acceptable use policy.

Under "Unacceptable Uses" is the phrase "Use for for-profit activities, unless covered by the General Principle or as a specifically acceptable use." This contains the good news and the bad news for businesses. The bad news is a very specific prohibition of for-profit activity; the good news is that for profit activities are acceptable if they relate to the "specifically acceptable" uses listed in the AUP under or the "General Principle" at the beginning of the AUP, including communication and exchange for professional development, and to debate issues in a field or subfield of knowledge.

The mid-level networks have increasingly experimented with, and developed a broader range of, "acceptable uses." This can be seen in some of their acceptable use policies. Michnet, for example, states in its AUP that "unsolicited advertising is not acceptable. Advertising is permitted on some mailing lists and newsgroups if the mailing list or newsgroup

(5) Use in applying for or administering grants or contracts for research or instruction, but not for other fund raising or public relations activities.

(6) Any other administrative communications or activities in direct support of research and instruction.

(7) Announcements of new products or services for use in research or instruction, but not advertising of any kind.

(8) Any traffic originating from a network of another member agency of the Federal Networking Council if the traffic meets the acceptable use policy of that agency.

(9) Communication incidental to otherwise acceptable use, except for illegal or specifically unacceptable use.

UNACCEPTABLE USES:

(10) Use for for-profit activities, unless covered by the General Principle or as a specifically acceptable use.

(11) Extensive use for private or personal business.

This statement applies to use of the NSFNET Backbone only. NSF expects that connecting networks will formulate their own use policies. The NSF Division of Networking and Communications Research and Infrastructure will resolve any questions about this Policy or its interpretation.

explicitly allows advertising. Announcements of new products or services are acceptable." Many other network AUPs mention that they support "economic development," but it is usually unclear how broadly they define this. JvNCnet's AUP has as a goal to "promote and facilitate innovation and regional and national competitiveness," but it is unclear whether this is in addition to, or only in support of, another goal, which is to "provide the highest quality and optimum access of networking services to the research and educational community." Because some of these statements obviously allow some business activity, and sometimes because of confusion about how to interpret some of the AUPs, businesses have developed some presence on these networks. There is considerable debate about acceptable use, and changes in the various AUPs are expected in the near future.

The real growth of businesses on the Internet, however, has come through commercial Internet access providers who offer so-called "AUP-free" access to the Internet (most actually have AUPs, but they allow commercial activities). For example, two providers, UUNET and PSInet, started offering network access to businesses and later to individuals in the late 1980s.

While these networks could offer commercial-friendly AUPs for traffic within their own network, any data transferred on the NSF backbone or through other more restrictive networks had to abide by the more restrictive rules. To avoid those restrictions, several commercial networks started transferring data directly among themselves while maintaining full access to the NSF backbone and the rest of the Internet. The Commercial Internet Exchange (CIX), a nonprofit trade association, for example, now links more than 18 commercial access providers allowing flow of "AUP-free" data, while retaining the ties to the vast research and communications links of the rest of the Internet.

Even within this commercial environment it is not acceptable to send unsolicited advertising. ANS CO+RE, for example, a provider of commercial network links, has in its AUP the statement: "Advertising may not be broadcast or otherwise sent on an intrusive basis to any user of the ANS CO+RE network or any directly or indirectly attached network."

When looking for an Internet access provider, whether for a dial-up, SLIP, or node connection, check on what the access provider's AUP says. Before starting to build an Internet business presence, you need to be sure that the Internet access provider you select has a business-friendly AUP.

"Giving Back to the Internet"

As you can see, even on the most commercially oriented networks, unsolicited advertising, or junk e-mail, is prohibited. This leaves one primary mode of advertising: attracting potential customers to connect to your virtual storefront or other online presence (Gopher site, BBS, etc.). A business can attract people to its advertisements by providing free information, databases, software, or other goods and services along with the information about its business and products.

Creating a Business Presence

Techniques for creating a business presence and attracting Internet users are discussed in Chapters 5, 11, and 12. This "giving back to the Internet" is not only a useful business practice, it is the accepted norm on the Internet. Most of the millions of files available via the Internet were offered voluntarily to the public. A business that only provides information about its company and products will be perceived very negatively—and bad PR spreads very quickly and widely on the Internet.

To keep up-to-date on attitudes on the Internet about advertising, and to contribute your own ideas to the discussion, join the Coalition for Networked Information's discussion group called cni-modernization by sending an e-mail message to **listserv@cni.org**, with the body of the message **subscribe cni-modernization** *yourfirstname yourlastname*. Two other groups that discuss these issues are **com-priv@psi.com** and **ritim-l@uriacc.uri.edu** (See Chapter 7 for instruction on joining discussion groups.)

WAYS TO GET INTO (AND STAY OUT OF) TROUBLE

As with any group or community, the Internet has some common practices, customs, conventions, and expectations. On the Internet these are often referred to as "netiquette" (net etiquette). Being aware of these will help make you look less like a "newbie" and also help in getting more and better responses to your requests for help. It is also valuable to be aware of what is considered inappropriate behavior.

Unsolicited E-Mail

Never, under any circumstances, send unsolicited e-mail to a list of Internet users. The Internet cannot be used as an alternative method of sending card decks, flyers, and other advertisements. If, however, you have a request for information about your products or company, you can respond with a "canned" e-mail advertisement. (Tips on how to get requests for your advertisements are presented in several later chapters.)

Hacking

Hacking has a variety of meanings relative to the Internet. To some, hacking is a positive activity which involves the use of software and networks in new, creative ways, or a virtuoso demonstration of technical genius (even if what was accomplished was of limited actual value). Most people, however, refer to the negative aspects of using these technical skills: gaining unauthorized entry into private computer systems, damaging computer files, software, or communications systems, or causing disruption of other network activities. Obviously, this is unacceptable activity, and will probably result in your Internet access provider dropping your account. In some situations, at state and federal levels, hacking is a crime.

Passwords and some of the strange, convoluted logins are measures taken by system administrators to protect their systems from hackers. Also, files can be protected from changes, and directories can be protected from having new files put in them by unauthorized people. Due to these various safeguards, hacking is usually not a big problem on the Internet (though each incident gets lots of publicity).

Those new to the Internet are often amazed at how many networks and computer systems *are* open to the Internet public. Unless you've played "let's try 250 passwords" to get into a system, or you see warnings that you have reached a private system not open to the public, the system is probably intended to be open to the public and you are welcome.

Overloading

The computer systems on the Internet that offer information and services to the public usually do so on a voluntary basis. These computer systems usually also have some other primary reason for being there—as campus academic and administrative computers, as corporate computer systems, as research computers, or as government agency computers. This means that many systems offer the public resources as a secondary function of their computer systems. During normal business hours these systems may be used heavily and begin to respond to their primary tasks more slowly. Despite this, most sites do not shut off the Internet community even during peak hours—but they do request that people voluntarily limit the number and length of connections during these peak hours. So far this voluntary system has worked quite well, so few system administrators have had to "pull the plug" on the Internet community.

For a business, this doesn't mean avoiding these services entirely during the day, but just doing a little planning if you have a computer-intensive or long job for the remote computer. For instance, if you are on the East Coast of the United States, you could use the services of some West Coast sites before 11 A.M. Eastern time, so you would be finished before West Coast users got to work at 8 A.M. Pacific time. Also, after 11 A.M., the workday is over in Europe, so it is a good time to connect to European sites. If your demands on the remote system are light, it is fine to connect any time, but if it is a time-consuming job, give scheduling some thought.

Opinions and Flaming

With over 9,000 discussion groups on the Internet, just about every topic imaginable (or absolutely unimaginable) is discussed. These discussions sometimes provide more heat than light. Something about the nature of the network communications seems to lead some people to lose perspective and respond in overly harsh ways (a good psychological study is to be had here). These incendiary reactions are called "flames" or "flaming" on the Internet. Some who have strong opinions but have retained perspective will, in jest, write "set flame on," then proceed to have their say, followed by the words "set flame off," just to let you know that they feel strongly about the subject, but are still open to reason. It is good for the newcomer to be aware of flaming so as not to take it too seriously—and end up responding with flames.

In addition to the normal social reasons for not flaming, there are two Internet-related reasons to limit flaming. First, your communications on discussion lists are available worldwide—whichever group, individual, or institution you are flaming is probably reading the flame. Second, most discussion groups archive (keep) their past messages so that newcomers to the discussion can see what has been going on; therefore, others may still be reading your ill-advised words worldwide, three years down the road.

When sitting alone at your computer, writing to a discussion group may give the impression of anonymity, but it may be one of the most public things you ever do.

Passwords

A password will protect your account with an Internet access provider. This is important to protect the privacy of your account; and if you pay for your account by credit card or a checking account automatic withdrawal, it will protect you from someone running up large connect time charges or using extra cost services available at your access provider's site. In addition, with access to your account, someone could post messages and send e-mail in your name in a manner that could damage your reputation, or he or she could destroy or change information that you have stored. Generally this has not been a large problem, but you can do two things to help secure your account: First, store reminders of your password in a location separate from your account's user ID and, second, change your password frequently so that if someone does get it (e.g., through some sort of hacking), he or she will have a limited time to use it.

To protect yourself from hackers, select passwords that are not real words nor anything someone who knew a little about you could guess, such as your street name, hobby, or dog's name. A string of unrelated words and numbers or misspelled words are quite secure and easy to remember (e.g., "pencil7dog" or "bwerddog").

COMPUTER-MEDIATED COMMUNICATION (CMC)

The history of the Internet, the types of people who use it, the text-based nature of much of the communication, and the unique storage, search, and retrieval system available on the Internet have led to the development of customs and characteristics unique to the Internet.

The Great Equalizer

Because a person's gender, education, age, ethnic origins, appearance, handicaps, wealth, and social situation are not readily apparent in discussions and many e-mail exchanges, the Internet has become something of a leveler. It provides access to the world of information and ideas that often ignores the social restrictions put on each of these categories.

I have, for instance, heard of people getting extensive technical help from someone, only to find out later that the help was coming from a high school student or someone totally outside the field. Alternatively, many people get individual help in answering a question, and later learn that the help came from a nationally recognized expert in that field. It is much easier on the Internet to be evaluated for what you know, rather than for who you know or who you are.

Corporate CMC

This equalizing effect carries over to some extent to communications within a corporation. People seem freer at all levels, from CEO to mailroom clerk, to join in discussions about the business. Participating in e-mail discussion groups within a company can improve the sense of participation and openness within that company—like a giant corporate watercooler that can span all sites and divisions of a company.

Smiley Faces and Other Communicons: the New Internet Punctuation

Because it is difficult for the text-based messages on the Internet to express things like humor, sarcasm, surprise, anger, or bewilderment, a variety of symbols (*communicons*—communication icons) have evolved and come into popular use. One of the first of these communicons was the "smiley face," which was a combination of a full colon and a right parenthesis :) (just tip your head to the left to view). Other communicons were developed so that the reader would better understand the intent and context of the message, and message would therefore be less likely to be taken in the wrong way (see Table 4.1).

Another shorthand way of communicating on the Internet is through a set of commonly understood abbreviations such as those in Table 4.2.

Since fonts, italics, and other ways of highlighting are generally not available in discussion groups and e-mail, several common methods of showing emphasis have evolved:

Table 4.1 Communicons

Communicon	Meaning
:)	basic smiley—an expression of good will
:-)	another basic smiley
;>	mischievous smile
:]	goofy smile
;)	wink
8-)	smile with glasses
:-l	blank look
:-o	surprise
:-O	shock
:(	frown
:-<	sad face

pseudo-underlining	Using an underline character at the beginning and at the end of a phrase to be emphasized.
asterisks emphasis	Using stars at the beginning and end of the emphasized phrase.
ALL CAPITAL LETTERS	Overuse of all capital letters annoys some people and will often solicit responses such as "quit shouting!"

Table 4.2 Commonly Used Abbreviations

Abbreviation	Meaning
<g>	grin
AKA	Also Known As
BTW	By The Way
IMHO	In My Humble Opinion
IMO	In My Opinion
LD&R	Laughing
LOL	Laughing Out Loud
OTOH	On The Other Hand
SYSOP	SYStem OPerator
TIC	Tongue In Cheek

Another aid to communications used in discussion groups are parenthetical phrases that are intended to give some perspective to the text of
the message:

```
(as I rise to the soap box...)

--Here the author of the message makes his opinions
known.--

(stepping to the side of the soapbox I wait to see who
will join me)

Or someone might write: (hiding in my bunker, I throw
out this idea), and then continue with a controversial
statement.
```

Other Characteristics of CMC

Standard post office mail (known to the Internet community as "snail
mail") has privacy protections established in law. While there are a few
laws relating to the confidentiality of private e-mail, generally the level
of privacy is determined by the trustworthiness of the computer system
administrators. Ordinarily, e-mail communications are read only by their
intended recipients, but system administrators do, in most cases, have
access to private e-mail on their systems. On a day-to-day basis, the sheer
volume of e-mail traffic provides some privacy, but matters of a highly
sensitive nature should not be transferred on the Internet without encryption or other protection.

Many sites on the Internet keep log files of who used their systems
and what documents were accessed. Primarily these log files are used for
statistical purposes, to aid in planning which computer systems resources
are to be dedicated to Internet communication, and to help figure out
what is happening in case of network problems. They do, however, create
some issues of privacy. Librarians have a tradition and, in some states,
laws that prevent anyone from getting a record of what books another
individual has checked out. Increasingly Internet sites are starting to
provide privacy protections, but this is far from the norm. In day-to-day
activity on the Internet this is a relatively minor issue—just something to
be aware of.

FROM HERE . . .

With these cautions and clues to the unique character of the Internet in
mind, move on to Chapter 5 for some examples of how to create a business
presence on the Internet.

CHAPTER 5

Techniques for Creating a Business Presence on the Internet

Using the Internet as an entrepreneurial tool is an audience participation sport—two-way communication is the valued and expected norm. Here is an appropriate Internet advertising motto for you to follow:

Think Dialog, Not Monolog. Think *Information*, Not Hype.

Acceptable use policies and current practices have made the model of top-down delivery foreign to the Internet. The Internet encourages interaction, and encourages consumers to be providers as well. The "look and feel" of the Internet is normally friendly and casual, and despite having 15 million users, there is a sense of community. On the Internet, straightforward content-rich exchanges are the norm. Marketing on the Internet must also be creative, interesting, and constantly changing because you must make your information stand out.

The virtual community of the Internet has strong opinions about how the Internet should be used. To develop and maintain a positive image and customer acceptance, businesses need to be aware of the acceptable uses and customs of the Internet (as discussed in Chapter 4). It is very helpful to use the tools of the Internet—e-mail, FTP, Gopher, discussion lists, and so on—and get a sense of what is customary before jumping in. While a positive image of a company can spread network-wide quickly, so can a negative impression. Since broadcasting of advertising is restricted on virtually all networks, the only way a marketing plan will work is if the Internet community has a good impression of, and wants to come to, your company.

The denizens of the network are vocal, and will very quickly respond negatively to hype. The Internet is not a mass market—businesses market one on one, group by group, or to temporary groupings and virtual communities. Because of its global reach, the Internet is breaking down some of the traditional market segments such as urban and rural, local and global.

This virtual community is currently text-oriented, not image- or sound-oriented like the almost content-free advertising found on TV. Traditional "in-your-face" advertising is not successful on the Internet, and in fact, such activities garner considerable bad press. On the Internet, despite the fact that there are millions of users, is a small world when it comes to bad news.

"Giving back to the Internet" is an important concept for networkers. The Internet custom is that you can market your services and products if you return something of genuine value. A similar concept is "value added" services, again pointing to the idea of an obligation to provide something to the network. These kinds of contributions are needed in order to maintain goodwill and cooperation. The Internet is a place where valuable information and assistance is routinely given freely. This freely given information accounts for the vast majority of the information available on the Internet.

Although using the Internet to promote services and products is challenging, it is well worth the effort.

MARKETING VS. ADVERTISING

Advertising as practiced for the most part these days has an "in-your-face" attitude. You are bombarded with flashing images and loud sound and music, all designed to get your attention and sell the product. Almost none of this kind of advertising is content-rich. It is this noisy, intrusive, content-free nature of advertising that makes it unwelcome on the Internet.

As viewed on the Internet, advertising is intrusive, whereas marketing can be active and discourse-based, and can provide valuable information and services as part of its efforts to sell products and services. Businesses must be seen to be contributing back to the net. The key to living comfortably with network neighbors is to observe the simple rule that solicited information is good, but unsolicited is not. Businesses for the most part have to make a paradigm shift from something highly intrusive and image-oriented to something highly content-oriented.

Perhaps the most important concept in doing business on the Internet is that unsolicited information must be subtle and unobtrusive. Information that is requested, either through e-mail or because the individual accesses your business Gopher or FTP site, is then *solicited* and may be more detailed and more promotional.

> **Unsolicited E-Mail Ads**
>
> Never send mass unsolicited e-mailings to people on the Internet. This is the quickest, surest way to get into trouble.

The coin of the realm on the Internet is information. Overt hucksterism is met with flaming e-mail and virtual raspberries: You will receive irritated, pointed, negative messages demanding that you stop what you are doing. Don't even think about mass unsolicited e-mailings to the Internet. Acceptable use prohibits this in general terms, and inhabitants of the network will not tolerate it. On the other hand, if you provide something of genuine value, you will be met with collegiality.

What is needed then is for a business to create opportunities for interaction and the exchange of information: to create a business presence and, possibly, an information service on the Internet. This can require some ongoing labor—maintaining information, sites, and a list.

MODELS FOR CREATING A BUSINESS PRESENCE ON THE INTERNET

There are numerous ways to create a business presence on the Internet, and the choice among them depends upon your business goals, your marketing plan for the Internet, and the level of market penetration you wish to achieve. Taking advantage of the size and speed of the network, commercial ventures are finding a place for themselves where they can reach customers, promote their products, and provide information to others.

There are four most common models for creating a business presence on the Internet. You may want to start with one of these approaches, and then expand to another as you become accustomed to working on the Internet and have more resources to do so.

Billboard

The Billboard model is concerned with the posting of "come-on" kinds of information for others to read and take action on. These are visible, without being too obtrusive. The object is to place a small bit of your information in view, without coming on too strong. Usually these notices are for telling others where more complete information is available. People usually put notices in the following places (these methods will be explained later in this chapter):

- plan.txt, .plan, or .profile files
- Signature blocks (or .sig)
- E-mail headers or footers
- Greeting cards

Yellow Pages

The Yellow Pages approach is concerned with providing a directory or guide to information similar to the telephone yellow pages. Essentially, you create a menu, with each item on the menu pointing toward other sources and providing small bits of information. At the top of the menu you can advertise your company's name, and one or more of the menu items could contain advertisements and information about your products. By providing directory information and a useful service, you are definitely "giving back to the net," something your potential Internet customers will appreciate. You might use this approach on:

- Gopher servers (see Chapter 10)
- BBSs (see Chapter 8)
- Usenet News (see Chapter 7)
- WorldWideWeb and Mosaic (see Chapter 10)
- WAIS (see Chapter 10)

Brochure

The Brochure approach features the provision of information sheets, brochures, and informational items. For instance, you might offer a stock market "ticker tape" or worldwide weather information to anyone who wants it. The emphasis here is on the information itself, with only a small amount of promotional material. Some of the vehicles for brochures include:

- FTP archive (see Chapter 9)
- Gopher servers (see Chapter 10)
- BBSs (see Chapter 8)
- Usenet News (see Chapter 7)
- WAIS (see Chapter 10)

- WorldWideWeb and Mosaic (see Chapter 10)
- E-mail, particularly automated reply (see Chapter 6)

Virtual Storefront

The Virtual Storefront is a full information service designed to include the marketing of your services and products, and in some cases, to allow online purchasing, customer support, and more. It combines some of the activities from all of the other models, but in a more coordinated approach. A Virtual Storefront is:

- Usually created on Gopher, either your own or using "rented space" from an Internet provider, and
- Supported by e-mail, FTP, Usenet News, and the other tools already mentioned.

Choosing a Business Model

Each of these approaches is best suited to certain kinds of business ventures. In general, the Billboard approach works best for those just starting to use the Internet for business. It is a relatively low-cost strategy (in time, effort, and money) that can place your business information in view. This is a low-key approach, suitable for those with businesses that are traditionally outside of the Internet, and does not involve offering actual products or services over the network.

The Yellow Pages approach is a middle ground of involvement. It will require a heavier investment of time and money, but will create a higher profile for the business. This approach is good for those with some Internet experience, for products or services that are ready for Internet promotion, and for those with stable Internet access. The Brochure approach is similar, but with the added requirement that you maintain a good-sized inventory of useful information pieces, product information, and so on.

The Virtual Storefront should be approached cautiously by the Internet newcomer. It requires a fairly heavy investment of time and effort. A Storefront can be fairly costly if you maintain your own dedicated line and site, but it can also be maintained on a rental basis with a full-service Internet provider. This is a sophisticated approach and will call for a more substantial investment in planning as well. It is particularly suited to businesses that are information-based.

Overall, it is best to take a modest approach initially, since mistakes are broadcast to millions of users almost instantly—it is better to start slow and build from there. Chapter 11 on will assist you in making some of these decisions.

CREATING AN INFORMATION SERVICE: IF YOU BUILD IT, THEY WILL COME

Creating a business presence on the Internet can take many forms, from small tickler announcements as part of your e-mail signature file to the creation of a full-blown information service. Many regular business marketing activities can be adapted to Internet methods.

A quick example: It is popular these days for businesses to provide information to potential customers who have circled a number on a "Bingo Card" tipped into magazines. The potential customer circles the numbers on the card, mails it off, and some six to seven weeks later, receives the information through the mail. Using a Gopher server, that same customer will receive the information by way of e-mail or a file transfer in seconds—while his or her interest is still high.

What other kinds of traditional marketing strategies can be approximated on the Internet? These are a few examples:

- Product announcements
- Product flyers or introductory information
- Product specification and data sheets
- Pricing information
- Catalogs
- Events and demos
- Free samples
- Company contacts
- Customer support
- Promotional notices of special, sales, etc.
- Documentation and manuals
- Multimedia productions
- Marketing or customer surveys and needs assessments
- Product performance data
- Service evaluations
- Reviews and product commentary
- Customer service information and functions
- Job placement or recruitment notices
- Dialog with customers and others

Figure 5.1 rates each of the Internet tools with regard to its usefulness in providing marketing information.

	E-mail	.sig	.plan	Lists	Gopher	FTP	Newsletters	WWW	WAIS
Communication	x		x	x			x	x	x
Logistics	x			x	x	x			
Globalization	x			x	x	x	x	x	x
Competitive Advantage	x	x	x	x	x	x	x	x	
Cost Containment	x			x	x	x			x
Collaboration	x			x	x	x	x	x	x
Information	x	x	x	x	x	x	x	x	x
Marketing/Sales	x	x	x	x	x		x	x	x
Data Transfer	x		x		x	x	x	x	x

Figure 5.1 Internet Tools.

Some Internet Resources for Creating a Business Presence

Creating your own business presence on the Internet is a multifaceted undertaking. It can involve almost every Internet tool, but can also be based on a more modest approach, depending upon your resources and marketing plan.

E-Mail

E-mail is perhaps the most important tool for reaching out on the Internet to market services and products, or just to get your business some publicity. In addition to being the ubiquitous communication tool of the Internet, it provides quick and easy ways to work with people and information. Some businesses and customers do not have access to full Internet services, so e-mail may be the only way of reaching them electronically.

Advertising Your E-Mail Address

Always put your e-mail address on all electronic and nonelectronic communications; put it on your business card, stationery, catalogs, ads, and all your e-mail.

In addition to traditional e-mail, most mail programs allow you to set up an automated reply mailbox, which will send out standard information in reply to a request for information. The addresses for automated reply mailboxes look something like this: **info@whippet.com**, or **info-request@whippet.com.** Replies to these mailboxes are automatically generated by the mail program, which grabs the sender's e-mail address and mails out a reply with a message you have stored for this purpose. Reply mailboxes need little human attention once they are set up. These mailboxes addresses might appear in a .sig file such as:

```
[[[[[[[[[[[[[[[[[[[[[[[[[=====]]]]]]]]]]]]]]]]]]]]]]]]]]]
[  Claire Fincher              Purebred Whippets   ]
[  Contact me for more information about Whippets   ]
[  1-555-555-555                 info@whippet.com   ]
[[[[[[[[[[[[[[[[[[[[[[[[[=====]]]]]]]]]]]]]]]]]]]]]]]]]]]
```

They also can be configured to store the address of the sender so you can follow up on the lead. Most mailers (mail software) can create a distribution mailing list through the use of address books or of group aliases. You can then create listserv-like e-mail "exploders" in order to set up your own discussion list, either for inside personnel working on a project together or for interested others. It is increasingly common to see notices like this included in both electronic customer information and paper-based materials

```
+++++++++++++++++++++++++++++++++++++++++++++++++++++++++
        Customer Relations Representatives
        If you have a questions, e-mail us!

                --------

    John Jones all products          jones@steel.com
    Mary Smith all queep products    smith@steel.com
    Bob James  all poketa products   james@steel.com
+++++++++++++++++++++++++++++++++++++++++++++++++++++++++
```

MIME (Multipurpose Internet Mail Extensions), which is now part of some mailer programs (such as Pine), allows you to e-mail even binary data such as image, word processing, or spreadsheet files. MIME is becoming more common, so you can expect that the uses of e-mail will expand.

Signature Blocks or .sig Files

Signature blocks, also called .sig ("dot sig") files are very short attachments or preformatted areas at the end of e-mail messages and Usenet postings designed to identify you. They should be limited to five or six lines at most, or you will risk getting flamed—also, some mailers will truncate these files if they are attachments. At least include your name and e-mail address, but you can also include an institutional or business affiliation, a "snail-mail" address, and/or a telephone number. Business users often include a small "ad," composed of a line or two of information on their product or services, such as "contact **mary-jones@starcomp.com** for information on CAD peripherals." Some .sigs even have a small embedded corporate logo.

Here are some examples of .sig files containing business information:

```
Vern Matthews      vmatthews@genes.hybrid.com          (__)
Hybrid Genetic Engineering Corporation                (oo)
Research Park                              /-------\/
E. Lansing, Michigan                      / |      ||
                                      *   ||----||
Contact me about do-it-yourself kits.      ^^      ^^
```

```
+=-=-=-=-=-=-=-=-=-=-=-=-=-=-=-=-=-=-=-=-=-=-=-=-=-=-=+
Harrison Wilson  TECHNOLOGY COMMUNICATIONS   HW@saturn.tc.com
Phone:555-555-5555    Cell:555-555-5555     FAX:555-555-5555
Are you looking for Communication Business Consulting?
We can provide a wide range of services.  info@jupiter.tc.com

+=-=-=-=-=-=-=-=-=-=-=-=-=-=-=-=-=-=-=-=-=-=-=-=-=-=-=+
```

```
****************************************   Drew Hardy
* ARE YOU LOOKING FOR A DATACRUNCHER? *   Marketing
*       I've got lots of experience.  *   HAL International
* Finger drew@dave.hal.com to see     *   Nederwald, IN
* my resume, or e-mail me for a copy. *   555/555-5555
****************************************
```

Each mailer program will support different methods for inserting these at the end of e-mail and Usenet messages. Before constructing your own .sig, look at examples from the discussion lists and from Usenet postings for ideas and for getting a sense of the discussion list and group norms.

Using Listservs

Listservs are popular for the distribution of information and the discussion of issues related to businesses. (You can find out more about these in Chapter 7.) The lists are a method for maintaining discussions and group conferencing, since they take each message and send it to all members automatically.

Some lists have been started to discuss a subject or product of interest, such as the new Soviet Union, polymers, or WordPerfect. The number of existing lists is in excess of 3,500, and like everything else on the Internet, that number is growing. Many companies have started discussion lists focusing on their industries as a way to invite discussion of important issues, government regulations, technologies, techniques, and so on. Some have even started lists focusing on a particular product.

Usually, individuals join lists of interest, both personal and professional, as a way of keeping up to date, taking the pulse of the industry, or just exchanging ideas. The best way to use lists for marketing is for marketing research and for making product announcements on appropriate lists that permit such announcements. Use caution in posting to new lists—you are better off maintaining an active membership before sending an announcement out. For example, an announcement like this would be generally well tolerated on a list with some kind of MIS focus:

```
**************** NEW BOOK ANNOUNCEMENT ****************
************** From Churchill Publishers **************
******* MANAGEMENT INFORMATION AND THE INTERNET: *******
******************* TOWARDS 2001 *******************

               edited by
      David Simmons, HAL Computer Corporation

Table of Contents and Order Form are attached below.

More information, including Preface, can be obtained via
   anonymous FTP from 2000.hal.com in the directory
         simmons/books as 2000.txt or 2000.ps
```

Usually an announcement like this will be 20–40 lines or so, and might, as in this case, include the Table of Contents, and—here is the angle—a handy e-mail order form. In addition to a single announcement to a few appropriate mailing lists, it is common for publishers to include a free chapter or section via the FTP site. Product specifications, for example, could be made available at an FTP site.

Active participation on appropriate lists can give your business good Internet visibility if you spend the time to make a useful contribution to the list with thoughtful postings. Remember to use a .sig mentioning your business and e-mail address.

To effectively use the mailing lists, it is important to sample many lists before deciding on a few to be an active participant. After you sign up for a list, all messages sent from the list will start arriving—as many as 30 or more a day for a high-volume list, a few messages a month for a low-volume list. Remember, many lists prohibit advertising, but will tolerate the short signature. Some interesting mailing lists are identified in Chapter 12, and information on subscribing to lists is found in Chapter 7.

Plan.txt, .plan, and .profile Files

Many sites connected to the Internet allow other users to obtain a small file of information about you by using a utility called "finger." If you finger someone's account, almost immediately you will receive back some information about that individual or business. Often this information will tell you the account owner's name ("real name"), login name, whether the account has mail waiting, and the time of last login. For example, finger **drew@dave.hal.com** would look for a user named Drew at the machine named dave at HAL Corporation.

Many businesspeople create a file to be sent with this basic information called a *plan file*, or *plan.txt file*, or *.plan* (said "dot plan") or *.profile*, depending upon the software. Job hunters have been known to put their whole resumes in their plan files; others put price lists or corporate information. A sample plan file might look like this (where the first three lines are automatically provided by finger):

```
-User--Real Name--------------------------------
drew    Drew Allen Arkins   Last Login Fri 6-May
10:01 AM from netnet.com

Plan:
        ***DAA and Associates Internet Training Services***

We specialize in services to small and medium sized
businesses who want to provide employee training on the use
of the Internet. We offer both on- and off-site training
with small classes, or on an individualized basis.

DAA and Associates is a group of 9 trainers with combined
expertise in all facets of the Internet. The DAA team can
help you.

*On Site Training: $500.00 per day, plus travel and
expenses for three trainers

*At our headquarters in San Francisco, $300.00 per day

Call 555/555-5555 for more information or e-mail me at
drew@dave.hal.com, FAX 555/555-5555
```

This kind of plan file provides information about the business, a little price information, and more about how to contact the business. The following plan file is more specific, and is basically a price list of specials.

```
              THE DYNAMIC COMPUTER EQUIPMENT CORPORATION^
                              17554 IH - 35 ACCESS^
                              SPRING, OKLAHOMA 12345^
     Voice: (555) 555-5555   (days, nights or weekends)^
                              FAX:    (555) 555-5555^
                              terry@sooner.dcec.com^


     ----------------------------------------------------------


     * NOTE: Some prices are dependent upon foreign suppliers,
     or on market prices so E-mail for a custom quote. Ask
     about any items that you don't see listed *

     %%% SPECIALS FOR JUNE %%%   June   %%% SPECIALS FOR JUNE %%%
     486-60hz CPU Heat Sink Fans                    Only $ 18!
     4Mb VESA Local Bus 24-bit SVGA Video Card      Only $195!
     Sound Galaxi BXII (100% Blaster Compatible)    Only $ 65!
     Pongate 3390A FASTEST 340Mb DRIVE              ONLY $300!
     Eastern Digital 340Mb IDE Hard Drive,3yr warranty ONLY $275!
```

Some finger files are designed to be news updates on products, people, and so on. These plan files are requested, so they may have more specific information and promotionally oriented material. Most individuals mention that the plan file is available via finger in their signature, in newsletters, or in most documents that they distribute. There are some animated finger files that can be constructed on UNIX machines. Check with your user services contact (often called in jest "sys$gods") to discuss the use of a plan file.

Greeting Cards

Greeting cards are relatively new, but are often considered just a variation on an e-mail message. Some companies are using them as mailings to current customers. They should not be sent out to individuals who do not already have a relationship with your business, but depending upon the content, they can be mentioned in a .sig file. Greeting cards usually look something like this:

```
         Grandstaff, Fincher and Harrison, Esq.
                   Attorneys-At-Law
       Wishing You a Happy and Prosperous New Year


              You are cordially invited
          to a Holiday reception at our Chicago offices
```

Friday December 31, 1994 from 6 to 8 P.M.

R.S.V.P. rsvp@lawlook.com

We will be upgrading our LawLook System in January
Request information from upgrade@lawlook.com

Gopher

Gopher is a system with menus of documents, images, software, and other material, and menus leading to other menus and resources. This system allows for searching, viewing, downloading, and e-mailing of files. Gopherspace—that is, the global collection of files available to Gopher servers—can be searched using a utility called Veronica, either by filename or by menu entry. (Gopher and Veronica are discussed more fully in Chapter 10.) Gopher is easy to use and by far the most popular and full-blown of the tools for creating a business presence on the Internet. The estimated growth rate for Gophers in 1993 was 997 percent.

Many businesses are setting up their own Gopher menus through their own sites or through one of the Internet access providers that will allow you to "rent" space on their Gophers. Pointers to your information are set up, allowing users throughout the world to access the items you have made available. The information can include product information, brochures, surveys, up-to-date price lists, catalogs, images, even binary files of software. Many sites provide sample products, services such as Usenet or Clarinet, access to other Gophers, and full text of important documents.

Below is a sample Gopher menu, from O'Reilly and Associates:

```
             O'Reilly & Associates (computer book publisher)


    1.   About O'Reilly & Associates.
    2.   News Flash! -- New Products and Projects/
    3.   Product Descriptions/
    4.   Ordering/
    5.   Complete Listing of Titles.
    6.   FTP Archive and Email Information/
    7.   Errata for "Learning Perl".
    8.   Bibliographies/
    9.   Feature Articles/
```

This is their root menu, with access to information about O'Reilly, a news flash of new products and projects, various detailed product descriptions, ordering information, information on titles, bibliographies, and full text of feature articles. Choosing item 2 brings up the next menu:

```
News Flash! -- New Products and Projects

   1. ORA T-Shirts Now Available.
   2. Software Development Conference and Exposition--San Jose.
   3. UniForum Conference and Exhibition--San Francisco.
   4. Beta Release of ViolaWWW.
   5. GNN's Education Issue Hits the Stand.
   6. System Administrator Openings.
   7. New Credit Card Ordering Number: 800-889-8969.
```

This menu outlines both products and information, from a T-shirt to a beta release of software. In addition, employment, conference, and ordering information have been placed on this menu. Following through the menus to the item called new books reveals:

```
An O'Reilly Buyer's Guide

   1.  Book Description and Information.
   2.  Table of Contents.
   3.  Book Cover [40k] <Picture>
   4.  Quotes and Reviews.
```

In this menu, there are choices for a full book description, a table of contents, reviews of the book, and a .GIF format picture of the book cover—a clever way of making sure that you can spot the book in the bookstore.

This is a virtual storefront, where each menu can be explored to locate information, opportunities, and products. O'Reilly & Associates is a leading publisher of books on UNIX, in business since 1978. It began as a technical writing consulting business, and started publishing books in 1985 with a series of "Nutshell Handbooks," later moving into full-fledged computer book publishing.

Now, it has created a very substantial Internet presence with a Usenet newsgroup, the Global Network Navigator, and this Gopher. O'Reilly has a full electronic store and information service. In addition to its Gopher, it offers program source codes at its FTP site, and provides electronic product updates.

In addition, O'Reilly's WorldWideWeb has a publishing activity called the Global Network Navigator (GNN). GNN is an interactive guide to the Internet that is part electronic magazine, part electronic catalog, and part field guide. The key feature is an expanded online version of the catalog section of *The Whole Internet User's Guide and Catalog* by Ed Krol, which locates information resources by category. Get information by e-mail from **info@gnn.com** or on its Gopher.

Using FTP to Create a Business Presence on the Internet

Many businesses are using an anonymous FTP site to provide information, product descriptions, price list updates, news releases, catalogs, demos, text files, and executable software files and demos for customer use. These archives are publicly accessible using the anonymous FTP protocol described in Chapter 9.

Users can FTP to your business archive site, look around a little, and download files (both ASCII and binary). Many businesses put a "banner" at the top of their listing to welcome you and give a bit of information about the archive. A typical listing might look like this one from The World Software Tool & Die:

```
FTP.STD.COM>
<Hello!
<
<This is the anonymous FTP area for world.std.com, a public
<access Unix system. Accounts directly on the system are
<available via telnet or direct-dial (617-739-9753, 8N1, V.32bis
<(14.4K), V.32 (9600), 2400, etc.), login as new (no password)
<to create an account. Accounts are charged at $5/mo+$2/hr or
<$20/20hrs/month, your choice. Grab the details in the
<world-info directory here if interested.
<
<<Please read the file README
<  it was last modified on Wed Apr 21 12:46:51 1993-329 days ago
<Guest login ok, access restrictions apply.
FTP.STD.COM>dir
<Opening ASCII mode data connection for /bin/ls.
total 388
-rw-r--r--  1 0      daemon 145157  May 28  1992 .find.codes
drwx------  2 114    daemon    512  Mar 15  1993 .obs
drwxr-xr-x  9 0      daemon    512  Feb 11 23:19 AW
drwxr-xr-x  7 2391   2391      512  Feb 28 17:37 Kluwer
drwxr-xr-x  3 0      daemon    512  Feb 11 22:32 OBS
drwxr-xr-x  5 1650   1650      512  Mar 11 16:25 Quantum
drwxrwxr-x  2 112    daemon    512  Jan 21 20:01 RAT-archive
-rw-rw-r--  1 0      src      1739  Apr 21  1993 README
drwxrwsr-x  2 1965   1965      512  Dec  3 14:36 SoFTPro
drwxrwxr-x  2 108    10        512  Feb 25 19:14 WWW
drwxrwxr-x  7 103    10        512  Aug 14  1993 amo
```

```
drwxrwxr-x  3 108    10         512 Oct 18 23:15 archives
lrwxrwxrwx  1 0      0            7 Mar 15 21:56 bcs -> amo/bcs
dr-xr-xr-x  2 0      daemon     512 Mar 16 03:52 bin
lrwxrwxrwx  1 0      0            8 Mar 15 21:56 bmug -> amo/bmug
drwxrwxr-x  4 103    10         512 Nov  1 22:30 consultants
drwxr-xr-x  2 0      0          512 Mar 15 21:25 customers
drwxrwxr-x 19 0      daemon     512 Feb 10 22:45 gopherdir
drwxrwxr-x  2 0      src        512 Nov 10  1992 info-futures
```

`<Transfer complete.`

This shows the opening banner, which is, in effect, a short ad for The World telling you to how to obtain an account. You can then ask for a directory listing of the files and subdirectories. (For more information on how to decipher this directory listing, see Chapter 7 on FTP.) There are sections, for example, on getting information on The World (*world-info*), public files (*pub*), periodicals, the Online Book Initiative (*obi*), and consultants. Under the periodicals subdirectory is a joint project with a local (traditional, paper-based) newspaper:

```
FTP.STD.COM>cd periodicals
<CWD command successful.
FTP.STD.COM>dir
<Opening ASCII mode data connection for /bin/ls.
total 52
drwxrwxr-x  11 1039  1039     512 Nov  5 21:49 Middlesex-News
drwxrwxr-x   9 2354  2354     512 Feb  9 21:19 Network-World
drwxrwxr-x   2 4766  4766   24576 Mar 16 03:17 rachel
<Transfer complete.
```

Further information is located in the next directory down:

```
FTP.STD.COM>cd Middlesex-News
<CWD command successful.
FTP.STD.COM>dir
<Opening ASCII mode data connection for /bin/ls.
total 26
drwxr-xr-x  2 1039  1039    512 Oct 18 16:09 .cap
-rw-r--r--  1 1039  1039   1997 Sep  2  1993 About_the_Middlesex_News
-rw-r--r--  1 1039  1039    339 Sep  2  1993 About_this_service
drwxr-xr-x  4 1039  1039    512 Sep 15  1993 Government
drwxr-xr-x  2 1039  1039    512 Sep  2  1993 MetroWest_Organizations
drwxr-xr-x  2 1039  1039    512 Sep  2  1993 Museums_and_nightclubs
drwxr-xr-x  3 1039  1039    512 Nov  2 22:29 calendar
```

```
drwxr-xr-x  8 1039  1039   512 Oct  7 17:36 columns
drwxr-xr-x  3 1039  1039   512 Oct 20 18:35 history
drwxr-xr-x  3 1039  1039  1024 Nov  5 18:21 movies
drwxr-xr-x  3 1039  1039   512 Nov  5 16:30 restaurant-reviews
-rw-r--r--  1 1039  1039   745 Nov 10 22:38 tomorrow
<Transfer complete.
```

You can then get files related to various of the subjects presented: calendars, columns, movies, tomorrow's headlines, and more.

The World maintains a Gopher, and this FTP archive supports that effort, and also allows any user to get a wealth of information both related and unrelated to the services that The World provides. The World assists businesses by renting space on its Gopher menus and FTP archives, and offers a corporate mailbox option (so that you too can look like a node). Information about this option is under the *world-info* subdirectory.

FTP sites are searchable using a utility called archie, which is described in Chapter 10. archie lets you search for files by name worldwide.

Newsletters and 'Zines

Electronic newsletters are used by businesses to provide information of all kinds to current and potential customers. These are usually targeted at a particular audience as a paper-based newsletter would be. As with traditional paper-based newsletters, the contents are a mix of articles about the business itself and other articles and information to keep the reader's attention. Successful Internet newsletters have a high percentage of information, articles, and features, and less advertising (high signal-to-noise ratio). The ease of purchasing by e-mail and Gopher makes these powerful sales vehicles. Most newsletters are distributed upon request through e-mail, listservs, or Gophers. Many are archived at FTP sites. Some newsletters are redistributed on Usenet or network information mailing lists.

Electronic 'zines are creative, small, often experimental magazines. A few companies have created 'zines in order to grab attention, particularly in industries that are on the creative cutting edge and want to be a bit *avant-garde*. Some businesses underwrite a newsletter and thus get a free blurb in each issue, something like:

```
Newsbytes is sponsored by TechnoWoofer Inc.
TechnoWoofer is a major producer of speech recognition hardware.
1/555-555-5555. info@bark.woofer.com.
```

The Library of Congress now issues International Standard Serial Numbers (ISSN) to electronic publications intending to publish on a regular basis. Telnet to **locis.loc.gov** and log in as **marvel** to get more information on this. (See Chapter 8 on how to use Telnet.)

Usenet Newsgroups

Usenet newsgroups are sometimes confused with the Internet itself, since they are distributed to so many sites. These newsgroups are just one application running on the network. Usenet is a distributed messaging interchange focused on topics. The groups number in the thousands, and range from the practical to the esoteric.

One business person wrote recently on the network: "I don't advertise, I post to Usenet." The newsgroups are very active venues for the exchange of ideas and information. These are very fluid, with some groups having hundreds of postings a day.

On Usenet, you will find numerous small to medium product announcements, press releases, and many signatures with business information. Under the *alt.* and *biz.* categories you will find commercial groups. Some companies such as Zeos and O'Reilly have created their own newsgroups. Each newsgroup has its own charter, so be sure to check for commercial or business restrictions. This is a sampling of the business-related groups available for exploration:

alt.business.misc

alt.business.multi-level

biz.americast

biz.americast...

biz.americast.samples

biz.books.technical

biz.books...

biz.clarinet

biz.clarinet...

biz.comp...

biz.comp.telebit

biz.comp.telebit.netblazer

biz.config

biz.control

biz.dec

biz.dec...

biz.dec.ip

biz.dec.workstations

biz.digex...

biz.jobs...

biz.jobs.offered

biz.misc

biz.next...

biz.oreilly...

biz.oreilly.announce

biz.pagesat

biz.pagesat...

biz.sco...

biz.stolen

biz.tadpole...

biz.test

biz.univel...

biz.zeos

biz.zeos...

misc.entrepreneurs

Some newsgroups are moderated, while others are not. Moderated groups are monitored by group administrator, who will, in some cases, screen posts for excessive flaming and appropriateness of content. Unmoderated groups are those where every message is posted as is—no changes.

Usenet is popular for postings of business networking opportunities, and there are opportunities to form business partnerships through the groups. For example:

```
Article #1119 (2045 is last):
Newsgroups: biz.comp.hardware
From: Alexandr Stepanovich <commerce@volga.compusoft.su>
Subject: Am looking for business partner in America
Date: Thu May 26 01:37:23 1994


Greetings to all BizNetters!


I have a really good firm from Moscow, Russia and am
looking for business partners in America.
```

```
We want to resell in Russia low-cost computer parts and
systems like 486/P2 motherboards, SIMM 4M & 8M, sound
cards, sVGA cards, hard drives & streamers, sVGA
monitors, high speed modems, 386 and 486 notebooks,
CDROMs, software under Unix, OS/2 and MS Windows, MS
Windows NT and so on. Used equipment will be good too.

At first sales volume can be $20,000 per month.
Please send us your suggestions.

Alexandr Stepanovich
<stephanov@volga.compusoft.su>
Director, CompuSoft Computing Equipment

FTP compusoft.su
voice 7-555-5555555 10:00-16:00 Moscow time
```

On most *biz.* groups, it is common to see price lists, brochures, product announcements, and all kinds of business-related information posted if those groups allow those postings.

```
Newsgroups: biz.comp.hardware,biz.comp.software
From: csquare@lobby.computersquare.com
Subject: Pricing on BNE products
Reply-To: gstone@office.computersquare.com
Date: Sat Sep 17 06:17:44 1994

NOTICE!!!!!!!!!!!!!!!!!!!!!!!!!!!!!!!!!!!!!!!!!!!!!!

Computer Square is pleased to announce significant price
reductions on BNE products currently in our warehouse.
We are offering a 25% automatic markdown for all
individuals who mention this ad in their price query.
Tell them you saw it on biz. Call our toll free order
line at 555-555-5555, or e-mail your query to
info@office.computersquare.com to get further ordering
information, or send it directly to me. George.
```

WorldWideWeb (WWW) and Mosaic

Both of these technologies are based on hypertext linkages. They allow you to browse Internet information, following up on items of interest. Many parts of each are "still under construction," but they are rapidly expanding.

Many businesses are creating documents with the HyperText Markup Language (HTML) so that WWW and Mosaic searches can find and use their documents. WWW is largely text-based, but some browsers such as Lynx can display the images and play the sound files. Mosaic is a graphical front end for these searches, and provides online images and sound to accompany formatted documents.

To provide information using WWW and Mosaic, you must create your documents with links and use a WWW server. This requires some higher-quality Internet access, and at present is not possible through non-SLIP dial-up. Some Internet providers are "renting" WWW space and services. For more information on WWW, Mosaic, and Lynx, see Chapter 10.

Wide Area Information Servers (WAIS)

WAIS is a distributed text-based tool which will let you search through Internet archives for articles containing groups of words. The system is based on the Z39.50 standard. Businesses are running WAIS servers with information on products and services. The information is indexed, using software called waisindex, and allows others to use your indexing to locate the information. WAIS is a relatively new Internet tool. More information on WAIS can be found in Chapter 10.

TIME, EFFORT, AND MONEY

These methods vary in their relative need for human and capital investment. The creation of .sig and .plan files requires little initial investment, and almost no ongoing maintenance. A couple of hours of planning and design with your .sig and .plan file is all that is needed. Once you have created the .sig file, just attach it to all your e-mail and you are up and running. A .plan file, once created in your account, is available to anyone who seeks it, and requires no further effort. Both kinds of files should be monitored for revisions when needed, but they are definitely low-cost/low-maintenance options.

Using discussion lists and Usenet newsgroups for *participation* will take some time and effort. You must read your e-mail frequently and take the time to respond in ways that benefit your business. Time and effort go into thoughtful participation, and in the placement of announcements. Depending on the level of participation, this could mean between 5 and 15 hours of effort a week.

To "own" or moderate a list or a newsgroup is a much more substantial commitment, usually requiring 20 hours a week or more depending upon the size and activity level of the list or group. To moderate a list or group also requires learning the software and locating a site for your list or group. Your local systems manager can help you set up a list on your site, or you can purchase services from your Internet access provider.

Making information available through Gopher, Telnet, FTP, WWW, and so on, requires a substantial investment in the planning, monitoring, and creation of materials. The materials must be kept current. If you provide feedback options, there is the need for a commitment to timely response, or you will defeat your purpose. After up-front development, these options typically require 5–6 hours of time a week in information maintenance, and another 5–20 hours of e-mail and request processing. Of course, this number could skyrocket if your efforts are attractive to customers!

Making use of an Internet access provider, setting up your information on existing servers such as Gopher, FTP, WWW varies tremendously in its costs. Some sites provide modest access to all of these resources for little more than disk storage fees ($5.00 a month), while others charge ten times that amount, and have development and one-time charges. Like anything else, the more you want to do with these tools, the more it will cost. Information about costs, both initial and ongoing, is best sought as part of your research for chosing service providers.

Setting up your own node and running your own server for Gopher, WWW, FTP, and so on is a big undertaking. The initial costs of equipment, configuration, and training are considerable, and these servers require monitoring and maintenance. This requires considerable technical know-how and, typically, a company planning for this large an investment hires a consultant to work with it in its planning and implementation.

Chapters 11 and 12 can assist you in creating your marketing plan using these tools.

UNDER CONSTRUCTION

There are some Internet tools that have yet to be fully utilized for businesses because they are relatively new and/or take considerable bandwidth (network resources) to use. Creatively used, one of these might prove to be the perfect vehicle for your business:

- IRC—Internet Relay Chat allows for real-time interactive text-based "conversations" where all parties are online together. This means that a business could directly interact with customers and potential customers, or provide an online expert to answer questions. Delphi recently began offering IRC to its subscribers.

- ITR—Internet Talk Radio from Carl Malmud uses direct linkages to the Internet to broadcast digital audio. Businesses could "broadcast" information with an advertising slant, provide added value by doing interviews, and so on.

- MUD—Multi-User Dialog/Dimension/Dungeons are text-based virtual environments allowing several individuals to interact in real time. Currently, these are often used for games. TinyMUD is used for social gatherings. These and other virtual environments will provide almost endless opportunities for businesses to create an entire community, store, or setting for customers to browse.

- MOO—MUD Object Oriented is a MUD based on an object-oriented language, and offers a richer experience than MUD.

- MUSE—Multi-User Simulation Environment is a facility that combines elements of Internet Relay Chat and role-playing games. Users create their own virtual reality, or can participate in existing scenarios. Currently this is being used for K–12 education, but it has possibilities for use by businesses.

- Mosaic/WorldWideWeb—Hypertext-based browsers are the fastest growing tools on the Internet. Businesses find them particularly attractive because they can provide an audio/visual approach to their materials, more familiar to them from the world of television and radio. (See Chapter 10 for more information on WWW and Mosaic.)

- Virtual reality—On the Internet, virtual reality will offer almost endless opportunities for customer interaction and enjoyment. Businesses can let customers try out a product, visit a virtual store, or play an adventure game.

WHERE FROM HERE?

As you can see, using the Internet to create a business presence can take many forms, from simple e-mail signatures to virtual storefronts. If you are new to the Internet, Chapters 6–10 will explain how to use the most popular Internet tools. If you already have mastered the Internet tools such as e-mail, Gopher, Telnet, and FTP, you can skip to Chapter 12, which will describe in detail some resources for doing business on the Internet, and then to Chapter 13 for information on specific online databases and libraries.

Internet Tools and Resources

CHAPTER 6

Electronic Mail

Electronic mail (e-mail) is the most popular of the Internet tools. It is also the easiest to use, and the most frequently used by businesses. It is the key Internet resource for most people, and may be the first reason for a business to get connected. E-mail is used for:

- Sending single or multiple messages to individuals.
- Sending single or multiple messages to several individuals, or to groups of associated users.
- Sending text files.
- Sending binary items (such as a spreadsheet or graphics).
- Distributing electronic newsletters, flyers, and magazines.
- Broadcasting notices or updates to a group of individuals.

I typically receive 80–100 e-mail messages a day. They include messages from various discussion lists that I have joined related to professional and personal interests. They also include communications with colleagues and companies that I am working with on a variety of projects. Other messages come from graduate students in the classes that I teach and from friends and relatives around the country.

OVERVIEW

In the electronic maze of the Internet, e-mail is perhaps the most facile tool for the business user to access and utilize in corporate communication. In addition, it is available on the greatest variety and number of computing systems, including commercial services. E-mail, like its counterpart, postal mail (often called "snail mail" on the Internet), can be used to send all manner of letters and documents.

It can be used to exchange not only messages, but almost any material that can be stored electronically on a computer. It makes the distribution of material to individuals or groups easy, and allows for impromptu, ad hoc group conferencing and working groups, making it a powerful tool for business and corporate users. It is also an increasingly popular format for customer feedback and technical support.

There are numerous advantages to e-mail communication:

- E-mail is fast: Messages are often delivered in minutes, as opposed to weeks in parts of Europe or months in parts of Central Asia and Africa when using "snail mail." You can exchange numerous messages in the time it would take to send one piece of mail via the post office or even via one of the express document delivery services. In fact, during times of low message traffic, delivery takes just a few seconds. If, by chance, the recipient of the message happens to be online at the time that your message is received, a response may be back in just minutes.

- Messages can often be sent for less that the cost of a first-class stamp, and with most Internet providers, the cost is the same for a message going across the street as for one to the far side of the world. With many Internet access providers, after you pay a monthly fee, all e-mail messages are free.

- E-mail is convenient, since mail can be read and sent at work, home, anywhere, and at any time that a computer can be hooked up to a phone line. Business travelers find this particularly useful.

- Because e-mail has become popular, many individuals are including their e-mail addresses on their business cards, letterheads, promotional pieces, and other communications.

You should be aware of some further characteristics of e-mail:

- E-mail is not a fully secure medium. Unlike postal mail, your messages can be read by others, such as system administrators or individuals with access authority, either intentionally or unintentionally. The confidentiality of the postal and telephone systems is established in law, but that of e-mail is still in flux. While this is not a big problem on the Internet, you can't assume confidentiality, so exercise caution in sending certain financial, personnel, or proprietary information. Encryption is a hot topic on the Internet, and you can expect new protocols and algorithms to be available in the near future which will make e-mail more secure and useful. A new version of the Mosaic software, for instance, has encryption built in.

- E-mail is a form of asynchronous communication: Information does not flow in both directions at once as it does in a telephone conversation. As with postal mail, a "conversation" is made up of a series of messages and replies. This asynchronous method makes communication across time zones much easier. E-mail, however, combines advantages of synchronous and asynchronous systems: Like letters, e-mail messages can be composed, sent, and read at any convenient time and at many locations; and, as on the telephone, messages travel quickly (sometimes they are delivered within seconds).

- The formality of e-mail varies according to your purpose. Some messages are very informal, and some emulate "snail mail" by having a letterhead and using formal formats, styles, and language.

- E-mail messages may be fugitive unless you make a point of downloading and saving them. Some mainframe systems, access providers, and mailer software will even delete messages if they are left in the electronic in- or out-box too long.

UNDERSTANDING E-MAIL ADDRESSES

To use e-mail, you need an account from an Internet access provider or from your company, and a computer address. That is to say, an e-mailbox is needed—a "place" to send and receive e-mail. Addresses for e-mail are like postal addresses in some ways. For example, a postal address might look like this:

John Grandstaff
New York Stock Exchange
Wall Street
New York, NY 12345

Via the Internet, John Grandstaff's address might be something like this:

jgrandstf@nyse.sec.com.

An Up-Close Look at Internet Addresses

The actual name of your correspondent has almost nothing directly to do with the automated network routing of the e-mail message—all of the routing information is embedded in the address itself. E-mail is called a *store and forward system* because it moves through the Internet by leaps and bounds, guided by the information in the header. Internet addresses typically have a form that looks like this:

m_smith@jupiter.cedar.com

You don't need to fully understand the components of Internet addresses to use them, but by learning about the components you will be better able to figure out things about the addressee and to handle errors or e-mailing problems that come up now and then. Here's a breakdown of the components of this sample address:

- **m_smith** This is the individual's name as known to the local computer that collects and processes his or her e-mail. Some systems allow users to use full first and last names, others confine the user to cryptic names such as **msmit01**. In all cases, however, there are no spaces allowed, so the underline or dash character is often used instead of a space. You will see syntax like this: **digi_com** or **oakridge-com**.

- **@jupiter** Like pets, ships, and big buildings, computers on the Internet have names. This is the name of the computer that collects m_smith's e-mail. In other words, m_smith is @ (at) jupiter.

- **.cedar** This represents the name of a group of computers (of which jupiter is one) that are connected together and operated by a group or organization. Often, computers in a cluster have related names, like saturn, mars, and pluto. (Or pluto, goofy, and mickey!)

- **.com** Within the United States, a three-letter designator usually identifies the type of Internet user. Table 6.1 shows Internet user types.

In addresses outside of the United States this three-letter domain name is usually replaced by a two-letter country designator. Some are easy to figure out, like .fr for France or .uk for United Kingdom, but some are more obscure, like .za for South Africa or .pn for Pitcairn Island.

Notice that the computer group name and the user type (or country code) are each preceded by a single period (usually said "dot"). Notice too, that the address is given in lowercase. Most systems on the Internet are case-insensitive for Internet traffic, though not all. It is best to observe carefully the case of any address you receive from others (for example, from the header of their message to you) but generally, using lowercase will work with most sites.

Return to Sender, Address Unknown

Just as with a phone number or a zip code, one wrong letter or number in an e-mail address could send your company's spreadsheet to someone who shouldn't have it, or could result in a "bounced message" returned to your e-mail box because it couldn't be delivered.

Table 6.1 Internet User Types

Abbreviation	Type
.com	Business and commercial users
.org	Organizations and nonprofit groups
.mil	Military-related groups
.gov	Nonmilitary government and related groups
.edu	Educational institutions
.net	Network providers

BITNET addresses have fewer elements, and might look like this: **jgrandstf@nyse.bitnet**. BITNET addresses are used almost exclusively for educational entities, and so they are rarely seen in the world of business. An individual may have several addresses: local, Internet, and BITNET. Obtain information on your own address from your corporate computer user services department or from your commercial service provider.

There are numerous conventions for mail addressing to commercial, European, and Asian sites which involve many other symbols and signs, leading Brendan Kehoe in *Zen and the Art of the Internet* to call this addressing "the symbolic cacophony." Some networks use exclamation marks (!), called "bangs," in their addresses. Information on the more unusual addressing schemes can be found in *!%@:: A Directory of Electronic Mail Addresses and Networks* (Frey and Adams, 1990).

E-mail travels well beyond the Internet backbone, to and from many associated nets and commercial services such as MCImail, America Online (AOL), CompuServe, SprintMail, and ATTmail. All these commercial services have different addressing conventions (see Table 6.2).

E-Mail on Commercial $ervices

Some commercial services charge their users for receiving mail (by item and/or by size), so be sure that the message will be useful and not too large.

More information on mail and gateways can be obtained via **FTP** to **ariel.unm.edu**, in the */library/network.guide* subdirectory, in a file called **internetwork-mail-guide**. This is *The Inter-Network Mail Guide* by John Chew (1993).

Table 6.2 E-Mail Addresses for Commercial Services

Service	Address example
America Online	**Maryjones@aol.com**
Applelink	**Maryjones@applelink.apple.com**
ATTmail	**Maryjones@attmail.com**
CompuServe	**12345.678@compuserve.com** (Note that the comma used on CompuServe user IDs should be changed to a period when e-mail is sent from an Internet address.)
Delphi	**Maryjones@delphi.com**
GEnie	**Maryjones@genie.geis.com**
MCI-mail	**Mary_Jones@mcimail.com**
Prodigy	**Maryjones@prodigy.com**
Sprintmail	**/PN=Mary.Jones/O=anycom/ADMD=** **telemail/ C=US/@sprint.com**
World Software Tool & Die	**Maryjones@world.std.com**

Locating E-Mail Addresses

Locating an e-mail address can be simple: Just call the individual on the phone and ask. This is not, however, the usual method, nor is it always feasible, so there are a variety of tools that have been developed for locating a person, machine, or node:

- White pages directories (essentially, electronically stored telephone books) are maintained by several groups, most notably the Knowbot Information Service, which maintains an online electronic white pages service that can be reached by **Telnet** to **nri.reston.va.us 185** (the space before **185** is unusual but needed in this case), and then by choosing White Pages at the menu.

- You can **Telnet** to **nic.ddn.mil** to use some of the services such as "whois" and, by following the prompts, locate e-mail addresses of many military personnel as well as those of prominent Internet personalities.

- Using Gopher (explained in Chapter 10), you can search for phone books, and you will be presented with a menu of electronic phone books from cities, campuses, organizations, and businesses. (A recent exploration of mine revealed over 500 phone books to search.)

- Netfind is a utility designed to locate machine and node names at institutions. To use it, **Telnet** to **bruno.colorado.edu** and log in as **netfind**. The utility will provide prompts to assist you in your search.

- Many systems allow for remote testing of an address, using a utility called finger. Finger will return information about the remote user and his or her login activity. Type **finger user@node** at your system prompt (for example, **finger jgrandstf@nyse.sec.com**). To use finger, you will need the node name; you can obtain it by using netfind.

- Most sites have an e-mail postmaster or a staff member who maintains the e-mail functions for the company or institution. You can send e-mail to **postmaster@address** with a request for assistance in locating someone. (Replace *address* with the specific Internet or BITNET address for example, **postmaster@nyse.sec.com**.)

- There is an address database generated from Usenet postings that can be queried using e-mail. Send an e-mail message addressed to **mailserver@pit-manager.mit.edu**. There is no need for a subject field entry. In the body of the message put: **send Usenet-addresses/name**, replacing name with the actual name you wish to locate. (Out of curiosity, I tried this out with my own name, and much to my surprise, I found myself!)

- Commercial providers such as Delphi and CompuServe will allow their own members to search a membership list. CompuServe, for example, will allow searches by last name, first name, state, and city.

- Jonathan Kames at MIT maintains a FAQ file called **finding-addresses**, which outlines various search strategies. It is available via **FTP** to **pit-manager.mit.edu**.

Using Telnet and FTP

You can find out how to use Telnet in Chapter 8, and FTP in Chapter 9.

HOW TO USE E-MAIL

There are numerous mail programs for a full variety of computing platforms. Different software requires different commands and processes. In the chapters on Telnet, FTP, and other Internet tools, it will be possible to give you step-by-step directions. For e-mail however, it will just be possible to give you a couple of examples and tell you about e-mail in general.

The particular commands and techniques that you will use when sending and receiving e-mail will vary depending upon the services and software that you use. Learning basic e-mail commands and techniques, however, will greatly enhance your understanding of what your particular e-mail host can be expected to do.

Sending and Receiving E-Mail

For many people, access to e-mail is gained through company or institutional computing systems, typically through VAX/VMS environments or UNIX systems. You may already have an e-mail address and not know it—call your computer user assistance staff and ask! These people are usually in the MIS department.

Getting online may mean learning to connect to a mainframe or UNIX box, and learning the arcane command languages of one or both. (See Appendix C for a brief summary of useful UNIX commands.)

E-Mail Software: Mailers

Any system that handles Internet mail will have a mail program installed. All mail programs have a set of commands that allow you to send and receive mail, but they vary in their capabilities to compose, edit, and manage messages. Some require that you compose the message as a file outside the mail program, and some will not let you edit it before sending. Others, however, provide much more user-friendly features such as full-screen editing, named electronic file folders for storing and organizing received messages, and various sort and search utilities to help you to manage your messages.

E-mail software often contains provisions for functions based on those of paper. You can carbon copy (cc) or blind carbon copy (bcc) someone, forward mail, and reply. The reply function will have a method for extracting the address of the sender, to help you to send a return message without having to type in the address or subject line. Use caution with this, since you may have received the message via a list or via another person, and the reply might go to the wrong person. Each mailer treats the reply function differently; some mailers will reply to the sender, others will reply to the address identified in the *From:* field. Read the program documentation for particular structures. The reply function will be particularly useful when managing discussion list messages. (See Chapter 7 for more information on the discussion lists.) Most mailers have commands like those shown in Table 6.3.

In addition, many mail programs will let you scan existing messages by subject and sender, print messages, and place messages in a wastebasket folder until you exit the program (as opposed to getting rid of them

Table 6.3 Mailer Commands

Command	Meaning
send	Send a message or a file (this usually starts the process of addressing).
reply	Reply to a message using address information from the received mail's header.
file save or extract	Convert the message(s) into a separate ASCII file for downloading individually or as a group.
delete	Erase a message.
forward	Send a received message to another user.
read	View a specific mail message.

instantly). Most mail systems also will alert you when you first log in that you have new mail waiting.

The specific command structure and mailing procedures differ depending upon the particular mailer provided by your local system or access provider, but the following procedure is typical of many VAX/VMS mailers (follow each command or typed-in response by pressing Enter):

1. At the system prompt (often $, %, or #), invoke the mail program by typing the name of the mailer (**Mail**, etc.).
2. Type **send** to begin the e-mail process.
3. Identify the recipient with the user's complete e-mail address when prompted by *To:*.
4. Enter the subject of the message when prompted.
5. Type in the message.
6. Signal the end of the message, often by typing Ctrl-Z on a separate line (hold down the Ctrl key and type **z**).
7. Exit the mail program by typing **exit** or **quit**.

The mail can be sent to individuals, such as **matt@northwest.com**, a program, such as **archie@sura.net**, or a mailing list, such as **compriv@psi.com**.

Make the subject entries descriptive. A subject that says "Re: your mail" is not very helpful to a busy person with dozens of e-mail messages to sort through, but one that says "Marketing meeting on Friday canceled" is much more useful and likely to be read.

A typical e-mail procedure using Pine, one of the more user-friendly mailers, would look something like this:

1. At the system prompt (often % or #), invoke the mail program by typing **pine**. The first Pine screen will appear as shown in Figure 6.1.

2. Type **C** to begin the e-mail process by composing a message, and the Compose Message screen shown in Figure 6.2 will appear.

3. In the *To:* field, identify the recipient with the user's complete e-mail address. At the Cc: prompt, you can also enter a carbon copy recipient. Some people cc themselves as they do with postal mail. (Don't you find the reference to carbon paper interesting in an electronic environment?)

4. Enter the subject description in the *Subject:* field.

5. Next, enter the message in the message pane. Notice that you have some options at this point—you can cut and paste text, spell check the message, read-in a file, cancel or postpone the message.

6. Signal the end of the message by typing **Ctrl-X**. The message will now be sent without further action on your part.

7. Exit the mail program by typing **Q** to quit.

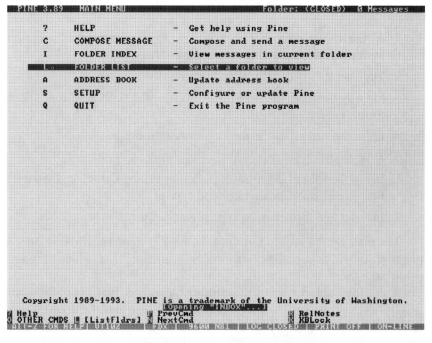

Figure 6.1 The Opening Screen of the Pine Mailer.

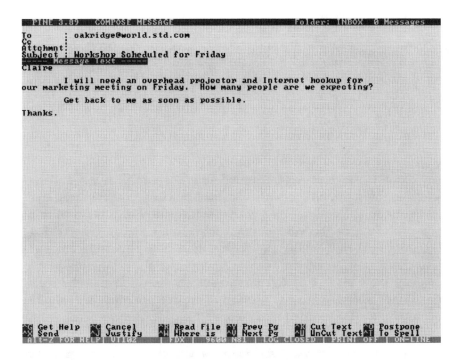

Figure 6.2 The Pine Compose Message Screen.

Sig Files

It is common to include what is called a sig (or .sig—said "dot sig") at the end of e-mail messages. This is a short identifier that may include your name, company name, e-mail address, and sometimes, a short quotation or thought. Sig files of more than five lines are considered to be a breech of etiquette, since many users pay for their e-mail based on the size of the messages they receive. Sometimes the sig file includes a small ASCII graphic, or a discrete advertisement, for example:

```
-=-=-=-=-=-=-=-=-=-=-=-=-=-=-=-=-=-=-=-=-=-=-=-=-=-=-=-=-
Harrison Grandstaff     GHG Computing     g01@greyhound.ghg.com
Business Phone: 555-555-5555                   FAX: 555-555-5555
Are you looking for Internet Business Consulting?
                                    We Provide Solutions!!!
Send an e-mail message to:          info@greyhound.ghg.com
-=-=-=-=-=-=-=-=-=-=-=-=-=-=-=-=-=-=-=-=-=-=-=-=-=-=-=-=-
```

E-Mail Management

Any system that handles Internet mail will have a mail program installed. Many mail programs allow you to create an address book. This is a vehicle for storing your frequently used addresses, and with those long cryptic strings of numbers and characters, it can be a real time-saver. These address books can also facilitate group messaging. The Pine mailer, among others, allows for an address book.

Many mail programs, such as Pine, provide for the arrangement of your messages in folders. See Figure 6.3.

E-mail message management will differ by user, platform, and system. Depending upon the particular mail services, you may read mail online, or download it for reading and management on a personal computer. Because of the volume of mail and files that is generated by becoming active on the Internet, information management becomes absolutely critical. Once the files are on your personal machine, it is best to organize the messages by category or subject thread, using subdirectories, floppy disks, and so on. Text and file search programs are valuable in making the downloaded files useful.

Figure 6.3 The Folder List in Pine.

One Very Small Caution

Not all e-mail messages are authentic. They may have been sent by someone other than the obvious sender, or the text may have been changed. This does not happen very often, but a small grain of salt with odd messages may assist you in sorting through it all.

Creating Emphasis in E-Mail

Generally, messages are sent in ASCII (7 bit), which contains upper- and lowercase letters, numbers, a few punctuation marks, and some control codes. Because the Internet involves millions of computers, messages must use this lowest common denominator to communicate. In practice, this means no elaborate underlining, fonts, formatting, or graphics. This can be a little frustrating at first. However, with some practice, you can accentuate words by using asterisks, dashes, or carets. For example, emphasis is usually expressed *this* way or as pseudo _underlining_. (See Chapter 4 for information on communicons.)

Don't Type E-Mail in All Capital Letters

Don't try to create emphasis or a sense of urgency in your e-mail messages by typing them in all capital letters. This is considered rude because it is the electronic equivalent of shouting.

Attaching and Sending a File

Most mailers will allow you to attach or include a file with your message. On a VMS system, for example, you would include a filename after the send command: **send** *example.txt*. In Pine, you would enter the *Compose Message* menu, and then type Ctrl-**R** to read in a file. In each case, the file needs to be uploaded to your mainframe first. Each mail program will have a slightly different method for accomplishing this task, so be sure to read the program documentation. See Appendix B for information about up- and downloading.

Understanding Message Headers and E-Mail That Strays

When Internet e-mail arrives, one of its most striking characteristics is that it has a long, complex header that seems to go on and on, with many lines iterating and reiterating the sender, the receiver, some intermediary routing information, when it was sent and received, and message identifications—for example:

```
To: vicepresident@whitehouse.gov
Received: from Jnet-DEAMON by vicepresident.gov (STMP V4.2-11
  #3491) id <01GZIK4GC8G9EDV2G@whitehouse.gov>
 Mon 27 Jun 1994 14:37:20 EDT
Received: From GWUVM1 (MAILER) by whitetrogan with Jnet Id
 5029 for vicepresident@whitehouse.gov; Mon 27 Jun 1994 14:37
Date: Mon 27 Jun 1994 16:28:00 -0400
From: Mikhail Gorbachev <mgorb@moscow-state.edu.ru>
Subject: Meeting December 1994
Sender: mgorb@moscow-state.edu.ru
Reply-to: mgorb@moscow-state.edu.ru
Message-id: <01GZIK4GC8G9EDV2G@whitehouse.gov>
Content-transfer-encoding: 7BIT


Al-
     When we meet in December, would it be possible for you
to bring your policies on information exchange ......
          M.
```

Headers can take 40 lines or more. Although they are complex and confusing at first, with practice, they become decipherable. Fortunately, you can ignore most of this information unless you need to do some troubleshooting. Most users need only to be concerned with the *Date:*, *From:*, and *Subject:* fields toward the bottom of the header.

From time to time, a piece of e-mail, like postal mail, is undeliverable. "Bounced mail" is e-mail that has been returned to the sender because of an incorrect address, an unknown host, an unknown user, faulty hardware or software, hardware or transmission lines that are malfunctioning ("down"), and so forth. It is here that the header becomes important in figuring out what happened. The first step in troubleshooting bounced mail is to check the exact spelling, case, and syntax of the address. The most frequent error that I make is typographical: Simply, the address was incorrectly transcribed. If the address appears to be in order, resend the message after a few hours, since the second most frequent problem is that the system linkages are temporarily down. Finally, the local sysop may be able to help, or a message to the postmaster at the remote site may help resolve errors.

Magic: How to Send Binary Information Via E-Mail

There are now some methods for sending binary information in regular e-mail messages, one called MIME, and the other UUENCODE. This is especially important, since business users often need to send formatted spreadsheets, graphs, and word processing files to colleagues. In addition, you can send images, sounds, and animated files using these programs.

Using UUENCODE and UUDECODE to Mail 8-Bit Files

A pair of programs exists that will allow you to send and receive 8-bit binary files on almost any system that can handle Internet e-mail: UUENCODE and UUDECODE. First, a few definitions:

- **UUENCODE**—This is a program that can convert binary (8-bit) files, such as word processor files, spreadsheets, computer programs, and graphics images, into ASCII (7-bit) files.
- **UUDECODE**—This is a program that can convert ASCII (7-bit) UUENCODEd files back into exact copies of the binary (8-bit) files that they came from.
- **ASCII**—When 7 binary bits of on/off data are sent as a group, there are 128 possible combinations. In the ASCII standard, each of these combinations is assigned a meaning, such as one of the uppercase letters, lowercase letters, numbers, punctuation marks, or symbols. The Internet uses this ASCII standard for transferring e-mail. These ASCII files are often called "text" files.
- **Binary**—While ASCII files are, in fact, binary, in the sense that they are made of groupings of binary numbers (0s and 1s), when you see the term "binary" it usually refers to 8-bit files—that is, files where eight binary numbers are sent as a group. Eight binary numbers in a group allow for 256 possible combinations. Unlike ASCII, however, binary code has no standard assignment for what each of these 256 numbers means—the meaning has only to do with their use with specific software programs. The number 212, for example, might mean "draw a blue dot" in a graphics program or "start showing letters in bold" in a word processor file. Examples of binary files include: spreadsheet and word processor files, graphics/picture images (such as .PCX, .GIF, etc.), some database files, and software programs.

While the Internet has devised several systems that allow transfer of binary files (such as FTP), the Internet e-mail system is based on ASCII. You can, however, send binary files through e-mail if you first convert them from binary to ASCII. Then, the recipient of your message converts the files from ASCII back into binary. A popular method for doing this is to use UUENCODE and UUDECODE.

Finding and Getting UUENCODE and UUDECODE

From the Internet, **uuencode.com** and **uudecode.com** are available by FTP from **wuarchive.wustl.edu** in the */mirrors/msdos/starter* subdirectory (see Chapter 9 for information on using FTP). If you can't locate these programs at that site, do an archie search for **uuencode.com** and **uudecode.com** (see Chapter 10 for information on archie searches). Also, since these programs are so popular, you can get them from most commercial services such as CompuServe and from many free local dial-up BBSs.

Using UUENCODE on Your PC

Suppose you want to send a spreadsheet file to a business associate. While some spreadsheets, databases, and word processors will allow you to save the data in ASCII format, you would lose all the special formatting, formulas, fonts, boldfacing, and other styling elements. Assuming the file you want to send is named **january.wks** located in the *c:\expenses\atlanta* subdirectory of your PC, taking the following steps will convert this binary file to a mailable ASCII file:

1. Change to the subdirectory where you have stored the UUEN-CODE program using the **cd** command. For example, if you've stored it in a directory called *convert* in your *utility* subdirectory, at the prompt, you would type in **cd c:\utility\convert**.

2. Now type **dir** at the prompt to confirm that the UUENCODE program is there.

3. To do the actual conversion, at the DOS prompt type **UUENCODE** followed by the full path and name of the file to be converted, followed by a space, followed by the full path of where you would like the converted file to be stored, including your new name for that converted file. If you want the file stored in the *temp* subdirectory and you want to call it **jan-exp.uu**, then the full command line would look like this:

```
C:\>uuencode c:\expenses\atlanta\january.wks c:\temp\
    jan-exp.uu
```

The original binary file itself is not moved or changed in any way by this procedure.

In a few seconds the DOS prompt will return, the conversion will be complete, and **jan-exp.uu** will be ready for uploading and e-mailing. You can take a look at this converted file if you want to, but if you use a word processor, be very careful not to alter the file in any way or to "save" it—just view the file and then close it without changes. What you will see when viewing the file is line after line of letters, numbers, and characters, without spaces, and in uniform length lines.

For details on how to upload this file to your Internet e-mail host computer, see Appendix B. For details on how to send an encoded or any other kind of ASCII file, see the information on sending files earlier in this chapter.

Using UUDECODE on Your PC

Looking at UUENCODEd files and becoming aware of their characteristic appearance is helpful, since you may get files or messages that are encoded without your correspondent or file source mentioning this. If you are not familiar with the file's appearance, you may think that your mail program has gone berserk. If you have the UUDECODE program on your PC and you download an encoded message or file, follow these steps to convert it:

1. Change to the directory where the UUDECODE program is stored—for example: **cd c:\utility\convert**.

2. At the prompt, type **UUDECODE** followed by the name of the ASCII file containing the encoded binary file, followed by the path to the directory where you want the binary file stored. No name is needed, since the binary file will have the same name that the original binary file had when it was converted. The full command line, along with the prompt supplied by your computer, might look like this:

```
C:\>uudecode c:\download\from-bob.txt c:\database\
```

This would convert the file **from-bob.txt** from ASCII to a binary file that will be stored in the *database* subdirectory.

Don't worry about any message headers, .sig files, or other text in the message as long as it comes either before the word "begin" or after the word "end." If, however, some lines of text have gotten into the encoded material, they will need to be edited out. It is best to use a simple editor that does not do formatting, rather than a full word processor, since many word processors change margins or add characters, even when they are directed to "save as ASCII."

Using UUENCODE and UUDECODE on Your Remote Account

The computer that holds your e-mailbox is quite likely to have encoder and decoder programs installed (especially if it is a UNIX system). You will probably be able to determine this by typing **help** at the main prompt for a list of commands or by checking with the computer system administrator.

The most likely syntax for encoding a file (once you have uploaded it from your PC to your Internet host computer) is: **uuencode** *original .name new.name*. For example:

```
uuencode january.wks january.uu
```

Putting **uu** after the dot is not required, just a good way of keeping straight which file is which.

To decode an e-mail message, you will need to convert the message to a file in your subdirectory. The technique used to do this varies between mail programs.

Now leave the mail program, and from the main computer prompt type **uudecode** followed by the name you just assigned to the file. You don't supply a name for the binary file that will result from the conversion, since it will be named exactly the same that the original binary file was called at the time it was converted. What you type in might look like this:

```
uudecode fromjohn.uu
```

More Info on Sending Files

For information on uploading and downloading files, see Appendix B. For information on common UNIX and other host computer commands, see Appendix C.

Encoding/Decoding for Mac Users

As a Mac user you can, of course, use any encoders/decoders available on your host machine, but you can also get programs for use on your personal machine such as uutool, which can be obtained by FTP from **sumex-aim.stanford.edu** in the */info-mac/util* directory.

MIME

This is not about Marcel Marceau. A special protocol called MIME (Multipurpose Internet Mail Extension, RFC 1341) can distribute and receive digitized pictures and executable programs if the MIME protocol is available on both the sending and receiving machines. Created in 1992 by the Internet Engineering Task Force (IETF), it is a set of information exchange standards for non-ASCII e-mail.

Not all mailers support MIME. When a mailer that does not support it receives a MIME message, it will display all of the ASCII information, but only a notation about the items that cannot be processed. The Pine mailer, among others, does support this protocol. MIME-capable mailers allow word processing documents, spreadsheets, images, audio, and other binary data to be attached to an e-mail message. Multimedia mail also allows for information in alternative formats to be attached at the same time, so that it can be read by a variety of mailers. Check with your correspondents to determine if they can receive MIME attachments.

SPECIAL E-MAIL APPLICATIONS

There area two specific applications of e-mail that have proven to be particularly useful to business users; automated e-mail (servers), and e-mail for work groups.

Automated E-Mail

Some e-mail addresses are not the addresses of an actual person; rather, they are addresses of what are called *servers*. Servers are special computer addresses that use software for automated file distribution. An example would be the server **almanac.@oes.orst.edu** maintained by the Oregon Extension Service, which maintains a large repository of files, among them Project Gutenberg's full-text books. Using your mail program, sending **almanac@oes.orst.edu** the message **send guten alice** would retrieve the full text of *Alice in Wonderland*.

Servers are very useful for setting up automated replies to requests for information. This means that your customers, or those interested in your products, can get information by reply mail. Check with your system operators about the availability of this kind of server on your system.

Using E-Mail with Workgroups

Using e-mail, large groups can be reached as easily as one person, so work groups can communicate at a distance despite varying physical locations and time zones. Most mailers will let you create group address entries; for example, one group address entry called **marketing** might have the addresses of all of the people working in the marketing department, or all of the people working in marketing at all locations worldwide. Or, you might create ad hoc short-term communications groups for work teams.

FINDING MORE INFORMATION . . .

What is the next step?

- Many of the items listed in Part IV, "Professional and Business Resources on the Internet," make use of these e-mail techniques.

- E-mail is particularly useful in creating a business presence on the Internet—Part II of this book will show you how to use e-mail in marketing, customer service, and other business applications.

- Chapter 4 will show you how e-mail can change corporate communications.

- Continue on to the next chapter to learn about one of the most popular uses of e-mail for getting up-to-date information on participating in discussions on thousands of topics.

CHAPTER 7

How to Use Discussion Lists

Early in the development of BITNET, e-mail–based discussion lists were created to provide the academic and research community with the ability to exchange ideas freely and quickly across long distances. These e-mail–based, subject-related exchange/distribution groups now number in excess of 3,500, and cover almost any subject you can imagine.

As with most Internet resources, the number of groups grows daily. These discussion lists have been compared to all kinds of things: meetings at the watercooler, discussions in employee lounges, presentations and conversations at conferences, and even talk radio. Each list has its own flavor—how frequently people post, how they post (formal, informal), how much flaming is tolerated, and other style issues. Reading the mail for a time is a good way to discover the customs and the "signal-to-noise ratio" of each list—that is to say, how many informative or interesting messages there are compared to the number of trivial or uninteresting messages.

USING THE INTERNET DISCUSSION LISTS

The discussion lists can focus on virtually any topic: popular TV shows, scientific and academic research, current Internet practices, business practices, anything. They are useful for obtaining up-to-date information, discussing current situations in organizations industries, networking with colleagues, getting assistance, and more.

After subscribing to (joining) a list, the listserver software will begin e-mailing copies of all messages posted to the list directly to the user. (We'll discuss exactly what a listserver is in the following section.) High-traffic lists can generate 30 or more messages a day, while low-traffic lists may generate one message every week or so. Subscribing to several high-volume lists could mean that you find 200 messages in your e-mailbox every morning! Try out a couple of lists before signing up for more, to be sure that the number of pieces of e-mail does not exceed the time you have available to read and process them. Often, the best way to get started with the discussion lists is to subscribe to one or two lists and read them for a while before jumping in with both feet. This helps you get a sense of the issues being discussed, the style, and level of formality of the group.

The lists are maintained, for the most part, by software that allows for automated message distribution, management, and retrieval. These programs are sometimes called mail exploders. Some of the most popular list management programs are LISTSERV by Eric Thomas; *ListProcessor*, a UNIX listserver by Anastasios Kotsikonas; Majordomo; and the Mailbase system in the United Kingdom. If you are interested in starting your own list, ask your Internet service provider about using a listserver with your account.

Some lists are moderated, while others are not. Most lists allow open, unmoderated posting, with all messages automatically sent to members of the list without screening. Review by a moderator before posting allows for the screening of long, off-topic, or offensive postings. Some moderators are *laissez-faire*, or choose to direct the list by suggestion or persuasion, while others will even edit messages or combine related messages. Most moderators see themselves as maintaining list civility and keeping it on track with its stated mission.

Open enrollment lists allow anyone to subscribe. An open list will let the user sign up via an automated system with no human intervention. Closed lists, on the other hand, are often exclusively for members of particular organizations or groups with screened subscriptions. There are, for example, lists that are maintained to support ongoing corporate or working groups, and other lists that serve as communication channels for specialized groups. These lists are typically private and may not be open for subscription without invitation.

Joining Lists

Signing up for, or subscribing to, lists requires an understanding of an important distinction between the listserver and the list itself. The listserver is the software that handles the tasks (administrivia) associated with list maintenance, including subscription processing, database management, and archiving. The list itself is the group of people who are currently subscribed.

The listserver software acts like an administrative secretary working for a group of, say, salespeople. The secretary handles administrative matters such as typing, filing, and making appointments. The *list* is the group of sales representatives themselves, who, assisted by the administrative secretary, communicate with each other by exchanging memos, messages, phone calls, and information.

Figure 7.1 first shows the traffic of the list, with messages going from one user out to all other members. Below that is the traffic from the user just to the listserver.

Often, messages sent to the listserv are read by computer, not human beings, so additional requests for help or additional information will be ignored or cause the request to be rejected. The software "knows" a limited number of commands that will carry out some basic instructions. To subscribe to a list, you send an e-mail request to the listserver, and if your request is accepted, you will be added to the list and begin receiving messages. Here is an example of a message sent to a listserv for subscribing to a list:

```
EMAIL>send
To: listserv@csncs.com
Subj: [leave this space blank]
Message:
subscribe htmarcom Meg Jones
^X[Ctrl-X, Ctrl-Z, or the usual way that the mailer ends a message]
```

This message to subscribe to the htmarcom (High Technology Marketing Communications) list is being sent to the address of the software that is managing the list, in this case **csncs.com**. Meg's e-mail address does not need to be typed in, since the listserv grabs her e-mail address from her message header. Meg has instructed the listserv to place her on the htmarcom discussion list, and has given the name she wants to be known by on this list. In some cases, the correct syntax to reach the listserv is to send the message to *listname*-**request** in **htmarcom-request@csncs.com** (try this second method, if the first method does not work).

When you first subscribe to a list, there are two messages that are typically received in reply. One of these is from the listserv automatic software, welcoming you or telling you that you have been added to the list. It often contains instructions for unsubscribing. The other message from "the system" details computer CPU use as well as the address that was extracted from your subscription request header. Always save both messages, so that later, the commands for leaving the list, suspending

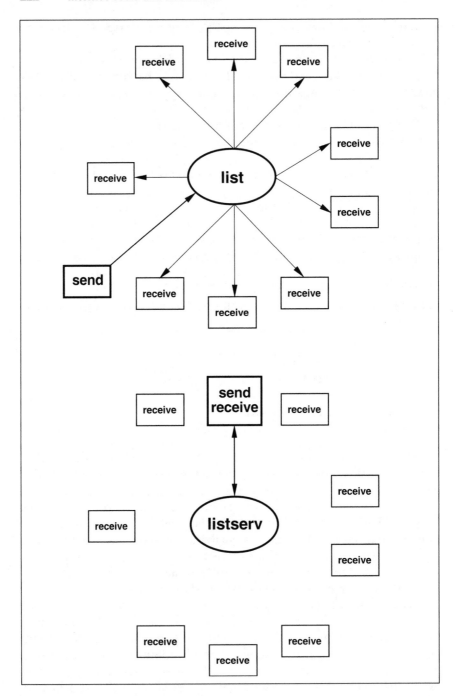

Figure 7.1 List Traffic

mail, or searching the archives can be used. These differ considerably, depending upon the list moderator or owner. Following is a subscription welcome from htmarcom. Notice that the list owner has outlined the purpose of the list, and in this case has specifically addressed issues concerning the use of the list for commercial purposes.

```
From: "Kim M. Bayne (kimmik@bayne.com)" <kimmik@cns.cscns.com>
Subject: WELCOME TO HTMARCOM
Sender: htmarcom@cscns.com
To: oakridge@world.std.com
Errors-to: kimmik@cscns.com
Reply-to: htmarcom@cscns.com
Message-id: <Pine.3.89.9403021848.B11992-0100000@cns>
Content-transfer-encoding: 7BIT
Originator: htmarcom@cscns.com
Precedence: bulk
X-Listserver-Version: 6.0 -- UNIX ListServer by Anastasios Kotsikonas
X-Comment: High Tech Marketing Communications


WELCOME TO HTMARCOM


Welcome to the HTMARCOM list. This list is modeled after
professional organizations and their monthly "brown bag
roundtable" discussions. Subscribers are invited to share
information and solve problems about different aspects of
marketing communications.


*** HTMARCOM FOCUS Marcom professionals have responsibilities in
such areas as advertising, collateral, public relations, trade
shows, sales support, and strategic and tactical marketing
communications. High tech marketing communications professionals
are involved in the marketing and sales of software,
peripherals, semiconductors, board-level products, cards, data
communications, systems, and other computer and electronics
technologies. Subscribers to this list may work for a company or
agency involved in high tech marcom. Others, such as editors,
publishers, analysts, academicians, or students may subscribe to
this list as well.


*** LIST ADMINISTRATION
On a regular basis, I'll upload information that will be of
interest to marcom professionals. This will be in the form of an
online newsletter (of sorts). Subscribers can read this
```

newsletter for discussion topics. The newsletter will include press list updates, services and resources, new technology, and anything else that I can gather in time for the newsletter. Submissions to the newsletter are encouraged. Email kimmik@cscns.com with suggestions. Please type "NEWSLETTER SUBMISSION" in your email subject header.

*** LIST GUIDELINES
While one of the purposes of this list is to expand your network of contacts beyond the traditional "print and meeting" world, please keep in mind that certain messages will 'congest' the traffic on this list and are therefore discouraged.

1) PLEASE DO NOT POST UNSOLICITED ADVERTISEMENTS TO THIS LIST. In a future newsletter, I will compile a list of subscribers who are offering their services. PLEASE WAIT UNTIL I send out a questionnaire on this one before you start emailing stuff to me.

Obviously, if your .signature file contains a few lines, as in a slogan, or your company name, that's not a problem (see my signature, for example). But please don't upload advertisements, sales letters, news releases and data sheets to broadcast to the entire list, or subscribers won't be able to sift through the clutter to get to the discussions.

If someone posts a specific problem and you wish to offer your (for hire) services, query the INDIVIDUAL first with a few lines stating that you can help, as in: "My company creates magic potions to transform bad product reviews. Please email PRflack@bluesky.com if you would like some more info." Make it clear to the reader in the subject header, as in: "SERVICES OFFERED: MAGIC POTIONS."

Another way to handle this is to create a .plan file (if you're on the Internet). For example, someone on the Internet who wishes to find out more about me and my company can type 'finger kimmik@cscns.com.'

2) PLEASE DO NOT POST UNSOLICITED RESUMES TO THIS LIST. While I understand about being out of work, please use the above procedure (query individuals first) before you send out your resume. I'll create a section in the monthly newsletter to post job offerings.

3) For those of you who have never been in a listserv before, it
will be easier for people to read their email messages if you:
use a subject header that is very clear ..don't include all
messages in all replies (be selective). I usually give up after
the third page if I receive a message within a forwarded message
within a forwarded message. (Yuck!) I'm not going to read all
that to get to the point!

Unless the message is long and you wish to address every point,
I suggest that you reply to most messages referencing the
previous message, like this: "In answer to your question about
Dataquest, here is their address."

One of the problems list subscribers run into is being unable to
understand what another subscriber meant. One cryptic message I
received broadcast to the entire list simply contained the
following text: "Yes, I agree. It's always been that way." Does
anyone really think I can decode that without a reference point?

*** SUGGESTIONS WELCOME
Suggestions for administration of this list can be emailed
directly to the list owner at kimmik@cscns.com. I'll review all
suggestions and consider adding them to this file. If you have
any questions, please feel free to email me directly at
kimmik@cscns.com. Thanks for your participation.

```
****************************************************************
   Kim Miklofsky Bayne, President        "For measurable results
   wolfBayne Marketing Communications     in high tech public
   P.O. Box 50287                         relations"
   Colorado Springs, CO 80949-0287
   Tel.  (719) 593-8032,  FAX   (719) 599-3175
   email:  kimmik@bayne.com, kimmik@cscns.com
****************************************************************
```

Posting a Message to All Members of a List

Now, to send a message to all of the list members, you would send out
something like the following, depending upon the mailer that you use:

```
MAIL>send
To: htmarcom@csns.com
Subj: Trade Shows
```

We have been invited to exhibit at the Office Product trade show
in Cobo Hall (Detroit) in November. Has anyone else been to this
show before? If you have, please contact me — I need some advice
about clientele and set-up. Thanks

<><><><><><><><><><><><><><><><><><><><><><><><><><><><><><><>
Meg Jones <mjones@sumaron.com>
Marketing   555/555-555
Sumaron Industries   FAX 555/555-555
<><><><><><><><><><><><><><><><><><><><><><><><><><><><><><><>

In posting to a list or sending an individual e-mail, use the reply
feature of your e-mail software carefully if you are replying to a message
from a list. If you intend the message for one person, do not use the reply
feature, or your message will go out to all and sundry on the list. Almost
every veteran list member can tell a story or two about a private message
that was broadcast to a list—some of these are fairly innocuous, but a few
have been embarrassing.

Listserver Commands and Protocols

Most listservers respond to a small group of common commands sent in
messages to them such as Meg's request to subscribe. This group of
commands depends upon which listserver is managing the list. There are
several popular listserver software packages currently in use on the
Internet. While they operate in a similar manner, there are some differences, based on both the software and the platform running the software.

For lists that began as a part of BITNET, the most popular software
is LISTSERV by Eric Thomas, which runs on UNIX, VAX, and IBM
platforms. If you send an e-mail message consisting of the word **help** to
the site serving the list that you are subscribed to (**listserv@kentvm
.bitnet**, for example), you will get back a quick reference guide to the most
common commands:

```
LISTSERV version 1.8a - most commonly used commands

Info       <topic|listname>        Order documentation
Lists      <Detail|Short|Global>   Get a description of all lists
SUBscribe  listname <full name>    Subscribe to a list
SIGNOFF    listname                Sign off from a list
SIGNOFF    * (NETWIDE              - from all lists on all servers
REView     listname <options>      Review a list
Query      listname                Query your subscription options
```

```
SET        listname  options       Update your subscription options
INDex      <filelist_name>         Order a list of LISTSERV files
GET        filename filetype       Order a file from LISTSERV
REGister   full_name|OFF           Tell LISTSERV about your name
```

There are more commands (AFD, FUI, PW, etc.). Send a message of
INFO REFCARD to the listserver for a comprehensive reference
card, or just INFO for a list of available documentation files.

Also in this message is information about getting a more complete
listing of the listserv commands.

Another popular listserver is ListProcessor by Anastasios Kotsikonas. Again, when you put **help** in the message to ListProcessor (**listproc
@nic.umass.edu**, for example), you will get a file of information:

```
                ListProcessor 6.0
```

Here is a brief description of the set of requests recognized by
ListProcessor. Everything appearing in [ ] below is optional;
everything appearing in <> is mandatory; all arguments are case
insensitive. The vertical bar ("|") is used as a logical OR
operator between the arguments. Requests may be abbreviated, but
you must specify at least the first three characters.

Keep in mind that when referring to a <list>, that list may be
of two kinds: local or remote, unless otherwise noted. When
referring to a local list, your request will be immediately
processed; when referring to a remote list (a list served by
another ListProcessor which this system knows about), your
request will be appropriately forwarded. Issue a 'lists' request
to get a listing of all local and known remote lists to this
ListProcessor.

Recognized requests are:

help [topic]

Without arguments, you receive this file. Otherwise gets
specific information on the selected topic. Topics may also
refer to requests. To learn more about this system issue a 'help
listproc' request. To get a listing of all available topics,
generate an error message by sending a bogus request like 'help
me'.
```
```

```
set <list> [<option> <arg[s]>]
------------------------------
```
Without the optional arguments, get a list of all current
settings for the specified list. Otherwise change the option to
a new value for that list. Issue a 'help set' request for more
information.

```
subscribe <list> <your name>
----------------------------
```
The only way to subscribe to a list.

```
unsubscribe <list>
signoff <list>
------------------
```
Two ways of removing yourself from the specified list.

```
recipients <list>
review <list>
-----------------
```
Get a listing of all non-concealed people subscribed to the
specified list.

```
information <list>
------------------
```
Get information about the specified list.

```
statistics <list> {[subscriber email address(es)] | [-all]}
-----------------------------------------------------------
```
Get a listing of non-concealed subscribers along with the number
of messages each one of them has sent to the specified list. If
the optional email addresses are given, then statistics will be
collected for these users only. For example:
```
        stat foo user1@domain user2@domain
```
will generate statistics about these two subscribers. "-all"
lists statistics for all users that have posted on the list
(whether currently subscribed to not).

```
run <list> [<password> <cmd [args]>]
------------------------------------
```
Run the specified command with the optional arguments and
receive the output from stdout and/or stderr. To get a listing
of all available commands to run, omit the arguments, i.e. issue
a 'run <list>' request. You have to belong to the specified
list, and must have obtained the password from the list's owner;

the owner's address may be found in the Errors-To: header line
of each delivered message. <list> may be local only.

lists

Get a list of all local mailing lists that are served by this
server, as well as of all known remote lists.

index [archive | path-to-archive] [/password] [-all]

Get a list of files in the selected archive, or the master
archive if no archive was specified. If an archive is private,
you have to provide its password as well.

get <archive | path-to-archive> <file> [/password] [parts]

Get the requested file from the specified archive. Files are
usually split in parts locally, and in such a case you will
receive the file in multiple email messages -- an 'index'
request tells you how many parts the file has been split into,
and their sizes; if you need to obtain certain parts, specify
them as optional arguments. If an archive is private, you have
to provide its password as well.

view <archive | path-to-archive>] [/password] [parts]

Same as "get" but in interactive mode just catenates the file on
the screen.

search <archive | path-to-archive>] [/password] [-all] <pattern>

Search all files of the specified archive (and all of its
subarchives if -all is specified) for lines that match the
pattern. The pattern can be an egrep(1)-style regular expression
with support for the following additional operators: '~'
(negation), '|' and '&' (logical OR and AND), '<' '>' (group
regular expressions). The pattern may be enclosed in single or
double quotes. Note: . matches any character including new line.

fax <fax-number> <archive | path-to-archive> <file> [/password] [parts]

Same as 'get', but it faxes you the files instead to the
specified number.

```
release
-------

Get information about the current release of this ListProcessor
system.


which
-----

Get a listing of local mailing lists to which you have
subscribed.
```

There are many other listservers. One is called Majordomo, by Brent Chapman. You can make a request for help from **majordomo@csn.org**.

In the United Kingdom, there is a listserver system called Mailbase. You can receive a lengthy description of how to use the service by sending the command **send mailbase user-card** in an e-mail message to **mailbase@mailbase.ac.uk**. If you require a comprehensive introduction to Mailbase, you may retrieve the user's guide by sending the command **send mailbase user-guide** in an e-mail message to **mailbase@uk.ac.mailbase**. For a list of online documentation about Mailbase, send the command **index mailbase** in an e-mail message to **mailbase@uk.ac.mailbase**.

Database/Archive Searching

Some lists make previous postings available in a variety of forms for both list members and nonmembers. The **index** command can be used to obtain these listings of archived information. Some lists group the postings by subject and then distribute them in digest format, while others maintain postings in chronological order. Archives of long documents or documents not sent out to the list members are often available, and some have frequently asked questions (FAQ) documents available for new or potential members. Archives can be searched for items to be retrieved by using the following search structure sent as the body of a message to the appropriate listserv:

```
MAIL> send
   To: listserv@ukanvm.bitnet
   Subj:
//
database search dd=rules
//rules dd *
search management in TQM-L
index
/*
```

This search will locate all messages that contain the word "management" in the archives of the Total Quality Management (TQM-L) list, located **@ukanvm.bitnet**, and return a listing of the files containing "management" to you as an e-mail message. To carry out another search, replace **management** with any keyword, **TQM-L** with the list name, and **@ukanvm.bitnet** with the address of the listserv. You can then request that the listserv get any files found in the search.

List and File Management

Some mailers aid the reader in keeping track of the subjects of the discussions by allowing for searching and/or sorting of the subject field. On most lists there are several topics being discussed simultaneously; for example, on one list there might be an ongoing discussion of advertising, acceptable use, and what AT&T and the telcos (telephone companies) are up to, all at once. Each of these subjects is called a thread. Some users prefer to follow the subject thread rather than read the messages chronologically as sent. Threads may be tracked, since they usually maintain identical wording in the subject line of each message.

FINDING APPROPRIATE LISTS

Finding interesting lists can involve getting several documents and listings. Arno Wouters has created a document called *How to Find an Interesting Mailing List*. To get a copy of this, e-mail a message reading **get new list wouters** to **listserv@vm1.nodak.edu** or to **LISTSERV@NDSUVM1 .BITNET**.

In addition, an annotated list of lists can be fetched via FTP from **ftp.nisc.sri.com** in the subdirectory */netinfo* with the filename **interest-groups** (note that the size of this file is currently almost 1 megabyte; see Chapter 9 for instructions on how to use FTP). It can also be obtained via e-mail: Send a message to **mail-server@nisc.sri.com** with the message **send netinfo/interest-groups**.

You can also FTP to **pit-manager.mit.edu**, and find files named **part1**, **part2**, **part3**, **part4**, **part5**, **part6**, **part7**, and **part8** in the *pub/usenet/news .answers/mail/mailing-lists* subdirectory, which contain a detailed listing of interest groups. To receive the latest information on new lists as they are formed, a user may subscribe to the mailing lists called **new-list@ndsuvm1** or to **interest-groups-request@nisc.sri.com**.

Marty Hoag has compiled a guide called *Some Lists of Lists* to help in the list hunt as well. This can be obtained by sending the message **get listof lists** to **listserv@vm1.nodak.edu**.

Dartmouth University maintains a merged list of the LISTSERV lists on BITNET as well as the Interest Group lists on the Internet. It is a large single file. It is also provided as a Macintosh Hypercard stack. These files can be obtained by anonymous FTP from **dartcms1.dartmouth.edu** **<129.170.16.19>** in the */siglists* subdirectory.

A keyword-searchable list is maintained on a Gopher entry called *Internet Dog-Eared Pages*. You can point your Gopher to **calypso-2.oit.unc .edu**, or search for **dog-eared** using Veronica. (See Chapter 10 for information on how to use Gopher and Veronica.)

Diane Kovacs maintains an extensive categorized list of lists, organized by subject. To get an index of the nine subject matter files and the hypercard stacks, send the e-mail message **get acadlist index** to **LISTSERV@KENTVM.BITNET** or **listserv@kentvm.kent.edu**. This is also available via FTP to **ksuvxa.kent.edu**, in the subdirectory */library*, as file *acadlist.index*.

A very large file containing a global list of BITNET lists can be obtained by sending an e-mail message as follows:

```
To: listserv@bitnic.educom.edu
    (or listserv@bitnic.bitnet)
Subj: [leave this blank]
```

```
list global
```

Here are some lists that are focused on discussions of business use of the Internet and marketing:

- **com-priv@psi.com** discusses all facets of the commercialization and privatization of the Internet.

- **cni-modernization@cni.org** focuses on a variety of issues and, in the past, has had lively discussions about advertising and use of the Internet.

- **htmarcom@cscns.com** is for professionals with interests in areas such as advertising, public relations, trade shows, sales support, and strategic and tactical marketing communications.

- **ritim-l@uriacc.uri.edu**, sponsored by the Research Institute for Telecommunications and Information Marketing, is a lively discussion list focusing on technology and marketing.

In addition to "serious" lists, there are hundreds of discussion lists on almost every facet of modern life. These use the same protocols and syntax as the other discussion lists. The lists cover politics, health matters, humor, hobbies, weather, and everything in between. Most subscription and unsubscription requests are processed automatically without human intervention. To reach a person related to a list, you can often send e-mail to **owner-***listname@address*.

USENET NEWSGROUPS

Usenet is an odd phenomenon—you almost always see a discussion of the blind men discussing the elephant when you hear talk of Usenet, because it is so large and diverse. Often no one has a full understanding of what Usenet is.

Usenet is a worldwide community of discussions called *newsgroups*. Each host on the network pays for its own transmission costs. No one "owns" Usenet—it is a self-regulating network of newsgroups. Some have said that Usenet is the CB on the Internet. It resembles the conferences found on BBS systems—both commercial and nonprofit. Usenet is a group of people posting public messages, often called articles, that are organized by subject category. They are tagged with a standardized set of labels for distribution from site to site.

Generally, Usenet does not allow commercial messages—though the discussion of products you have purchased and how you feel about them is okay as long as there is no financial gain. No unsolicited advertising is permitted. Some **alt.** groups have a specific charter stating that commercial messages are fine, and the **biz.** domain encourages commercial discussions (you will see **biz.** at the beginning of the name of the group: **biz.computers**).

The Usenet messages are organized into thousands of topical newsgroups (approaching 4,000 now). You read and post (contribute) at your local Usenet site. That site distributes the postings to other sites. The groups names are always in lowercase, separated by periods (said "dot"): **comp.fonts, misc.forsale, rec.skiing, sci.archaeology**, or **alt.fan.monty-python**. The group topics are organized hierarchically, going from the general level to the more specific level:

- rec
- rec.sports
- rec.sports.baseball

The first word in a Usenet name indicates the general topic of the list. Table 7.1 shows the Usenet naming scheme.

Outside of the regular Usenet hierarchies are some unregulated topics. Under unregulated hierarchies, groups can be formed without any regulation as to subject or commercial content and without a formal vote to approve the formation. Usenet has no "management." To start a group, you must poll the readers for permission (except in **alt.**, where you can

Table 7.1 Usenet Topic Names

Name	Topic
comp	All computer-related topics
misc	Things that do not fit elsewhere
news	Happenings around the Internet and networks
rec	Hobbies
sci	For all the sciences
soc	For social issues and culture
talk	Debate-oriented

start a group unimpeded). The groups organized under **biz.** and under **.biz** under some other classifications (e.g., **clari.biz**) are quite useful for business or commercial discussions and actual product information. The other groups are good for asking and answering questions, participating in discussion of interest, getting information on files, programs, and other resources. Table 7.2 shows a few of the unregulated Usenet topics.

There are special software packages needed for Usenet users and sites. The software for users, often called a newsreader, allows for thread tracking, and kill files to sort out what you *don't* want to read. Popular newsreaders are *rn, nn,* and *tin*. To read the news, you have to find a news site. Your Internet access provider may be a news site and may provide the needed reader software. Or you may have to Telnet to another site and use a newsreader there. You must locate an online source in order to gain access—there are "readers" available for your local PC, but they can only read the messages you have downloaded from a news site.

The best way to approach Usenet is to start reading some groups of interest. You will need to find out about your access to Usenet and your newsreader software from your Internet access provider. Many news-

Table 7.2 Unregulated Usenet Topics

Name	Topic
alt	Alternatives (highly unregulated)
biz	Business and commercial
clari	Claris Network
bit	BITNET
k12	Education

groups have a frequently asked questions (FAQ) document full of useful information about the newsgroup and its operation.

In Chapter 12 you will find out how businesses are using Usenet in creating a business presence on the Internet.

FREQUENTLY ASKED QUESTIONS DOCUMENTS

Many mailing and Usenet groups have what are called frequently asked questions (FAQ) documents. FAQs (rhymes with tacks) are structured as a list of common questions that a newcomer might have about the group and the subject of the group.

These are the "start here" documents of the Internet. They help avoid discussing the same old subjects over and over. Often these documents have evolved over time. They are created to answer the basic questions that are often asked about a group or subject. Usenet FAQs are maintained in the FTP archives at **pit-manager.mit.edu**. These are also available by mail, by sending e-mail to **mail-server@rtfm.mit.edu**, with a message of **help**. This is the first paragraph of a FAQ on WorldWideWeb:

```
comp.infosystems.www FAQ
************************


Contents
========


o 1. Recent changes to the FAQ
o 2. Information about this document
o 3. What are WWW, hypertext and hypermedia?
o 4. What is a URL?
o 5. How can I access the web?
o 5.1 Browsers accessible by telnet
o 5.2 Obtaining browsers
o 6. How can I provide information to the web?
o 7. How does WWW compare to gopher and WAIS?
o 8. What is on the web?
o 9. I want to know more.
o Z. Credits
```

In some cases on both the discussion lists and on Usenet, the FAQ document is posted at regular intervals, sometimes monthly or every two months (or when the moderator thinks the readers need a dose of getting organized).

WHERE FROM HERE . . .

To see how discussion lists and Usenet newsgroups can be used to help your business on the Internet, see Chapter 5. To learn about the very versatile and easy-to-learn Internet system called Telnet, continue on to the next chapter.

CHAPTER 8

How to Use Telnet— Remote Login

The Telnet system allows you to command your Internet access provider's computer to connect to another computer on the Internet. You can then operate that remote computer much as if you were directly connected to it. With the Telnet system you can use BBSs, databases, search tools, services, and files otherwise not available on your host computer. This means that if your Internet access provider offers Telnet, your business will have access to just about all of the resources of the Internet.

Beyond e-mailing, this is the most basic, must-know, Internet tool. And fortunately, it's easy to learn and easy to use.

TELNET COMMANDS AND TECHNIQUES

Telnet, also called "remote login," allows you to connect directly with other computers on the Internet. In order for you to use Telnet, both your service provider's computer and the remote computer that you want to access must have the Telnet software installed. Also, you must either have an account with the remote computer, or the remote computer must be set up to allow open access to some portions of its system.

If you are unsure if your Internet access provider offers Telnet service, log in to its computer and, at the main prompt (%, $, etc.) type **telnet** and press the Enter key. If the Telnet software is available, a new prompt will appear looking something like this: *Telnet>*. To return to your system's main command prompt, type **quit** and press the Enter key. (This is a quick way to check, but is not 100 percent accurate, since the software might have been installed on a host computer without a full Telnet-compatible

127

connection to the Internet). If Telnet doesn't seem to be working, check with your computer system's administrators.

There are two pieces of information that you will need to make a Telnet connection: the address of the Telnet site, and the login word (see a later section of this chapter for suggestions on where to locate this information).

The Plain Vanilla Telnet Session

The following example will show a Telnet session with MarketBase Online Catalog of Goods and Services, whose address is **mb.com** and whose login word is **mb**. To see how this works, follow this example which simply logs on to MarketBase's computer and then logs off. In the next section, Telnet will be explored in more depth.

At your main system prompt (in this example, *world%*) type **telnet** followed by a space and then the address of the site you would like to connect to, then press Enter. The computer will respond with *Trying*, and then you will see the numeric address of the site you are connecting to:

```
world% telnet mb.com
Trying 198.99.196.10...
```

If a connection is established, the two-line report shown below will be displayed, confirming connection to the address you requested, and displaying what the escape character is (its use will be explained in the next section of this chapter).

```
Connected to mb.com.
Escape character is '^]'.
```

These two lines are followed either by the *login*: prompt or by some announcements from the site itself—in this case, there is a note that **mb** is the login word to use.

```
login: mb
```

At this point, Telnet itself will be in the background, out of sight, shuttling data to and from the remote computer. All of the commands, announcements, menus, and anything else you see displayed will be unique to that site and the software it is running. In this case, MarketBase gives several welcome and information screens and then offers choices on how to access their products.

```
Welcome to the MarketBase(tm)

Online Catalog of Goods and Services
```

Each site will have its own commands for leaving; if they aren't obvious, typing a question mark or **help** will often result in the display of a list of commands. Usually, **x**, **exit**, **quit**, or **bye** will end the session. In this case, the command is **:q**.

```
Enter keyword followed by the return key: ?


                      MarketBase(tm) commands:
Note that most commands begin with a colon (':')

?, :h, or :help
     Print this screen.
:k or :keyword
     Specify a new keyword and execute a new search.
:q or :quit
     Terminate this MarketBase(tm) session
:r or :restart
     Return this MarketBase(tm) session back to the first screen.
:t or :terms
     View the terms and conditions of use of this system.

Please type one of the commands above when ready to continue, or
hit the return key to go back to the previous non-help screen: :q

              Thank you for using MarketBase(tm)

Connection closed by foreign host.
world%
```

After you enter the **:q** command, this site, as most sites do, sends commands to the Telnet software to disconnect and exit from the Telnet program, resulting in a return to the host computer's main prompt (in this case, *world%*).

A Telnet Session with a Few Bells and Whistles

Most Telnet sessions resemble the plain vanilla example, but at times you will want to use a few Telnet features that can help out in some problem cases. In this example, the session is with Book Stacks Unlimited, Inc. Its address is **books.com** and the login is accomplished just by pressing the Enter key one time.

A different method of connecting to a remote site than shown previously is preferred by some: First, type the command **telnet** and press

Enter. Your system's response is the *Telnet>* prompt. This indicates that the Telnet program is active and can accept Telnet commands. To connect to the remote site, type **open** followed by a space and then the address. The connection will be made in the same manner as in the plain vanilla example.

```
world% telnet
Telnet> open books.com
Trying 192.148.240.9...
Connected to books.com.
Escape character is '^]'.

Book Stacks Unlimited, Inc.
Cleveland, Ohio  USA

The On-Line Bookstore

Modem    : (216)861-0469
Internet : Telnet books.com

Enter your FULL Name (e.g SALLY M. SMITH):
```

If, instead of getting connected, nothing happens, or you receive a response such as *host unavailable,* the remote computer or some links may not be working at the moment. Wait a while and try again. If, instead of getting a connection, you receive a response such as *host unknown*, the most likely problem is a misspelled address, although it is possible that the remote computer has been removed from the Internet.

Telnet Addresses

There are two ways that an address may vary in appearance from those used in the examples:

- The address may be followed by a space and a number—for example, **books.com 3000**. If the number, called a port number, is shown with the address, it has to be used.
- The address may be in the form of numbers and dots—for example, **192.148.240.9**. You can use this form of address in the same manner as the alphanumeric addresses.

Sometimes, due to hardware or software problems, you may not be sure if you're connected to the remote computer. You can use the **status** command to check. To use this command, the first step is to get back to Telnet's command mode. This is accomplished by holding down the CTRL key and then pressing the right bracket key (]). This key combination varies from system to system. To know which keys to use for escape, be sure to read the initial connect messages. In this example, the line after *Connected to books.com* tells you that the *Escape character* is *^]* (the caret ^ symbol represents the CTRL key).

In this case, when you hold down the Ctrl key and press], the Telnet prompt will appear. Now you can type the command **status** to see if you are connected to the computer you want to access:

```
Telnet> status
Connected to books.com.
Operating in single character mode
Catching signals locally
Remote character echo
Local flow control
Escape character is '^]'.
```

After each command Telnet returns to the "input" mode—in other words, whatever is typed in now will go directly to the remote computer. To use another Telnet command, use the escape character again. To see which Telnet commands are available, use the escape character and type in a question mark. Some common Telnet commands are shown in Table 8.1.

The display command (?) allows you to view all of Telnet's current settings. It is good to know how to view these settings if you are having a recurring problem with Telnet, but don't be concerned with deciphering this report now.

If you cannot find the remote site's exit command, you can use Telnet's **close** command. First use the escape character, and then at the *Telnet>* prompt, type **close**. This will disconnect your host computer from the remote computer, but leave you in the Telnet program.

```
Telnet> close
Connection closed.
```

Since your host computer is no longer connected to the remote computer, a *Telnet>* prompt appears—you do not need to use the escape character again. The fact that the computers are disconnected can be confirmed with the **status** command:

```
Telnet> status
No connection.
Escape character is '^]'.
```

The **quit** command can be used to leave Telnet and return to your host computer's prompt. The **quit** command could have been used above instead of **close** in order to disconnect the computers and leave Telnet in one step.

```
Telnet> quit
world%
```

If Your Computer Is Not Responding

Occasionally your computer might get locked up during a Telnet session in such a way that pressing the Telnet escape character will not put Telnet back into command mode. In this case, sometimes pressing Ctrl-C (or whichever key your host system considers its Break key) will return you to your system prompt. It is not good practice to force your software to hang up the phone line in this situation, since it may leave the remote computer and your host computer connected for an extended period of time. This is bad netiquette and also may cause extra charges for you if you pay for your access based on connect time. Check with your host system administrators for advice on how to best handle such lockups.

POPULAR USES OF TELNET

The Telnet commands and protocols are, as you can see, quite simple and easily learned. The challenging parts of using Telnet are, first, to find out where the sites are, and second, to learn the variety of different commands needed to use the many services at these remote sites. The following are some examples of ways to find Telnet sites and information on several interesting sites.

Hytelnet

Hytelnet provides a database of Telnet sites. It contains address, login, and other information about Telnet-accessible libraries, BBSs, Freenets, Gophers, and other resources. The information is presented in a hypertext format: Each document, including the opening screen, has highlightable words; moving the cursor to a highlighted word and pressing Enter will take you to other documents.

Table 8.1 Telnet Commands

Command	Meaning
close	Close current connection.
logout	Forcibly log out remote user and close the connection.
display	Display operating parameters.
mode	To enter line or character mode (**mode ?** for more information).
open	Connect to a site.
quit	Exit Telnet.
send	Transmit special characters (**send ?** for more information).
set	Set operating parameters (**set ?** for more information)
unset	Unset operating parameters (**unset ?** for more information).
status	Print status information.
toggle	Toggle operating parameters (**toggle ?** for more information).
slc	Change state of special character (**slc ?** for more information).
z	Suspend Telnet.
!	Invoke a subshell.
environ change	Environment variables (**environ ?** for more information).
?	Display help information.

In practice, it works this way: After Telneting to Hytelnet, read the screen and find an item of interest. Use the up and down arrow keys to move the reverse video cursor up and down the screen until it is on the item you have chosen. Now use the right arrow to get a document on that subject. This new document may itself have highlightable words that you can choose with the up and down arrow keys and get more information on by using the right arrow key. At any time, if you want to go back to the previous document, press the left arrow key and you will go back up one step per key press.

Table 8.2 shows other Hytelnet commands.

Hytelnet can be installed on DOS-based computers, as well as Macintosh, UNIX, and VMS systems. It is also available by Telneting to any one of the sites shown in Table 8.3.

Table 8.2 Hytelnet Commands

Command	Meaning
m	Go directly back to the introductory screen.
+	Go forward a page within a document.
-	Go back a page within a document.
?	Help.
q	Leave Hytelnet.
/	Start a search of the Hytelnet keyword index for documents containing a particular word, which you are prompted to type in.

Table 8.3 Hytelnet Sites

Site	Address	Login
Columbia Law School	lawnet.law.columbia.edu	lawnet
El Paso Community College	laguna.epcc.edu	library
Manchester Computing Centre	info.mcc.ac.uk	hytelnet
Oxford University	rls.ox.ac.uk	hytelnet
University of Adelaide	library.adelaide.edu.au	access
University of Arizona	info.ccit.arizona.edu	hytelnet
University of CA, San Diego	infopath.ucsd.edu	infopath
University of Saskatchewan	access.usask.ca	hytelnet
University of Denver	du.edu	atdu

Multiservice Sites Available Via Telnet

There are some multiservice sites with lots of programs, documents, and links to other services. These supersites are constantly adding items, so they are worth many return visits. Two of the best supersites are described here.

Washington and Lee Law Library

While this site has a large amount of material for the legal profession, that is just the tip of the iceberg. It is a huge site providing access to just about everything publicly accessible on the Internet. The menu lists approximately 3,000 different resources and services including the search tool archie, the search and retrieval tools, Gopher, WWW, Lynx, and resources such as indexes, databases, and libraries. The menu program is easy to understand and use, and includes a search feature.

Address: **liberty.uc.wlu.edu**
Login: **lawlib**

WorldWindow—Washington University Libraries

This is another multiservice site with an easy-to-understand menu interface. All of the standard Internet tools and resources are available including WorldWideWeb, Gopher, archie, WAIS, and Hytelnet. There is also access to Freenets, libraries, and many Campus Wide Information System sites.

Address: **library.wustl.edu**
Login: Press the Enter key to confirm use of standard VT 100 terminal type and then press Enter again to confirm guest status.

BBSs

BBS software provides an easy method for offering databases, e-mail, topical conferences, and file distribution. While BBSs are generally thought of as small amateur systems with names like "The Pink Slime-Mold" or "The Dungeon of Demented Wizards," BBS software can be used for the distribution of business and scholarly material. There are many BBSs available on the Internet via Telnet. Since there are many different BBS programs available and each can be configured in many ways, you will need to read introductory screens and other announcements in order to navigate well. Fortunately, most are menu-driven and have a common "look and feel," so after using several, others will usually be quickly learned.

There are thousands of BBSs that you can explore through the Internet. For current lists of BBSs, check these two FTP sites:

Address: **wuarchive.wustl.edu**; Directory: *systems/msdos/msdos/bbs*
Address: **aug3.augsburg.edu**; Directory: *files/bbs_lists/*
Get files: **nal008.txt** and **Yanoffs_inet_list**

For discussions of new and current BBSs, read the Usenet Newsgroups **comp.bbs.misc**, **alt.internet.services**, or **alt.bbs.internet**. The FAQ file from the **alt.bbs.internet** group is available via FTP from **rtfm.mit.edu** in the directory *pub/usenet/news.answers/* under the filename **inet-bbs-faq.Z**.

Some of the specialized BBSs will be mentioned in Chapters 13 and 14, but the following sections will give you an idea of what's out there.

Business Start-Up Information Database

This site, operated by the Michigan Department of Commerce, contains the following choices on its welcome screen:

1. Licensing Information for Specific Types of Business
2. Checklist for Starting a Business
3. Information for Employers
4. List of Business Development Centers
5. Business Financing Information
6. Help— How to Use NEWBIZ

Address: **hermes.merit.edu**
Login: Respond to *Which Host?* prompt with **mdoc-vax**, and respond
to the *Username:* prompt with **NEWBIZ**.

Fedworld: National Technical Information Service

This is a system for providing U.S. federal government information, public mail, forums, gateways to other government information sources and agencies, government document archives, teleconferencing, and federal job announcements.

Address: **fedworld.doc.gov**
Login: **new**

Book Stacks Unlimited, Inc.

This is an online bookstore with over 240,000 titles. You can search for books by author, title, or subject and then place an order online for books to be shipped to you. There is also a message and conference area for discussing book-related topics.

Address: **books.com**
Login: Press Enter key one time.

MarketBase Online Catalog of Goods and Services

Marketbase provides businesses with virtual storefronts. Potential customers can browse the goods and services for free. Vendors pay a fee to maintain their product information listings.

Address: **mb.com**
Login: **mb**

University of Illinois Division of Environmental Health and Safety BBS

This BBS primarily handles databases of Material Safety Data Sheets (MSDS). Part of the database provides information on suppliers of MSDSs for each chemical; another part of the database has full-text

MSDSs showing chemical properties, hazards, safe use, and emergency procedures.

Address: **romulus.ehs.uiuc.edu**
Login: Contact **mandel@romulus.ehs.uiuc.edu** for authorization
    and login information.

Biotechnet Electronic Buyer's Guide

This site has databases of specific products in the areas of chromatography, electrophoresis, liquid handling, apparatus and instruments, and molecular biology. Specific products can be found, along with the names and addresses of the manufacturers of these products.

Address: **biotechnet.com**
Login: **bguide** (prompt will be for "password")

OAQPS Technology Transfer Network

This site gives users access to a network of over a dozen BBSs which provide documents and messages regarding control of air pollution (including information on Clean Air Act amendments), compliance information, emission measurement technical information, and the Office of Air Quality Planning and Standards.

Address: **ttnbbs.rtpnc.epa.gov**
Login: Press the Enter key.

Window on State Government—Texas Comptroller of Public Accounts

This is a state-run BBS with Texas economic data and tax information, and a section on state and federal grants. An additional feature is the "dial out" service which can connect you to state agency BBSs such as those offered by Parks and Wildlife, Technology Assessment Center, Employment Commission, and the Ethics Commission. In addition, you can connect to the Texas Marketplace BBS.

Address: **window.texas.gov**
Login: **new**

Texas Department of Commerce Bulletin Board

The main menu for this BBS lists these choices:

```
TEXAS COMPANY DIRECTORIES
TEXAS INFORMATION SYSTEM (TEXIS)
TEXAS BUYER/SUPPLIER PRODUCT MATCHING SYSTEM
```

```
INTERNATIONAL TRADE
THE WASTE EXCHANGE
TEXAS STATE PROCUREMENT OPPORTUNITIES
BUSINESS DEVELOPMENT CALENDAR
RURAL DEVELOPMENT
```

Address: **texis.tdoc.texas.gov**
Login: **guest**

Texas Innovation Network

In addition to university library and Gopher connections, this site lists these services: TechTalk Bulletin Board, High-Tech Texas, Faculty Profiles, Research Centers, Government Grants and Contracts, and the NASA Regional Technology Transfer Center. There are connect charges of 35¢ per minute (55¢ per minute for some services) and a $9.95 minimum monthly charge.

Address: **puma.dir.texas.gov**
Login: At Username: prompt, type INNOVATE; at the Password
        prompt, type INNOVATE.

Hawaii FYI

This BBS's information is quite varied, but has one common theme: life in Hawaii. Topics include Hawaii's fishing limits, news from the governor, Hawaii INC BBS, landlord-tenet code, tax information, septic tank information, and veterans' services. Select *Directory of Categories* from the main menu to get to the *Business and Finance* section.

Address: **fyi.uhcc.hawaii.edu**
Login: Press the Enter key two times.

Freenets and Community Computer Systems

Freenets and Community BBSs provide free dial-up access to large BBSs. Increasingly, these BBSs are getting connected to the Internet—usually first with e-mail connections and access to Usenet News, and then with FTP, Telnet, and Gopher access. These are voluntary groups that depend on donations of time, money and equipment.

The bulletin boards with the name Freenet share a common style and philosophy with the Cleveland Freenet, which was the first and is now the largest Freenet. Many of the community bulletin boards use the metaphor of a city to organize their services and files. As an example, here is the opening screen of the Cleveland Freenet.

```
                              / \
WELCOME TO THE...        _!   !_
                        _!__   __!_
          __            !         !
    _!  !_              !   !  !   !
    !      !   / \      !   !  !   !
    !      !  ! !       !   !  !   !___
    !      ! ! !  !     !   !  !   !    !
    !      !_!_  !   !   !  !   !    !
    !      !   ! !     !   !  !   !    !
   _!      !   !_!_  !             !   !_
   !       !      !_!             !      !
  !                                       !
  !          CLEVELAND FREE-NET           !
  !      COMMUNITY COMPUTER SYSTEM        !
  !_____!
```

```
            brought to you by
       Case Western Reserve University
      Community Telecomputing Laboratory
Are you:
            1. A registered user
            2. A visitor
Please enter 1 or 2: 2


[[[ CLEVELAND FREE-NET DIRECTORY ]]]

   1 The Administration Building
   2 The Post Office
   3 Public Square
   4 The Courthouse & Government Center
   5 The Arts Building
   6 Science and Technology Center
   7 The Medical Arts Building
   8 The Schoolhouse
   9 The Community Center & Recreation Area
  10 The Business and Industrial Park
  11 The Library
  12 University Circle
  13 The Teleport
  14 The Communications Center
  15 NPTN/USA TODAY HEADLINE NEWS
--------------------------------------------------
```

How Your Business Can Get Involved

Many of these community sites currently have only a small amount of business-oriented information (though most do have a business section). They are not suitable for any heavy-duty marketing or sales. There are, however, three ways that businesses can get involved:

- Donating time, equipment, and/or expertise to set up a Freenet in your community provides a highly visible way of developing name recognition and a positive public image. Sponsoring a community computer system provides a way to continue this high visibility.

- Maintaining information files or databases (especially those connected with the expertise of your business) can provide an ongoing business presence, public goodwill, and recognition of your company's knowledge and skills. For instance, on the National Capital FreeNet in Ottawa, a local TV station posts its evening news scripts each day.

- Since a community system can offer whatever services it wants to, a system could be set up by several businesses in an area with a strong local business component as well as the other community service features.

Some of the larger community bulletin boards are listed in Table 8.4. For a current list of BBSs, check the following FTP directory:

Site: **alfred.carleton.ca**
Directory: *pub/freenet/*

Table 8.4 Major Community Bulletin Boards

Name	Address	Login
Buffalo Freenet (Buffalo,New York)	**freenet.buffalo.edu**	freeport
Cleveland Freenet (Cleveland,Ohio)	**freenet-in-a.cwru.edu**	2
	freenet-in-b.cwru.edu	2
	freenet-in-c.cwru.edu	2
Columbia Online Information Network (Columbia,Missouri)	**bigcat.missouri.edu**	guest
Denver Freenet (Denver, Colorado)	**freenet.hsc.colorado.edu**	visitor

Table 8.4   (Continued)

Name	Address	Login
Heartland Freenet (Peoria, Illinois)	**heartland.bradley.edu**	bbguest
Lorain Country Freenet (Elyria, Ohio)	**freenet.lorain.oberlin.edu**	guest
National Capital Freenet (Ottawa, Ontario)	**freenet.carleton.ca**	visitor
Tallahassee Freenet (Tallahassee, Florida)	**freenet.scri.fsu.edu**	visitor
Vaasa FreePort BBS	**garbo.uwasa.fi**	guest
Victoria Freenet (Victoria, BC, Canada)	**freenet.victoria.bc.ca**	guest
Youngstown Freenet (Youngstown, Ohio)	**yfn.ysu.edu**	visitor

Alternate Sites for Search Tools

Many of the search tools used on the Internet, such as Gopher and archie, are used as programs installed on your service provider's computer. If these programs are not installed on your host, you can Telnet to another computer and use its search programs. Sometimes, even if your host has these tools, you will find that there are better features in the software at another site which make it easier to use or more efficient. Chapter 10 discusses each of these tools and lists Telnet sites for them, and Chapters 12, 13, and 14 present many other Internet resources which can be reached via Telnet.

More Info on Telnet

For more information on using Telnet, see *The Internet Navigator,* Second Edition, by Paul Gilster (published by John Wiley & Sons).

CHAPTER 9

How to Use FTP to Transfer Files

Thousands of the computers on the Internet have files available free to the public. These may range from a dozen assorted files available from one location to an in-depth collection of thousands of software programs or business-related files at another location.

The most commonly used Internet tool for getting copies of these files is FTP (File Transfer Protocol). The FTP system will transfer both ASCII and binary files of almost any size and type: data files from spreadsheets, CAD, word processors, databases, photo images, and desktop publishing, as well as software and plain text files. This FTP system for file transfer is very powerful, but can seem a little cryptic.

HOW TO USE ANONYMOUS FTP

Each of the sites that offer files in this manner has the FTP software installed. In order to use this transfer system, the host computer (your Internet service provider's computer) must also have the FTP software installed. If you are in doubt as to its availability, you can check with your system administrator or your system's documentation and help files. Another quick way to find out if your system is FTP-ready is to just type **FTP** at your system's main prompt (%, $, etc.). If FTP is installed, you will receive a new prompt: ftp> (to get back to your main system prompt, type **quit** and press the Enter key).

FTP is usually used when you already have these three pieces of information:

- The address of the site where the file you are interested in is stored.
- The directory (subdirectory) in which the file is stored at that site.
- The name of the file.

These three pieces of information may be obtained in a variety of ways—for example:

- Using one of the search tools discussed in Chapter 10.
- From messages others have posted to discussion or Usenet groups that you are a member of.
- From one of the many lists of FTP sites and files that are maintained in discussion group archives and at FTP sites themselves.
- From the README or INDEX files found at most FTP sites, often in the *pub* directory.
- From many places throughout this book, especially Chapters 12, 13, and 14.
- From the guides listed in Chapter 10.

A Plain Vanilla File Transfer

Let's assume that you have come across a list that mentions that there is a file for new Internet users that answers commonly asked questions. The list says the file's name is **fyi_04.txt**, that it is located at **nic.merit.edu**, and that it is in the *documents/fyi* directory. Now you want to find the file and transfer it to your computer so that you can read it. Here's what a typical FTP session seeking that file would look like (in this example, *world%* is the system prompt from the Internet service provider, and the **boldface** items are typed in from the user's keyboard).

```
world% ftp nic.merit.edu
Connected to nic.merit.edu.
220 nic.merit.edu FTP server (SunOS 4.1) ready.
Name (nic.merit.edu:oakridge): anonymous
331 Guest login ok, send ident as password.
Password:
230 Guest login ok, access restrictions apply.
ftp> cd /documents/fyi
250 CWD command successful.
ftp> get fyi_04.txt
200 PORT command successful.
150 ASCII data connection for fyi_04.txt
   (192.74.137.5,3672) (98753 bytes).
226 ASCII Transfer complete.
```

```
101220 bytes received in 4.4 seconds (22 Kbytes/s)
ftp> bye
221 Goodbye.
world%
```

Whew! Now, let's break this down into its components and see how that collection of cryptic characters actually can get the file to your computer.

First, obviously, get online with your access provider and get to the main prompt, which will often be a % or $ (the prompt provided for my account at World Software Tool & Die is *world%*). Next type in the **ftp** command and address:

```
world% ftp nic.merit.edu
```

You will get the following response from your host computer:

```
Connected to nic.merit.edu.
220 nic.merit.edu FTP server (SunOS 4.1) ready.
Name (nic.merit.edu:oakridge):
```

Now, type in the word **anonymous** and the host computer will respond with a request for a password:

```
331 Guest login ok, send ident as password.
Password:
```

If Your Computer Doesn't Respond

If now or at any other point in the FTP session the system seems to stop working correctly, try pressing Ctrl-C key to escape from FTP.

The password is your e-mail address. I would, for instance, type in **oakridge@world.std.com**. As the address is being typed in, it will not be echoed back; that is, you will not see what you are typing appear on the screen. When you've typed in your e-mail address as your password and pressed Enter, the host will respond with anything from one line to a full screen of information about that FTP site, notices, rules, and other information. In this case, the response is:

```
230 Guest login ok, access restrictions apply.
```

Now the directory information comes in to play: type in **cd**, then a space, then a forward slash (/, not \), followed by the full string of directory names:

```
ftp> cd /documents/fyi
```

The host computer will respond with the line shown below and another *ftp>* prompt. Now type in the command **get** followed by a space and the filename:

```
250 CWD command successful.
ftp> get fyi_04.txt
```

FTP Filenames

Filenames are case-sensitive at FTP sites. Copy the upper- and lowercase letters just as they were shown in your original source of information about this file. **Index**, **index**, and **INDEX** would be considered three different filenames.

After you press the Enter key, several transfer status lines like those shown below will appear. If your system has "hash" turned on you will also see, for each block of data transferred, a "#" character printed to the screen.

```
200 PORT command successful.
150 ASCII data connection for fyi_04.txt (192.74.137.5,3672)
    (98753 bytes).
226 ASCII Transfer complete.
101220 bytes received in 4.4 seconds (22 Kbytes/s)
ftp>
```

When the new *ftp>* prompt appears, you can finish the process by typing in **bye**; being polite, FTP will respond by saying *Goodbye* and returning you to your host system's prompt:

```
221 Goodbye.
world%
```

The file you requested is now in your account's subdirectory in your access service provider's computer (or if you changed to another subdirectory before using the FTP command, it will be in that subdirectory). Appendix B explains how to download the file from the host computer to your personal computer.

File Transfers with All the Bells and Whistles

Getting a simple text file may only involve the steps just shown, especially if the site address, directory, and filenames were exactly correct. But those who maintain files may update them and change their names, or they may decide to group them differently in different directories. The FTP system has several commands and functions that help deal with these and several other problems.

The following is an FTP session that will get two more files that were in the same directory as the file obtained in the preceding example. Only the steps that are different from those in the preceding example will be discussed. The session begins as before, by making a connection and logging in:

```
world% ftp nic.merit.edu
Connected to nic.merit.edu.
220 nic.merit.edu FTP server (SunOS 4.1) ready.
Name (nic.merit.edu:oakridge): anonymous
331 Guest login ok, send ident as password.
Password:
230 Guest login ok, access restrictions apply.
ftp>
```

At any FTP prompt, the current directory can be listed to your screen. If you do this before using any **cd** (change directory) command, the top directory available to the public will be shown:

```
ftp> dir
200 PORT command successful.
150 ASCII data connection for /bin/ls (192.74.137.5,4847) (0 bytes).
total 58
-rw-r--r--  1 nic       merit      21219 Feb 11 02:30 INDEX
-rw-r--r--  1 nic       merit      16326 Oct 22 23:18 READ.ME
drwxr-sr-x  2 nic       merit        512 Sep 15  1992
    acceptable.use.policies
drwxr-sr-x  2 root      system       512 Sep 15  1993 bin
drwxr-sr-x  3 cise      nsf          512 May 12  1993 cise
drwxr-sr-x  4 nic       merit        512 Oct 31 20:59
    conference.proceedings
dr-xr-sr-x  2 root      staff        512 Aug  6  1993 dev
drwxr-sr-x  9 nic       merit        512 Nov 30 22:37 documents
drwxr-sr-x  2 root      system       512 Aug  6  1993 etc
drwxr-sr-x 12 nic       merit        512 Jan  7 19:24 internet
drwxr-sr-x  3 nic       merit        512 Nov 30 21:04 internet.tools
drwxr-sr-x  2 nic       merit       1024 Mar 11 12:03
    introducing.the.internet
drwxr-sr-x  2 root      staff        512 Aug  6  1993 lib
drwxr-sr-x  2 nic       merit        512 Oct 13 19:26 maps
```

```
drwxr-sr-x  9 nic      merit      512 Mar  3 19:25 michnet
drwxr-sr-x  7 nic      merit      512 Oct 14 23:39 newsletters
drwxr-sr-x  7 nic      merit      512 Jan 10 17:53 nren
drwxr-sr-x 13 nic      merit      512 Oct 13 23:13 nsfnet
drwxr-sr-x  2 omb      omb        512 Sep 10 1993 omb
drwxr-sr-x  5 nic      merit      512 Mar 17 1993 resources
drwxr-sr-x  4 nic      merit      512 Jul 26 1993 statistics
drwxr-sr-x  3 root     system     512 Jun 12 1993 usr
drwxr-sr-x  3 nic      merit      512 Jul 15 1992 working.groups
226 ASCII Transfer complete.
ftp>
```

As you can see, the directory listing looks rather cryptic, but there are several useful pieces of information you can pull out of the alphabet soup:

- A line that begins with the letter *d* is a directory. For instance, nearly halfway through this directory listing, you will see a line that starts with *d* and ends with the word *document*. If you typed in **cd documents** and pressed Enter, and then **dir** and pressed Enter, you would see a directory listing with *d* at the beginning of the line and *fyi* at the end. This shows in several steps what was accomplished by the command **cd documents/fyi** in the previous session.

- A line that begins with a dash (-) is a file, which is usually available to you for downloading.

- The number just before the date shows the size of the file in bytes. File transfers on the Internet itself are so fast that file size is rarely a concern in terms of Internet time. But you should be aware of the file size in case your Internet provider has restrictions on how much you can store. Another point to consider about file size: Downloading the file from your access provider's computer to your own computer can consume quite a bit of time and cost a lot in phone charges. A 500,000-byte file downloaded on a 2,400-baud modem using Kermit would take about and hour and fifteen minutes (though a good quality 14,400-baud modem using Zmodem protocol would only take around six minutes). See Appendix A for information on modems and downloading.

- At the end of the line is the name of the file or subdirectory. These names contain no spaces, so characters.like_these-will_be--used_to _link_words_together.

An alternative to **dir** is **ls**. Using **ls** provides a list of just the file and directory names, with no other information. This may be of some value if you are using a slow modem and the directory is very large.

Files intended for the public are often in the directory *pub* (though not in this example). Directories marked *system* (in the column near the middle of the screen), such as *etc* and *bin* in this example, have to do with the remote system's operation, and will generally not contain public files. A file named **ls-lR** in the top directory lists every file in the system at some sites (no descriptions). This is usually a huge file.

After moving to the *fyi* directory using the **cd** command, you can call for a directory listing again to see if the file **fyi_04.txt** is there.

```
ftp> cd documents/fyi
250 CWD command successful.
ftp> dir
200 PORT command successful.
150 ASCII data connection for /bin/ls (192.74.137.5,4894) (0
bytes).
total 1640
-rw-r--r--  2 nic     merit         4723 Feb 22 16:24 INDEX.fyi
-rw-r--r--  4 nic     merit         7722 Mar 25  1990 fyi_01.txt
-rw-r--r--  4 nic     merit       308528 Jun 24  1993 fyi_02.txt
-rw-r--r--  5 nic     merit        95238 Aug 19  1990 fyi_03.txt
-rw-r--r--  5 nic     merit        98753 Mar 11 11:49 fyi_04.txt
-rw-r--r--  4 nic     merit        18175 Aug 22  1990 fyi_05.txt
-rw-r--r--  4 nic     merit         3547 Jan 11  1991 fyi_06.txt
-rw-r--r--  4 nic     merit        32829 Feb 28  1991 fyi_07.txt
-rw-r--r--  4 nic     merit       254910 Jul 22  1991 fyi_08.txt
-rw-r--r--  4 nic     merit        92119 May 28  1992 fyi_09.txt
-rw-r--r--  5 nic     merit        71176 Jan 14  1993 fyi_10.txt
-rw-r--r--  4 nic     merit       132147 Jan  3  1992 fyi_11.txt
-rw-r--r--  4 nic     merit        29135 Feb 25  1992 fyi_12.txt
-rw-r--r--  4 nic     merit         9392 Mar 13  1992 fyi_13.txt
-rw-r--r--  4 nic     merit        35694 Mar 13  1992 fyi_14.txt
-rw-r--r--  4 nic     merit         8858 Aug  3  1992 fyi_15.txt
-rw-r--r--  5 nic     merit        53449 Aug 14  1992 fyi_16.txt
-rw-r--r--  4 nic     merit        48199 Oct  7 17:14 fyi_17.txt
-rw-r--r--  5 nic     merit       104624 Jan  7  1993 fyi_18.txt
-rw-r--r--  5 nic     merit         7116 May 27  1993 fyi_19.txt
-rw-r--r--  5 nic     merit        27811 May 27  1993 fyi_20.txt
-rw-r--r--  4 nic     merit        34883 Jul 22  1993 fyi_21.txt
-rw-r--r--  4 nic     merit       113646 Feb 22 16:10 fyi_22.txt
226 ASCII Transfer complete.
```

Before actually getting the file, you might decide to take a look around at what else this site has stored under the *documents* directory. Since the *documents* directory is one step up the directory tree from *fyi* (*documents/fyi*), the command **cd ..** can be used (that's cd, followed by one space, followed by two periods). To move two steps up the tree, type in **cd ../..** (three steps, **cd ../../..** etc.). After pressing Enter, you can again use **dir** to see the directory.

If You're Lost in the Directories

If you are not sure where you are in the directory tree, type **pwd** for a list of directories above the one you are in.

```
ftp> cd ..
250 CWD command successful.
ftp> dir
200 PORT command successful.
150 ASCII data connection for /bin/ls (192.74.137.5,4910) (0
   bytes).
total 57
-rw-r--r--  1 nic    merit    2300 Jul 31  1992 INDEX.documents
drwxr-sr-x  2 nic    merit     512 Mar 11 12:03 fyi
drwxr-sr-x  3 iesg   ietf     2048 Mar 17 08:12 iesg
drwxr-sr-x154 iesg   ietf     3584 Mar 17 08:13 ietf
drwxr-sr-x  2 iesg   ietf    24576 Mar 17 08:14 internet-drafts
drwxr-sr-x  2 nic    merit     512 Jul 15  1992 michnet.tour.guides
drwxr-sr-x  2 nic    merit   19968 Mar 14 15:05 rfc
drwxr--sr-x 2 nic    merit    1536 Mar 14 15:17 std
226 ASCII Transfer complete.
```

You can now go back to the *fyi* directory by typing **cd fyi**. Notice that the whole directory path statement (*documents/fyi*) is not needed, since the move is from *documents* to *fyi*, not from the top directory to *fyi*.

```
ftp> cd fyi
250 CWD command successful.
ftp> dir
200 PORT command successful.
150 ASCII data connection for /bin/ls (192.74.137.5,4929)
   (0 bytes).
total 1640
```

```
-rw-r--r--  2 nic      merit         4723 Feb 22 16:24 INDEX.fyi
-rw-r--r--  4 nic      merit         7722 Mar 25  1990 fyi_01.txt
-rw-r--r--  4 nic      merit       308528 Jun 24  1993 fyi_02.txt
-rw-r--r--  5 nic      merit        95238 Aug 19  1990 fyi_03.txt
-rw-r--r--  5 nic      merit        98753 Mar 11 11:49 fyi_04.txt
-rw-r--r--  4 nic      merit        18175 Aug 22  1990 fyi_05.txt
-rw-r--r--  4 nic      merit         3547 Jan 11  1991 fyi_06.txt
-rw-r--r--  4 nic      merit        32829 Feb 28  1991 fyi_07.txt
-rw-r--r--  4 nic      merit       254910 Jul 22  1991 fyi_08.txt
-rw-r--r--  4 nic      merit        92119 May 28  1992 fyi_09.txt
-rw-r--r--  5 nic      merit        71176 Jan 14  1993 fyi_10.txt
-rw-r--r--  4 nic      merit       132147 Jan  3  1992 fyi_11.txt
-rw-r--r--  4 nic      merit        29135 Feb 25  1992 fyi_12.txt
-rw-r--r--  4 nic      merit         9392 Mar 13  1992 fyi_13.txt
-rw-r--r--  4 nic      merit        35694 Mar 13  1992 fyi_14.txt
-rw-r--r--  4 nic      merit         8858 Aug  3  1992 fyi_15.txt
-rw-r--r--  5 nic      merit        53449 Aug 14  1992 fyi_16.txt
-rw-r--r--  4 nic      merit        48199 Oct  7 17:14 fyi_17.txt
-rw-r--r--  5 nic      merit       104624 Jan  7  1993 fyi_18.txt
-rw-r--r--  5 nic      merit         7116 May 27  1993 fyi_19.txt
-rw-r--r--  5 nic      merit        27811 May 27  1993 fyi_20.txt
-rw-r--r--  4 nic      merit        34883 Jul 22  1993 fyi_21.txt
-rw-r--r--  4 nic      merit       113646 Feb 22 16:10 fyi_22.txt
```

Often each directory listing will have a file called INDEX, or README, or something similar. These files usually contain information about the other files in that directory. They may briefly describe each file, or may give some background as to the source and nature of the files. Such index files are especially important in figuring out which of dozens of cryptically named files to get. (Note that each of the three directories in this example has an INDEX file.)

Dealing with Long FTP File Listings

To read a text file, you can download it, but then you must exit FTP and read the file using your host computer, and then FTP to the site again to get the file(s) you selected. This is a reasonable solution if the INDEX file is really large, or it will require a lot of time to figure out which files you want.

FTP software provides a faster method to look at any text file such as INDEX.fyi while you are online. This is accomplished by using the ¦**more** (said "pipe more") command in conjunction

> with the **get** command. This will print the file, one page at a time, to your screen. After reading each page, press a key, and the next page will be displayed. To use this feature type **get**, followed by a space, then the filename (copy upper- and lowercase letters exactly), followed by a space and then ¦ **more**.
> Note: Some FTP sites use **tt:** instead of ¦ **more**.

```
ftp> get INDEX.fyi ¦more
200 PORT command successful.
150 ASCII data connection for INDEX.fyi (192.74.137.5,2444)
(4723 bytes).
 <NIC.MERIT.EDU> /internet/documents/fyi/INDEX.fyi       22
February 1994


                    Merit Network Information Center Services
                               NIC.MERIT.EDU
                               FTP.MERIT.EDU
                             FTP.MICHNET.NET
                               NIS.NSF.NET
                               (35.1.1.48)


     fyi_01.txt      F.Y.I. on F.Y.I.:   Introduction to the F.Y.I.
                     Notes
                     Malkin, G.S.  (rfc1150.txt)
                     227 lines  7722 bytes


     fyi_02.txt      FYI on a Network Management Tool Catalog:
                     Tools for Monitoring and Debugging TCP/IP
                     Internets and Interconnected Devices
                     Enger, R., J. Reynolds   (rfc1470.txt)
                     10754 lines  308528 bytes


     fyi_03.txt      FYI on Where to Start:  A Bibliography
                     of Internetworking Information
                     Bowers, K.L.  (rfc1175.txt)
                     2412 lines  95238 bytes


     fyi_04.txt      FYI on Questions and Answers:  Answers to
                     Commonly asked "New Internet User" Questions
                     Malkin, G.S., A. Marine   (rfc1325.txt)
                     1795 lines  71232 bytes
```

```
fyi_05.txt    Choosing a Name for Your Computer
              Libes, D.  (rfc1178.txt)
              451 lines  18175 bytes


fyi_06.txt    FYI on the X Window System
              Scheifler, R.W.  (rfc1198.txt)
              171 lines  3547 bytes


fyi_07.txt    FYI on Questions and Answers:  Answers to
              Commonly asked "Experienced Internet User"
              Questions
--More--
```

Merit's Network Information Center host computer, accessible via anonymous FTP, contains a wide array of information about the Internet, NSFNET, and MichNet.

Notice the *--More--* that appears at the bottom of the screen after each page is displayed. This lets you know that there is more to the document which you can read by pressing any key. The number of lines displayed depends on how your account is configured on your Internet access provider's computer. The number of lines can be set to match whatever your communications software needs.

FTP can be set to transfer files in binary or ASCII mode. ASCII files are normally plain text files of letters, numbers, and symbols with no special fonts or formatting (except what can be accomplished with carriage returns and blank spaces). They can be read on most word processors and editors. Binary files may be program files, or they may be the data files from particular programs that can only be used by compatible programs: spreadsheets, CAD files, word processing files, configuration files of various types, digitalized pictures and sound files, and so on.

Whether a file is ASCII or binary can often be determined by looking at the filename extension, which is the group of letters after the last period in the filename (for example, **txt** in the filename **fyi_04.txt**). Some common ASCII filename extensions are **txt, doc, asc, uu, hqx**, and **bsc**. Some common binary filename extensions are **exe, com, zip, bin, sit, arc, tar, z, arj, gif, pcx**, and **jpg**; they may be the extensions assigned to data files designed to work with particular programs. Not all filenames have extensions.

While ASCII files will transfer well in both the binary and ASCII modes, binary files must be sent with the FTP software set to binary. Most FTP sites now make their default setting binary, but just to be sure, you can do the setting yourself. At any *ftp>* prompt, type in **binary** and press Enter. The response will say *Type set to I*. That's okay—"I" stands for Image, which is what the FTP program calls this type of file.

```
ftp> binary
200 Type set to I.
```

To find out which directory on you host computer FTP is going to send the file to, use the **lcd** command. The directory shown will be the place to look for your new files when you finish with the FTP session.

```
ftp> lcd
Local directory now /home/foyer/oakridge
```

The status of some of the features that the FTP user can change are shown in a report which is available at any *ftp>* prompt just by typing in **status** and pressing Enter. Note the report *Type: binary*—this is the file type setting which was just done.

```
ftp> status
Connected to nic.merit.edu.
No proxy connection.
Mode: stream; Type: binary; Form: non-print; Structure: file
Verbose: on; Bell: off; Prompting: on; Globbing: on
Store unique: off; Receive unique: on
Case: off; CR stripping: on
Ntrans: off
Nmap: off
Hash mark printing: off; Use of PORT cmds: on
```

To explore further some of these status report items or to get a list of all of the possible FTP commands, type **help** at the *ftp>* prompt and press Enter.

```
ftp> help
Commands may be abbreviated. Commands are:
```

!	debug	mget	pwd	status
$	dir	mkdir	quit	struct
account	disconnect	mls	quote	system
append	form	mode	recvs	unique
ascii	get	modtime	reget	tenex
bell	glob	mput	rstatus	trace
binary	hash	newer	rhelp	type
bye	help	nmap	rename	user
case	idle	nlist	reset	umask

cd	image	ntrans	restart	verbose
cdup	lcd	open	rmdir	?
chmod	ls	prompt	runique	
close	macdef	proxy	send	
cr	mdelete	sendport	site	
delete	mdir	put	size	

You can select any item on the screen to get help on. Just type in **help** and then any one of the words shown in the help list. As an example, help for **runique** is obtained by typing **help**, then a space, then **runique**.

```
ftp> help runique
runique    toggle store unique for local files
```

In other words, **runique** can protect files in your home directory from being overwritten with newly downloaded files that might happen to have the same name. This feature will rename the new file with most of the original name and a number. In fact, the status report above shows that this feature is on. Shown here is how it could be turned on if it isn't on by default at your site:

```
ftp> runique
Receive unique on.
```

In the first example of an FTP session shown in this chapter, the **get** command was used. A similar command, **mget**, allows you to download several files at one time, without having to type in each filename separately. For example, if files **fyi_21.txt** and **fyi_22.txt** were of interest, you could type in **mget**, followed by a space and then **fyi_2*.txt**. The * is a *wild card* which tells FTP to download all files whose name starts with **fyi_2** and ends with **.txt**. In this particular case, that would be the last three files in the directory: **fyi_20.txt**, **fyi_21.txt**, and **fyi_22.txt**. When each file is ready for transfer, the FTP program prompts you for a **y** or an **n** (Yes or No) as to whether you want that particular file sent. In the example below, I only wanted 21 and 22, so I responded with **n** for 20 and **y** for 21 and 22.

```
ftp> mget fyi_2*.txt
mget fyi_20.txt? n
mget fyi_21.txt? y
200 PORT command successful.
150 Binary data connection for fyi_21.txt
    (192.74.137.5,1260) (34883 bytes).
226 Binary Transfer complete.
34883 bytes received in 2.9 seconds (12 Kbytes/s)
mget fyi_22.txt? y
```

```
200 PORT command successful.
150 Binary data connection for fyi_22.txt
    (192.74.137.5,1270) (113646 bytes).
226 Binary Transfer complete.
113646 bytes received in 5.6 seconds (20 Kbytes/s)
```

FTP allows the user to rename a file at the same time it is being retrieved. In this example, the INDEX file displayed during this session showed that the file **fyi_04.txt** had to do with answers to questions that new users have about the Internet. To make this file easier to find after it is transferred to your computer, you might rename it **new-user.txt**. To do this, type in the **get** command, followed by a space, followed by the name of the file exactly as shown at the FTP site, followed by another space and the new name for the file. Changing the name is also helpful in reducing the filename to the 8-plus-3 character size of DOS filenames, allowing you to provide filenames that are easier to understand than those produced by letting your communications software chop the name down to size.

```
ftp> get fyi_04.txt new-user.txt
200 PORT command successful.
150 Binary data connection for fyi_04.txt
    (192.74.137.5,1158) (98753 bytes).
226 Binary Transfer complete.
98753 bytes received in 3.1 seconds (32 Kbytes/s)
ftp> bye
221 Goodbye.
world%
```

For information about how to download these new files from your Internet access provider's computer to your own personal computer, see Appendix B.

Exiting FTP

If you still have an *ftp>* prompt after FTP has said *Goodbye*, then type **quit** and press Enter to get back to your system prompt.

Many FTP sites also allow uploads of files (usually to a particular directory called something like *in.coming*, where files are checked by system administrators before they are offered to the public). To upload files, use the same logon, change directory, and other procedures as outlined previously, but use the command **put**, followed by the name of the file that you want to send (**mput** with the wild card character * can also be used in a manner similar to **mget** for sending multiple files).

FTP can also be used as a private system for transferring files between various sites. For this purpose the FTP software is configured to accept connection only with people who have the correct user names and passwords.

E-MAIL ACCESS TO FTP FILES

Several methods have been devised to help those with e-mail access to the Internet, but not FTP access. These methods are not as convenient or fast as direct FTP, but if your only access to the Internet is through e-mail, they provide an opportunity to use the many hundreds of thousands of files at FTP sites throughout the world.

Instead of linking directly to an FTP site, using FTPmail you can send e-mail messages to a special mail server, which then interprets your message as a script and connects to the FTP site to make your requests. The mail server then gets the information or files you requested and sends them back to you in an ordinary e-mail message.

Requesting a Directory Listing from an FTP Site

Using the same example as in the previous section, you might get a copy of the file **fyi_04.txt** via FTP mail. The first step could be to examine the directory that the file is supposed to be in, to see if it is still there and whether it is of a manageable size.

Refer to Figure 9.1 for each of these steps:

1. First, log on to your host computer and bring up your mailer as usual. (See Chapter 6 for a full explanation of how to send and receive e-mail.)

2. In the *To* field, type **ftpmail@decwrl.dec.com**. This address will be the same, no matter which site the FTP files are on, since it is the address of the mail server that will *process* your message.

3. In the *Subject* field, type in any name that will remind you of what is being requested. If you have several requests out at one time, this helps keep track of which request is being responded to. The mail server doesn't look at this line.

4. In the body of the message, type **reply**, a space, and then your full e-mail address.

5. On the next line, type **connect**, space, and the name and address of the FTP site where the files you are seeking are stored.

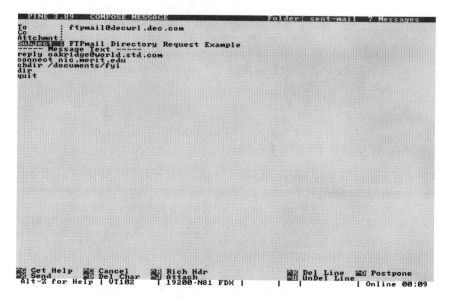

Figure 9.1 FTPmail Request for a Directory Listing. This example shows the message being written using the Pine mailer.

6. On the next line, type **chdir**, space, forward slash (/), and the name of the directory where the files are stored.

7. On the following line, type **dir**. This is a request for the FTPmail to send the directory listing for the current directory.

8. On the last line, type **quit**.

9. Now send the message in the usual manner.

You should get a message back, with the directory listing in the body of the message. This can take anywhere from one minute to several days, depending on how busy the mail server is.

Requesting an ASCII File from an FTP Site

Refer to Figure 9.2 for each of these steps involved in retrieving an file via FTPmail:

1. Fill out the *To* and *Subject* fields as described previously when requesting the directory listing.

2. In the body of the message type in the **reply, connect,** and **chdir** lines just as before.

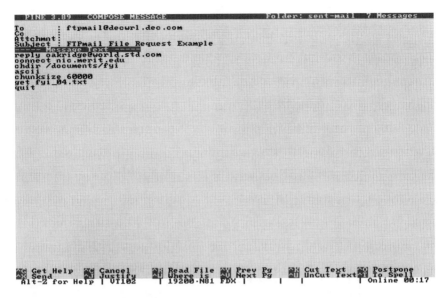

Figure 9.2 An E-mail Message Ready to Send as a Request for an ASCII (Text) File Stored at an FTP Site.

3. On the next line type **ascii**. This forces the FTP site to send in ASCII mode, which is appropriate for this text file. If the FTP site sent the file in the binary mode, the file would be damaged. This is different from a direct connection to an FTP site in which both binary and ASCII files can be sent in the binary mode.

4. On the following line, type **chunksize**, followed by a space, and then the maximum number of bytes your Internet access provider allows incoming mail messages to be. If you are uncertain, try 32,000, which should be acceptable on almost all systems. The **chunksize** command tells the mail server to break down large files into pieces of the size that you specify, and send them to you in a series of messages.

5. Now, the file can be requested with the **get** command. Type **get**, then a space, and then the full filename.

6. Finish the message with **quit** as the last line.

7. Send this message as a normal e-mail message.

The file will come to you as a normal e-mail message—or messages— with the file's contents as the body of the message.

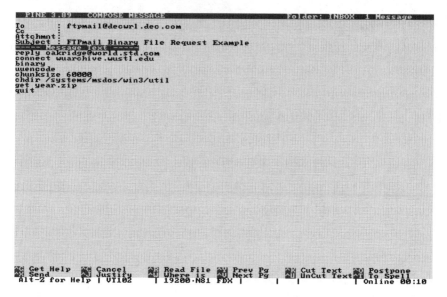

Figure 9.3   An E-mail Message Ready to Be Sent as a Request for a Binary File.

Requesting a Binary File from an FTP Site

In the following example, a calendar program that is in the compressed file *year.zip* is retrieved from the *systems/msdos/win3/util* directory at the **wuarchive.wustl.edu** FTP site. Refer to Figure 9.3 for each of the following steps involved with retrieving a binary file:

1. Fill in the *To* and *Subject* fields in the same way you did previously.
2. Type in the reply line with your address as in the preceding examples.
3. Type in **connect**, a space, then the address of the FTP site—in this case, **wuarchive.wustl.edu**.
4. Type **binary** on the next line. This command needs to be followed by a line telling which type of binary to ASCII conversion should be applied to the file—either **btoa** or **uuencode**. In this example, **uuencode** is used. See Chapter 6 for information on how to use UUDECODE to convert the ASCII messages back into a binary file.
5. The **chunksize, chdir, get**, and **quit** lines are used in the same manner as in the ASCII example.

After UUDECODing the file, you may also need to decompress it.

FILE DECOMPRESSION—.Z, .ZIP, .ARC

Many of the files at FTP sites will be compressed in order to save storage space and increase the speed of file transfers. Compression programs are also used because they can store a group of files (even dissimilar types of files) inside one file. Thus, a program, its support files, data files, and documentation files can all be stored and moved together as a single file.

There are dozens of compression systems, using a variety of methods for compressing and storing files. Therefore, you will need to determine whether the file is compressed, and if so, which system was used, so that you can use the appropriate program to decompress the file. Usually you can determine both whether and how the file was compressed by looking at the filename extension (the characters after the dot).

Here are the most commonly used compression systems listed alphabetically by filename extension. Also listed are files that contain compression and decompression programs which can be found at various FTP sites (the search tool archie discussed in Chapter 10 can be used to locate these files).

- **.arc**

  DOS: The programs ARC and PKARC compress files; ARCE and PKXARC decompress files.
  Software—**pk361.exe, arc602.exe**
  UNIX: Software—**arc521e.tar.z, arc.tar.Z**
  Mac: The program ArcMac compresses, and MacARC decompresses.
  Software—**Stuffit Deluxe and MacARC (commercial packages, not available via FTP)

- **.arj**

  DOS: The program ARJ compresses files and ARN decompresses.
  Software—**arj230ng.exe, arj239f.exe, unarj230.zip**
  UNIX: Software—**unarj230.tar.Z**
  Mac: Software for decompressing—**unArjMac**

- **.exe**

  DOS: Software for making self-extracting files—**pklte115.zip, lzexe91e.zip**

Several compression programs will, in addition to making normal compressed files, make a "self-extracting" file. Such a file will have an extension of **.exe** or **.com**. The INDEX or README files at the FTP site may help in determining whether the file you have received is a single program file or a self-extracting file. To use a self-extracting file, move it to a separate subdirectory, and then run it as you would any other program. It will then decompress and separate the file(s) that are stored in it. You will usually see status reports on the screen while it is decompressing.

- **.F**

  UNIX: A relatively new compression program called freeze. Currently only available for UNIX.

- **.hpk**
  DOS: Software—**hpack78.zip**
  UNIX: Software—**hpack78scr.tar.Z**

- **.hqx**

  Mac: A Macintosh format that uses BinHex to decompress.

- **.lzh**

  DOS: Use LHARC to both compress and decompress files.
  Software—**lha213.exe, lha255b.exe**
  UNIX: Software—**lha-101u.tar.z**
  Mac: Both compress and decompress with MacLHa.

- **.SHAR**

  UNIX: A UNIX format that uses unshar for decompressing files.

- **.Sit**

  Mac: A Macintosh format that uses Stuffit for both compression and decompression.

- **.sqz**

  DOS: Software—**sqz1083e.exe**

- **.tar**

  DOS: Software—**tar4dos.zoo**
  UNIX: .tar is primarily a UNIX compression method. Often, after a file is compressed with .tar, it is compressed again with .Z, so you will need to go through at least two steps to get the file(s) you want.
  Software—standard on UNIX systems

- **.Z**

  This compression is primarily used on UNIX systems. Note that the compression system denoted by this uppercase Z is not the same as the system denoted by the lowercase z.
  DOS: Software—**comp430d.zip**
  UNIX: Software—standard on UNIX systems

- **.z**

  DOS: Software—**gzip107.zip**
  UNIX: Software—**gzip-1.0.7.tar**, pack (on UNIX systems)

- **.zip**

  By far the most popular compression system; software is available for many types of computers.
  DOS: Software—**pk204g.exe, unz50p1.exe, zip19p1x.zip**
  UNIX: Software—**unz50p1.tar.Z, zip19p1.tar.Z**

- **.zoo**

  DOS: Software—**booz20.zip, zoo210.exe**
  UNIX: Software—**booz20.tar.Z, zoo210.tar.Z**

As you can see, there are many compression systems and even more compression programs. Each program has its own unique way of operating which is described in the program's documentation, but there are enough similarities that you can often decompress a file without having to dig too deeply into the instructions. Generally the syntax for decompressing a file looks like this:

```
decompression-program  switches  name-of-file-to-decompress
```

For example, to decompress the file *year.zip* with the **pkunzip.exe** program, move to the directory where *year.zip* is stored. Assuming that **pkunzip.exe** is stored in a subdirectory called *compress*, this is how the command to decompress would appear:

```
c:\compress\pkunzip -o  year.zip
```

In this example, the "switch" **-o** is used so that the program will automatically overwrite existing files of the same name. The list of switches that allow you to change various characteristics of the program can often be displayed to the screen, by changing to the directory where the compression program is stored and just typing the program's name. If this doesn't work, type the name followed by a space and one of these: **?** or **/?** or **/h** or **-?** or **-h** or **help**.

GOING ON FROM HERE

As you can see, FTP works well for getting a specific file when you already have the site address, directory, and filename, but is a slow and hit-or-miss way to search for files of interest. Fortunately, there are several search tools available that will scan Internet-wide file storage sites. The next chapter explains how to use several of the more powerful of these tools.

CHAPTER 10

How to Use the Internet's Searching Tools

The Internet has an enormous reservoir of information, resources, and files on more than 20,000 remote computer sites. Finding information at all of those sites can be difficult, but the search is made easier by a group of searching tools:

- Gopher
- Veronica
- archie
- WorldWideWeb (WWW)
- Lynx
- Mosaic
- WAIS
- CWIS

In addition to these tools, there are a number of useful guides which can be obtained through the Internet to help you in your search for useful information.

GOPHER

The Gopher system provides an easy-to-use, standardized user interface for finding and retrieving files of all kinds from all over the world. The basic feature of Gopher is that every Gopher session starts with a menu from which files, services, Internet tools, or other menus can be chosen. Some of the menu choices on this top menu screen lead to other menus, which lead to submenus, which can lead to more submenus. Using

Gopher menus means that you (and your customers) don't have to deal much with cryptic UNIX commands.

This huge linked system of menus with services and files is often called gopherspace. Because of the incredible growth in the use of Gopher and the intensive interlinking of Internet services and resources to the Gopher system, Gopher comes as close as anything on the Internet to one-stop shopping.

Gopher is based on what is called a "client-server" system. That is, client software running on many machines interacts with a smaller number of remote computers running the server software. If you are using a personal computer and a dial-up Internet access provider, you will just need your normal telecommunications software; the Gopher client software is installed on your access provider's machine for all of its customers to use. Check with your Internet access provider to make sure they offer Gopher.

Why the name Gopher? Gopher was invented in the "Gopher State" (Minnesota) at the University of Minnesota whose sports teams are called the "Golden Gophers"; and "go-fer" is a word for an assistant that finds and delivers things and does all sorts of jobs.

Using Your Access Provider's Gopher

If you are unsure whether your access provider offers Gopher service, you can do a quick check by typing **gopher** at your system's main command line prompt ($, %, >, etc) and then pressing Enter. If you get a menu similar in style to the one shown in the next section of this book, then you probably have a configured working Gopher client.

A Plain Vanilla Gopher Session

Many gopher sessions will be as simple as the following one in which gopher is used to find and read a text file. To start a Gopher session, type **gopher** at your access provider's main system prompt and press the Enter key. At my access provider world.std.com (World Software Tool & Die) the following screen is displayed (your screen might look different at your access provider, but they do all look quite similar):

```
             Internet Gopher Information Client v1.13
                 Root gopher server: gopher.std.com


       1.   Information About The World Public Access UNIX/
 -->   2.   The World's ClariNews AP OnLine & Reuters Newswire Index/
       3.   OBI The Online Book Initiative/
       4.   Internet and Usenet Phone Books/
```

```
 5.  Shops on The World/
 6.  Commercial Services via the Internet/
 7.  Book Sellers/
 8.  Bulletin Boards via the Internet/
 9.  Consultants/
10.  FTP/
11.  Government Information/
12.  Internet Information and Resources/
13.  Libraries/
14.  Membership and Professional Associations/
15.  News and Weather/
16.  Non-Profit Organizations/
17.  Other Gopher and Information Servers/
18.  Periodicals, Magazines, and Journals/
19.  Usenet Newsgroup and Mailing List Archives/
20.  University of Minnesota Gopher Server/
21.  software/


Press ? for Help, q to Quit, u to go up a menu        Page: 1/1
```

The arrow --> indicates which item is highlighted (selected). The first time you see a menu, the arrow will be pointing to item 1. By pressing the up and down arrow keys you can move to different items on the menu. To select an item, press the Enter key. Selecting 2. *The World's ClariNews AP OnLine & Reuters Newswire Index/* in our example would cause the following submenu to be displayed:

```
              Internet Gopher Information Client v1.13
         The World's ClariNews AP OnLine & Reuters Newswire Index


--> 1.  Information About These AP OnLine and Reuters Newswire Indexes.
    2.  Search ClariNews AP OnLine Newswire Index <?>
    3.  Search Reuters newswire index <?>



Press ? for Help, q to Quit, u to go up a menu        Page: 1/1
```

To read the file *Information About These AP OnLine and Reuters Newswire Indexes*, press the Enter key and the file will be displayed on your screen:

```
The World provides full-text search and retrieval of Associated
Press OnLine and Reuters newswire feeds for the last seven
calendar days. These indexes are updated four times daily.
```

```
You will be prompted for words to search for. You can respond
with one or more words, any articles which contain these words
will be listed for viewing by headline. You can combine more
than one search word with the word "and" in order to limit
matches to articles which contain both words, or "or" for all
articles that have either word. For example, "bill and clinton"
would only match articles which contain both the words "bill"
and "clinton" (note that searches ignore upper/lower case.) If
you do not specify "and" or "or" then "or" is assumed.

Send e-mail to "staff" if you have any questions or problems.
->Spike
Press <RETURN> to continue, <m> to mail, <s> to save, or <p> to print:
```

To leave Gopher after reading the file, just press the Enter key and then type in the letter **q**. You will be asked if you really want to leave Gopher with this prompt:

```
Really quit (y/n) ?
```

Since Yes is the default answer, all that needs to be done is to press the Enter key, and your access provider's main prompt will be displayed again. For just finding and reading a simple short text file, that's all there is to it!

A Gopher Session with Some Very Useful Bells and Whistles

Gopher can do a whole lot more than just finding and displaying a text file. When its other features are utilized, it can connect to other sites and services and find and download binary files of sound, graphics, and other data. This time we'll give Gopher a little more exercise and examine the screens more carefully.

As was done in the plain vanilla example, at your host system prompt type **gopher** and press the Enter key. Looking more carefully at the first menu screen at world.std.com, note that the first line tells which client software is running (since there are a lot of small differences in how Gopher clients operate, knowing which software is running can be helpful). The second line states: *Root gopher server: gopher.std.com*. This lets you know that this is the top menu (the menu from which all others can be reached) at this site. From wherever you are, in any menu, you can return to this top menu by pressing the **m** key.

The diagonal bar / at the right end of a menu item indicates that it leads to another menu rather than directly to a text file. In this example, all of the menu items lead to other menus, and most of those menus lead to still further menus.

```
               Internet Gopher Information Client v1.13
                  Root gopher server: gopher.std.com

       1.   Information About The World Public Access UNIX/
       2.   The World's ClariNews AP OnLine & Reuters Newswire Index/
  --> 3.   OBI The Online Book Initiative/
       4.   Internet and Usenet Phone Books/
       5.   Shops on The World/
       6.   Commercial Services via the Internet/
       7.   Book Sellers/
       8.   Bulletin Boards via the Internet/
       9.   Consultants/
      10.  FTP/
      11.  Government Information/
      12.  Internet Information and Resources/
      13.  Libraries/
      14.  Membership and Professional Associations/
      15.  News and Weather/
      16.  Non-Profit Organizations/
      17.  Other Gopher and Information Servers/
      18.  Periodicals, Magazines, and Journals/
      19.  Usenet Newsgroup and Mailing List Archives/
      20.  University of Minnesota Gopher Server/

  Press ? for Help, q to Quit, u to go up a menu        Page: 1/1
```

Selecting Menu Items

As an alternative to using the up and down arrow keys to select a menu item, you can simply type the number of the menu item you want, and then press Enter.

Remembering Where You've Been with Bookmarks

With thousands of menus leading from one to another, it is very easy to get lost, or to find an excellent resource and then forget how to get back to it at a later date. To deal with this, Gopher has a system called "Bookmarks" which allows you to record important resources in a custom menu that you create.

In the following example, I will create several bookmarks. Then you'll see how to display a menu of bookmarks so that you can quickly jump to the menus you've marked. First I'll go to *OBI The Online Book Initiative/* menu by selecting item 3. The name of this new menu is *The Online Books*. To create a bookmark for *The Online Books*, type Shift-**A** and the box shown in the center of the screen below will appear. To accept this as a bookmark entry with the name shown, press the Enter key.

```
                Internet Gopher Information Client v1.13
                           The Online Books


    -->  1.   Welcome to OBI.
         2.   A. Hofmann/
         3.   A.E.Housman/
         4.   ACN/
         5.   ATI/
         6.   Access/
         7.   Aesop/
         8.   Algernon.Charles.Swinburne/
         9.   Ambrose.Bierce/
        10.   Amoeba/
        11.   Anarchist/
        12.   Andrew.Marvell/
        13.   Anglo-Saxon/
        14.   Anonymous/
        15.   Ansax/
        16.   Antarctica/
        17.   ArtCom/


    +-------------------------------------------------------------+
    |                                                             |
    | Name for this bookmark?  The Online Books                   |
    |                                                             |
    |                        [Cancel ^G] [Accept - Enter]         |
    |                                                             |
    +-------------------------------------------------------------+

    Press ? for Help, q to Quit, u to go up a menu        Page: 1/6
```

Navigating Long Menus

Note that in the lower right corner of the screen *Page: 1/6* indicates that this is page 1 of 6 pages. The other pages of menu choices can be reached by using the + and - keys to move up and down the pages. (See the "Summary of Commands and Symbols" later in this chapter for variations on which keys different Gopher clients use for this.)

By default, the program names the new *Bookmarks* menu item with the name of the current menu. You can, however, change the name to something that will help you better remember what was important to you about the menu. After you type Shift-**A**, the Bookmark entry box will be displayed. Now, you can enter a new bookmark name by using the Backspace key to erase the existing name; then type in the new name, and press Enter. In the following example, I'll place a bookmark and change the name from *Government Information* (the current name of the menu) to *Census, Fed gophers, etc.*

Entering Bookmark Names

Instead of using the Backspace key to delete a bookmark name, you can type Ctrl-U to erase the entire name all at once. Then type in a new name and press the Enter key.

```
            Internet Gopher Information Client v1.13
                      Government Information


   -->  1.   Americans Communicating Electronically/

        2.   Clinton Speeches and Position Papers/

        3.   Clinton's Economic Plan/

        4.   Internet Sources of US Government Information.

        5.   Library of Congress - Marvel/

        6.   NSF's list of U.S. Government Gopher Servers/

        7.   North Atlantic Treaty Organization.

        8.   Resources for White House Information.

        9.   U.S. House Gopher/

        10.  U.S. Senate Gopher/

        11.  United States Bureau of the Census/

        12.  United States GOVERNMENT Gophers/

        13.  White House Press Release Service/
```

```
+------------------------------------------------------------------+
|                                                                  |
| Name for this bookmark?    Census, Fed gophers, etc              |
|                                                                  |
|                            [Cancel ^G] [Accept - Enter]          |
|                                                                  |
+------------------------------------------------------------------+
```

Another example of a menu item that would be good for a *Bookmarks* menu is a frequently changing database such as the new search services shown below. No matter how far down the menu tree this item is, with it in the *Bookmarks* menu you will have direct access to it.

```
              Internet Gopher Information Client v1.13
          The World's ClariNews AP OnLine & Reuters Newswire Index


  --> 1. Information About These AP OnLine and Reuters Newswire Indexes.

      2. Search ClariNews AP OnLine Newswire Index <?>

      3. Search Reuters newswire index <?>
```

```
+------------------------------------------------------------------+
|                                                                  |
| Name for this bookmark?  ClariNews AP OnLine & Reuters...        |
|                                                                  |
|                            [Cancel ^G] [Accept - Enter]          |
|                                                                  |
+------------------------------------------------------------------+
```

You have now created your own *Bookmarks* menu with three entries. To view this menu, press the **v** key and a menu similar to that shown below will be displayed. This custom menu can be used like any other ready-made Gopher menu that you find on the Internet.

```
              Internet Gopher Information Client v1.13
                            Bookmarks


  --> 1. The Online Books
      2. Census, Fed gophers, etc/
      3. ClariNews AP OnLine & Reuters Newswire Index/
```

Any time you want to use this *Bookmarks* menu, just press the **v** key. To return to whatever menu you were using when you pressed the **v** key, press the **u** key (if you are several levels down in menus that started from one of your Bookmark items, you may need to press the **u** key several times to get back to the *Bookmarks* menu before pressing the **u** key again to escape from the *Bookmarks* menu.

To delete any item from the *Bookmarks* menu, just use the up and down arrow keys to move the - -> pointer to the item to be deleted, then press the **d** key. Caution: There is no prompt asking if you really want to delete this item; it will immediately be deleted when the **d** key is pressed.

Shift-**A** is used to make bookmarks for menu items that lead to other menus or to searches. The lowercase **a** is used for menu items that are files. You might, for instance, want to repeatedly come back to one file that is changed frequently—possibly a weather forecast or stock information file.

To make this *Bookmarks* menu the top menu that shows up first when you start Gopher, invoke Gopher with the command **gopher -b**.

Searching Large Gopher Menus

When you encounter a Gopher menu as large as the one excerpted below (this is page 1 of 34 pages), it is often easier to do a search than to use the + and - keys and read all of the entries. To do a search, press the / key and a box will be displayed in the center of the screen:

```
               Internet Gopher Information Client v1.13
                 All the Gopher Servers in the World


  --> 1.   Search Gopherspace using Veronica/
      2.   ACADEME THIS WEEK (Chronicle of Higher Education)/
      3.   ACM SIGDA/
      4.   ACM SIGGRAPH/
      5.   ACTLab (UT Austin, RTF Dept)/
      6.   AMI -- A Friendly Public Interface/
      7.   AREA Science Park, Trieste, (IT)/
      8.   ARPA Computing Systems Technology Office (CSTO)/
      9.   AT&T Global Information Solutions (formerly NCR) Info Server/
      10.  Academic Position Network/
      11.  Academy of Sciences, Bratislava (Slovakia)/
      12.  Acadia University Gopher/
      13.  Action for Blind People/
      14.  Advantis Global Network Services, Applications & Outsourcing/
      15.  AgResearch Wallaceville, Upper Hutt, New Zealand/
      16.  Agricultural Genome Gopher/
      17.  Alabama Supercomputer Network/
```

```
+-----------------------------------------------------------------+
|                                                                 |
| Search directory titles for  Texas                              |
|                                                                 |
|                          [Cancel ^G] [Accept - Enter]   |
|                                                                 |
+-----------------------------------------------------------------+
```

Type in the word or phrase that you expect would be in Gopher menu items of interest to you. The search is case-insensitive, so capitalization doesn't matter. Partial words are often best: For example, using **electron** as the search word would find menu items with "electron," "electronics," "electronically," and so on. After the search term is typed, in this case **Texas**, press the Enter key and the pointer will move to the first menu item it finds that has your search word in it. To find the next menu item that contains the search term, press the **n** key.

```
                  Internet Gopher Information Client v1.13
                     All the Gopher Servers in the World


       1.   Search Gopherspace using Veronica/
       2.   ACADEME THIS WEEK (Chronicle of Higher Education)/
       3.   ACM SIGDA/
       4.   ACM SIGGRAPH/
       5.   ACTLab (UT Austin, RTF Dept)/
       6.   AMI -- A Friendly Public Interface/
       7.   AREA Science Park, Trieste, (IT)/
       8.   ARPA Computing Systems Technology Office (CSTO)/
       9.   AT&T Global Information Solutions (formerly NCR) Info Server/
       10.  Academic Position Network/
       11.  Academy of Sciences, Bratislava (Slovakia)/
       12.  Acadia University Gopher/
       13.  Action for Blind People/
       14.  Advantis Global Network Services, Applications & Outsourcing/
       15.  AgResearch Wallaceville, Upper Hutt, New Zealand/
       16.  Agricultural Genome Gopher/
       17.  Alabama Supercomputer Network/
       18.  Alamo Community College District/
       19.  Albert Einstein College of Medicine/
       20.  Alderson-Broaddus College/
       21.  Algonquin College of Applied Arts & technology, Nepean,
            ON, Ca/
       22.  Alpha Phi Omega/
```

```
      23. American Chemical Society/
      24. American Demographics/
      25. American Institute of Physics (AIP)/
      26. American Mathematical Society /
      27. American Philosophical Association/
      28. American Physiological Society/
      29. American Political Science Association/
      30. American Quarterly Magazine/
      31. American University/
      32. Americans Communicating Electronically/
      33. Amherst College/
      34. Andrews University/
      35. Andrews University School of Business/
      36. Anesthesiology Gopher /
      37. Appalachian State University/
      38. Apple Computer Higher Education gopher server/
 -->  39. Applied Research Laboratories, The University of Texas
          at Austin/
      40. Aquanaut (SCUBA Diving Forum)/
      41. Arabidopsis Research Companion, Mass Gen Hospital/Harvard/
      42. Arbornet/
      43. Arizona Board of Regents/


 Press ? for Help, q to Quit, u to go up a menu         Page: 1/34
```

Viewing and Downloading Gopher Text Files

Text files are often much larger than the few paragraphs seen in the plain vanilla example. Gopher therefore provides several methods for moving around within a document and several ways of downloading the document to your access provider's computer or directly to your personal computer. In this example the *GOES Data User's Guide* is selected to be read:

```
                Internet Gopher Information Client v1.13
              NOAA Geostationary Satellite Data Active Archive


   -->  1.  GOES Data User's Guide.
        2.  Information about the Browse Images.
        3.  GOES Browse Images/
        4.  Global Composite Geostationary Browse Images/
        5.  Information about the CRAS Forecast Images.
        6.  CRAS Forecast GOES Images/
        7.  Other NOAA Gopher Servers/
```

Gopher displays enough of the file to fill the screen, then stops and, at the bottom of the screen, displays the word *more* and the percentage of the document that has been displayed. In this case *8%* was displayed on this one screen, so the full document is probably about 12 or 13 pages long.

```
            Geostationary Operational Environment Satellite (GOES)
                          Data User's Guide
                            (preliminary)


I. INTRODUCTION

    The GOES system includes the satellite (with the GOES
instrumentation and direct down-link data transmission
capability), the NESDIS facility at Wallops Island, Virginia
(that receives the direct transmission and generates the
"stretched VISSR" transmission), and the ground systems at
NESDIS and at the University of Wisconsin - Madison's (UW) Space
Science and Engineering Center (SSEC).

A. The GOES Satellites

    The original GOES instrument was the Visible and Infrared Spin
Scan Radiometer (VISSR), which was an outgrowth of the spin scan
radiometer flown aboard several of the Applications Technology
Satellite series of NASA research satellites. The VISSR was first
flown aboard SMS-1 and SMS-2 (Synchronous Meteorological
Satellite), also NASA satellites, that were turned over to NOAA
for operational use. GOES-1, GOES-2, and GOES-3 were operational
satellites that flew the original VISSR instrument. GOES-4,
GOES-5, GOES-6 and GOES-7 where flown with a modified instrument
package called the VISSR Atmospheric Sounder (VAS). A set of
infrared sensors were added to provide an atmospheric sounder
capability. Details of these instruments are provided below.

    The data from these satellites have been archived at the
University of Wisconsin - Madison (UW) from 1978 to the present.
The holdings at the UW are currently about 120 terabytes. Data
from the archive are available through the National Oceanic and
Atmospheric Administration (NOAA) National Environmental Satellite
Data Information Service (NESDIS) facility at 301-763- 8111.
1. Visible and Infrared Spin Scan Radiometer (VISSR) Instrument

--More--(8%)
```

When a prompt such as --More--(8%) is shown, there are several options for moving around in the document (see the "Summary of Commands and Symbols" later in this chapter for the many variations on this among Gopher clients): To see the next page, press the Spacebar; to see the previous page, press the **b** key; to search for a word or phrase in the document, type the forward slash / followed by the word or phrase and then press the Enter key. Usually this search *is* case-sensitive, so you may need to try the word in several forms such as **house** or **House** or **HOUSE**.

If you want to leave the document before getting to the end of it, press the **q** key. If the document is too large to read at one time, or you want a copy in your personal computer for searching or printing out, there are several ways to get the file. One straightforward but not too elegant way is to turn on your communication software's "log" function, which saves to a file everything that is displayed to your screen. Once it is turned on you can repeatedly press the Spacebar and quickly page through the document. This does, however, mean the prompts such as *--More--(8%)* will appear on every page. This is fine for a short to medium-sized document that you just want for a quick look.

A good alternative for getting a full copy of the document without these problems is to mail the document to your e-mail account. To do this, at any time while viewing the document press the **q** key and the prompt shown at the bottom of the screen below will be displayed.

```
       Geostationary Operational Environment Satellite (GOES)

                        Data User's Guide

                          (preliminary)


I. INTRODUCTION


The GOES system includes the satellite (with the GOES

instrumentation and direct down-link data transmission

capability), the NESDIS facility at Wallops Island, Virginia

(that receives the direct transmission and generates the

"stretched VISSR" transmission), and the ground systems at

NESDIS and at the University of Wisconsin - Madison's (UW) Space

Science and Engineering Center (SSEC).


Press <RETURN> to continue, <m> to mail, <s> to save, or <p> to print:
```

Now press the **m** key and press Enter. A box will appear in the center of the screen as shown below:

```
+-------------------------------------------------------------+
|                                                             |
| Mail current document to:                                   |
|                                                             |
|                             [Cancel ^G] [Accept - Enter]    |
|                                                             |
+-------------------------------------------------------------+
```

Type in your full e-mail address and press Enter. The words *Mailing File* will appear for a short time at the bottom of the screen.

```
+-------------------------------------------------------------+
|                                                             |
| Mail current document to:  oakridge@world.std.com           |
|                                                             |
|                             [Cancel ^G] [Accept - Enter]    |
|                                                             |
+-------------------------------------------------------------+
```

```
                                             Mailing File..|
```

An alternative to mailing is saving. The file you are viewing is saved to your home directory on your Internet access provider's computer. You can then use an editor on the access provider's computer to read the file or download the file to your personal computer. (See Appendix B for details on this procedure.)

To save a file, press the **q** key while viewing the file. This will provide the prompt at the bottom of the screen as shown above. Now press the **s** key and hit Enter. A box will appear in the center of the screen with the current file's name. All that needs to be done now is to press Enter—you will briefly see the message *Saving File...* at the bottom of your screen.

```
+-------------------------------------------------------------+
|                                                             |
| Save in file:   GOES-Data-User-s-Guide                      |
|                                                             |
|                             [Cancel ^G] [Accept - Enter]    |
|                                                             |
+-------------------------------------------------------------+
```

```
                                             Saving File..|
```

If you plan to download the file to a personal computer which does not allow such long filenames (such as an MS-DOS system, which is limited to eight characters plus a three-character extension), you can change the file's name now. Type Ctrl-U to erase the current name. Now type in the new name for the entry and press Enter. The file will be saved to your home directory with the new name.

```
+---------------------------------------------------------------+
|                                                               |
| Save in file:    goes-wx                                      |
|                                                               |
|                             [Cancel ^G] [Accept - Enter]      |
|                                                               |
+---------------------------------------------------------------+

                                             Saving File..|
```

There are a variety of error messages that may be displayed from time to time. After you read them they can usually be removed from the screen by pressing the Enter key. If this doesn't work, hold down the Ctrl key and tap the **g** key.

In this example an attempt was made to get the *U.S. Weather Map <Picture>*. The error message says *Connection refused by host*. This refusal may be due to faulty information in the Gopher's configuration files or, more likely, to the remote computer's being too busy at that moment to connect with a new user.

```
              Internet Gopher Information Client v1.13
                          Art and Images


        1.   ASCII Clipart Collection/
        2.   DOS and Mac viewing software/
        3.   TAEX Clip Art Collection (TIFF)/
  -->   4.   U.S. Weather Map <Picture>
        5.   Entertainment Images from Texas A&M (GIF)/
        6.   Entertainment Images from U Michigan (GIF)/
        7.   WUARCHIVE Collection (GIF)/
        8.   WUARCHIVE Collection (JPEG)/
        9.   - - - - - - - - - - - - - - - -.
        10.  Search for Pictures/Images in all of GopherSpace <?>
        11.  - - - - - - - - - - - - - - - -.
        12.  Animals, Plants, Scenic Beauty from U of Indiana/
        13.  ArchiGopher: Images from U of Michigan/
        14.  Architectural Projects from Johns Hopkins U/
        15.  Art Gallery (from University of Vermont)/
        16.  Astronomical Images (from U of Arizona)/
```

```
17. As+-------------------Network Error-------------------+
18. Bi|                                                   |
19. Bi| Cannot connect to host wx.atmos.uiuc.edu, port 70. |
20. Bi|                                                   |
21. Bo|  Connection refused by host.                      |
22. Ca|                                                   |
23. Ca|                        [Cancel - ^G] [OK - Enter] |
24. Ca|                                                   |
25. Ca+---------------------------------------------------+
26. Central American Images/
27. Centre for Innovative Computer Applications (Indiana Univ.)/
```

Press ? for Help, q to Quit, u to go up a menu Receiving Information.

Downloading Binary Gopher Files

The document files described above are ASCII files (also known as 7-bit or text files). Binary files (also know as 8-bit files) can be spreadsheets, formatted word processing files, desktop publishing documents, CAD files, sound files, picture and graphics files, software, and hundreds of other types of files. Binary files can't be downloaded to your personal computer by any of the techniques described so far. Gopher provides another technique for these binary files. This method also provides another way of getting ASCII files.

In this example the picture file 2. *Fluid Dynamics 2 (8-bit GIF image)* *<Picture>* will be downloaded directly from Gopher to your personal computer. Start by using the arrow keys to move the --> pointer to the item of interest.

```
            Internet Gopher Information Client 1.2VMS p10
                        Fluid Dynamics (list)


       1.   Fluid Dynamics 2 (24-bit RLE image) <Picture>
  -->  2.   Fluid Dynamics 2 (8-bit GIF image) <Picture>
       3.   Fluid Dynamics 2 (text description).


Press ? for Help, q to Quit, u to go up a menu          Page: 1/1
```

Now type Shift-**D**. A box will be displayed in the center of the screen providing choices of downloading protocols. You must select the same protocol as you have your communications software in your personal computer set for. If your software has Zmodem available, it is a good choice due to its speed. Type in the number of your protocol choice.

```
Internet Gopher Information Client 1.2VMS p10


                    Fluid Dynamics (list)


     1.   Fluid Dynamics 2 (24-bit RLE image) <Picture>
-->  2.   Fluid Dynamics 2 (8-bit GIF image) <Picture>
     3.   Fluid Dynamics 2 (text description).


                 +---Fluid Dynamics 2 (8-bit GIF image)----+
                 |                                         |
                 |  1. Zmodem                              |
                 |  2. Ymodem                              |
                 |  3. Xmodem-1K                           |
                 |  4. Xmodem-CRC                          |
                 |  5. Kermit                              |
                 |  6. Text                                |
                 |                                         |
                 |  Choose a download method:              |
                 |                                         |
                 |  [Cancel ^G]   [Choose 1-6]             |
                 |                                         |
                 +-----------------------------------------+


Press ? for Help, q to Quit, u to go up a menu        Page: 1/1
```

The screen will clear and prompt you to give your communications software the command to begin receiving a file. (The particular command varies greatly among communications program, so you will need the software's documentation.) After the prompt, various lines of seemingly random characters will be printed on the screen.

```
Start your download now...
è*_B00000000000000
```

Move quickly to get your software into receive mode, because after sending several of these lines, Gopher will stop trying to send the file. After the file has been successfully sent, an additional two-line report will be displayed on the same screen.

```
Download Complete. 109184 total bytes, 1186 bytes/sec
Press <RETURN> to continue
```

Press Enter and you will be back to the Gopher menu.

Searching a Gopher Database

A Gopher menu item that ends with a bracketed question mark <?> will perform a search of the indicated database. In the following example, a database of news articles is searched for particular words in the texts of Reuters articles. The search starts by first moving the pointer down to 3. Search *Reuters newswire index* <?> and then pressing Enter.

```
            Internet Gopher Information Client v1.13
        The World's ClariNews AP OnLine & Reuters Newswire Index


    1. Information About These AP OnLine and Reuters Newswire
       Indexes.
    2. Search ClariNews AP OnLine Newswire Index <?>
-->  3. Search Reuters newswire index <?>


Press ? for Help, q to Quit, u to go up a menu        Page: 1/1
```

This will be a case-insensitive search, meaning that if you search for **CAR** you will find any occurrences of **CAR**, **Car**, and **car**. You can use full words, partial words, or phrases. **AND**, **OR**, and **NOT** can be used as logical operators to further refine the searches. (Words separated by a space are considered to be linked by **AND**, so a search for articles about the **White House** may also yield some articles about a **house** next to the **White** River, or the **House** of Representatives.) Use **AND** between pairs, then **OR** to connect pairs or single terms. In the search shown below, articles are sought that have somewhere in them either **stocks** or **bonds**. **OR** is not the "exclusive or"; in other words, this search will provide:

- All articles with the word **stocks** in them.
- All articles with the word **bonds** in them.
- All articles with both the words **stocks** and **bonds**.

```
            Internet Gopher Information Client v1.13

        The World's ClariNews AP OnLine & Reuters Newswire Index


    1. Information About These AP OnLine and Reuters Newswire
       Indexes.
    2. Search ClariNews AP OnLine Newswire Index <?>
-->  3. Search Reuters newswire index <?>
```

```
+-----------------Search Reuters newswire index----------------+
|                                                              |
| Words to search for  stocks or bonds                         |
|                                                              |
|                         [Cancel ^G] [Accept - Enter]         |
|                                                              |
+--------------------------------------------------------------+
Press ? for Help, q to Quit, u to go up a menu        Page: 1/1
```

Note: Gopher in general is case-insensitive so that **AND, OR,** and **NOT** may be entered in lowercase or uppercase. After typing in the search words, press Enter. The results will be presented as another Gopher menu from which you can select, read, mail, download, and so on. The following is the first of four pages of menus.

```
                Internet Gopher Information Client v1.13
                Search Reuters newswire index: stocks or bonds


 -->  1. _stocks-week_ Stocks expected to resume rally after freefall   ..ks/.

      2. _stocks_ Wall street stocks pause after recent recovery   ../stocks/.

      3. _stocks-overseas_ London stocks end slightly lower, tokyo ri   ..ks/.

      4. _stocks-close_ Stocks close higher on lower rates   ../Apr 7/stocks/.

      5. _stocks-canada_ Toronto stocks close stronger on canadian do   ..ks/.

      6. _stocks_ Wall street stocks sharply lower at midday   ..pr 8/stocks/.

      7. _stocks_ Blue-chip stocks dip, weighed down by high-tech sha   ..ks/.

      8. _stocks-asia_ Tokyo stocks end mixed; hong kong market rises   ..ks/.

      9. _stocks-week_ Stocks expected to resume rally after freefall   ..rt/.

     10. _stocks-asia_ Tokyo stocks end higher on late index-linked b   ..ks/.

     11. _stocks-asia_ Tokyo stocks close lower on arbitrage selling   ..cks/.

     12. _stocks_ Wall street stocks pause after recent recovery   ..-report/.

     13. _stocks-close_ Blue-chip stocks end higher   ..94/Apr/Apr 11/stocks/.

     14. _stocks-canada_ Toronto stocks end sluggish session lower on   ..ks/.

     15. _stocks-japan_ Tokyo stocks take hosokawa's resignation in s   ..ks/.

     16. _stocks-close_ Wall street stocks cut losses   ..4/Apr/Apr 8/stocks/.

     17. _stocks-canada_ Toronto stocks close slightly lower on canad   ..ks/.

     18. _stocks-actives_ Most active stocks on nyse and amex   .. 11/stocks/.

     19. _stocks-changes_ Stocks leading percentage gains and losses   ..cks/.

     20. _stocks-mexico_ Mexican stocks fall to lowest close this yea   ..ks/.

     21. _stocks-nasdaq_ Most active stocks in nasdaq trading   .. 11/stocks/.

     22. _stocks-actives_ Most active stocks on nyse and amex   ..r 8/stocks/.

     23. _stocks-changes_ Stocks leading percentage gains and losses   ..cks/.

     24. _stocks-nasdaq_ Most active stocks in nasdaq trading   ..r 8/stocks/.

     25. _stocks-mexico_ Mexico stocks chalk up biggest weekly loss t   ..ks/.
```

```
26. _stocks-changes_ Stocks leading percentage gains and losses  ..cks/.
27. _stocks-actives_ Most active stocks on nyse and amex  ..r 7/stocks/.
28. _stocks-mexico_ Mexican stocks close higher on rebound  ..7/stocks/.
29. _markets_ Stocks and bonds rise for third straight day  ..s-report/.
30. _stocks-overseas_ London stocks end slightly lower, tokyo ri  ..rt/.
```

```
Press ? for Help, q to Quit, u to go up a menu          Page: 1/4
```

If you find the response is too large, examine the list and decide how to redefine the search. In this example, since there is obviously a lot of Japanese stock market activity, the object of the search might be changed to "stocks in Japan." It can also be seen from the original list that some articles mention Tokyo, but may not use the word Japan; therefore combinations of **OR** and **AND** are used.

```
             Internet Gopher Information Client v1.13
        The World's ClariNews AP OnLine & Reuters Newswire Index


   1. Information About These AP OnLine and Reuters Newswire
      Indexes.
   2. Search ClariNews AP OnLine Newswire Index <?>
-->  3. Search Reuters newswire index <?>


+----------------Search Reuters newswire index----------------+
|                                                             |
| Words to search for  stocks and japan or stocks and tokyo   |
|                                                             |
|                   [Cancel ^G] [Accept - Enter]              |
|                                                             |
+-------------------------------------------------------------+
```

```
Press ? for Help, q to Quit, u to go up a menu          Page: 1/1
```

The resulting list of this more limited search is smaller and more to the point.

```
             Internet Gopher Information Client v1.13
   Search Reuters newswire index: stocks and japan or stocks and tokyo


-->  1. _stocks-japan_ Tokyo stocks take hosokawa's resignation in s  ..ks/.
     2. _stocks-asia_ Tokyo stocks end higher on late index-linked b  ..ks/.
     3. _stocks-asia_ Tokyo stocks end mixed; hong kong market rises  ..ks/.
     4. _stocks-japan_ Tokyo stocks take hosokawa's resignation in s  ..rt/.
     5. _stocks-asia_ Tokyo stocks end higher on late index-linked b  ..rt/.
```

```
 6. _stocks-asia_ Tokyo stocks end mixed; hong kong market rises   ..rt/.
 7. _stocks-overseas_ Closing stock market indices   ..Apr/Apr 8/stocks/.
 8. _stocks-overseas_ Closing stock market indices   ..pr/Apr 11/stocks/.
 9. _stocks-asia_ Tokyo stocks close lower on arbitrage selling   ..cks/.
10. _stocks-overseas_ London stocks end slightly lower, tokyo ri   ..ks/.
11. _japan-investors_ Foreign investors remain bullish on japan   ..ort/.
12. _stocks-asia_ Tokyo stocks close lower on arbitrage selling   ..ort/.
13. _stocks-overseas_ London stocks end slightly lower, tokyo ri   ..rt/.
14. _markets_ Stocks, bonds rise   ..ta/1994/Apr/Apr 11/business-report/.
15. _stocks-overseas_ Closing stock market indices   ../business-report/.
16. _stocks-overseas_ Closing stock market indices   ../business-report/.
17. _cocoa-japan_ Japan's cocoa imports seen stuck in slump   ..-report/.
18. _bizschedule_ Bc-bizschedule   ..ata/1994/Apr/Apr 8/business-report/.
19. _bizschedule_ Bc-bizschedule   /Reuters-data/1994/Apr/Apr 8/biz/.
20. _7apr06-bizsummary_ Morning business summary   .. 7/business-report/.
21. _bizschedule_ Bc-bizschedule   ..ta/1994/Apr/Apr 12/business-report/.
22. _bizschedule_ Bc-bizschedule   /Reuters-data/1994/Apr/Apr 12/biz/.
23. _markets_ Stocks and bonds rise for third straight day   ..s-report/.
24. _8apr06-bizsummary_ Morning business summary   .. 8/business-report/.
25. _markets_ Stocks and bonds end three-day rally, dollar up   ..eport/.
26. _8apr12-bizheadlines_ Midday business headlines   ..business-report/.
27. _markets-asia_ Asian markets mixed in cautious trade   ..ess-report/.
28. _11apr06-bizsummary_ Morning business summary   ..1/business-report/.
29. _12apr06-bizsummary_ Morning business summary   ..2/business-report/.
30. _12apr12-bizheadlines_ Midday business headlines   ..usiness-report/.
31. _8apr07-headlines_ World headlines   ..ata/1994/Apr/Apr 8/headlines/.
```

Press ? for Help, q to Quit, u to go up a menu   Page: 1/1

Restricting Your Searches with NOT

NOT can also be used to define a search. For example, searching for **cycle not bicycle** could find articles about business and stock cycles without getting articles about bicycle races. Searching for **bear not Chicago and bear not stock** would search for articles about the big mammals without having lots of sports stories and articles about worried stock market analysts.

To leave Gopher, **q** can be used as mentioned before, but to avoid the *Really quit (y/n) ?* question, type Shift-**Q** and you will be immediately returned to your access provider's system prompt.

Summary of Commands and Symbols

Commands do vary from site to site, but the commands listed in Table 10.1 are a good starting point. If no directions are given for viewing a list of the commands available for a particular Gopher, type ? and press Enter.

Table 10.1 Gopher Commands

Key	Command
Up arrow key (or **k** key)	Move the highlight/pointer up the menu.
Down arrow key (or **j** key)	Move the highlight down the menu.
Left arrow key	Go back up to the previous menu.
Right arrow key	Display currently highlighted item or menu.
Enter key	Display currently highlighted item or menu.
u	Go back to the previous menu.
m	Go back to the top (first) menu.
=	Display information about the current item.
> or **+** or **f** (also try Spacebar and the Enter key)	Display the next page within a document.
< or **-** or **b** (Some sites have no way to move back up in a document)	Display the previous page within a document.
s	Save the current file to your directory on the Internet access provider's computer.
D (Shift-**d**)	Download the currently highlighted file directly to your PC.
/	This initiates a search by prompting you to type in a word to search for.
n	After the search has found one menu item with the word you were searching for, use **n** to find the next menu item containing that word.
?	Display list of available commands.
q	Leave the Gopher (prompts with *Really quit (y/n)?*).
Q (Shift-**q**) (or Crtl-**z**)	Same as **q** but does not display a prompt asking whether you really want to quit.

Table 10.2   Common Gopher Symbols

Symbol	Meaning
/	This item is another menu (subdirectory).
.	This item is a readable text file.
<?>	This item will initiate a full-text index search by prompting you to type in a word or phrase to look for.
<TEL>	Selecting this item will initiate a Telnet session with the named remote service.
<)	This symbol (representing a speaker) indicates an audio data file.
<PICTURE>	This is a graphics/image data file.

At the end of the line following each menu item there is often some sort of symbol indicating what type of file that item is. These vary a great deal from site to site, but are usually consistent within a site. Table 10.2 lists the most common ones. An ongoing source of information about the current Gopher system and software is the FTP site **boombox.micro.-umn.edu** in the **/pub/gopher directory**.

Using Gopher to Explore Other Gopher Sites

Each site on the Internet that installs the Gopher client software configures it, by default, to link to a particular Gopher server. When you start Gopher you can, however, "point" the Gopher to another site so that you can explore more information on the Internet. Once you have pointed the Gopher to another site, you will see a new Gopher menu—this will be the top menu of that other Gopher site. Your Gopher client software will operate just as before, but you will have available a different set of menu choices reflecting the information available at this new site.

To point the Gopher, you need to know two things: the other Gopher's address and port number. (See the "Useful Guides" section in this chapter for information on where to get lists of Gopher sites.) If the port number is not given with the information you have about the Gopher site, assume that it is the very common 70. The command for pointing the Gopher takes this form:

```
gopher server-name port-number
```

For example, the Gopher server at the University of Illinois's Department of Atmospheric Sciences has an address of **wx.atmos.uiuc.edu**. In most lists of Gopher servers, no port number is listed for this site, so assume that it is **70**. The command typed at the system prompt would be:

```
gopher wx.atmos.uiuc.edu 70
```

Using a Remote Gopher

If a Gopher client is not available at your access provider's site, you can Telnet to any of hundreds of other sites that allow remote access to their Gopher client software. (See the "Useful Guides" section of this chapter for information on getting lists of these sites.)

The University of North Texas, for example, has a Gopher client available by way of Telnet; the address is **gopher.unt.edu** and the login is **gopher**. Therefore, to use this Gopher client, at your Internet access provider's system prompt type:

```
telnet gopher.unt.edu
```

Press the Enter key and wait for the connection to be established. When prompted for *Login:* type in **gopher** and press Enter. The top (root) Gopher menu at the University of North Texas will now be displayed.

GopherMail

For those with access to e-mail, but not to Telnet or a Gopher client, there is a service that allows use of Gopher via e-mail messages. It is much slower than normal Gopher, but it is much better than having no access to Gopher.

To use GopherMail, first send an e-mail message to **gopher@dsv.su.se** with nothing in the *Subject:* field and nothing in the body of the message. A message will be returned with a top Gopher menu. If, for example, you are interested in menu items 4 and 7, type **x4** and **x7** on separate lines at the top of the body of the message, and use your mail program's reply procedure to send the message back to **gopher@dsv.su.se**. Keep repeating these replies to follow various menu paths to the menu choices of documents you are interested in. If you specify a menu choice that is a search of a database, put the **x** and the menu item number in the message as usual, and place the words you are looking for in the *Subject:* line of your message. Binary files can also be requested. They will arrive as uuencoded files.

To get a detailed help file on how to use GopherMail, send an e-mail message to **gopher@dsv.su.se** with the word **help** in the *Subject:* field and with nothing in the body of the message. The publishers of *Wired* magazine also provide e-mail access to Gopher through their "infobot" system. Get more information on this by sending an e-mail message to **infobot-@wired.com** with the word **help** as the text of the message.

VERONICA

Gopher allows searching for keywords within menus, but only within the menu that you are currently viewing. Veronica, however, maintains an index of thousands of Gopher menu items from many Gopher server sites, and can search them all at one time, thus the somewhat strained acronym Veronica—Very Easy Rodent Oriented Net-wide Index to Computerized Archives.

Veronica, like Gopher, has client software installed at many sites and server software installed at a few sites. The server software has features that allow it to collect an index of all Gopher menu items on all Gophers known to it (Gopher servers registered with the "mother" Gopher at University of Minnesota or those that appear as a menu item on one of those registered Gophers). The index is updated approximately once a week.

The Veronica client software is installed at sites with Gophers and appears to the user as a normal Gopher menu item. At most sites, the top menu will have a menu choice such as *Gophers and other information servers*, or *Internet resources and services*. Try these and you are likely to find a menu choice such as *Search titles in Gopherspace using veronica/*. (If you are unable to locate Veronica, use one of the Telnet sites mentioned in Table 10.4.) A typical Veronica menu looks like the one below: some general background and instruction files, several places to do Veronica directory searches, and several sites for Veronica gopherspace searches. Each of these sites may be using the same index, so if you get the message *Too many connections*, you can try the next closest site to you.

```
            Internet Gopher Information Client v2.0.12
             Search titles in Gopherspace using veronica


      1.
-->   2.  FAQ:  Frequently-Asked Questions about veronica
      3.  How to compose  veronica queries (NEW June 24) READ ME!!
      4.  Search Gopher Directory Titles at PSINet <?>
      5.  Search Gopher Directory Titles at SUNET <?>
      6.  Search Gopher Directory Titles at U. of Manitoba <?>
      7.  Search Gopher Directory Titles at University of Cologne <?>
      8.  Search gopherspace at PSINet <?>
      9.  Search gopherspace at SUNET <?>
      10. Search gopherspace at U. of Manitoba <?>
      11. Search gopherspace at University of Cologne <?>


    Press ? for Help, q to Quit, u to go up a menu  Receiving Information...
```

In this example, a gopherspace search will be performed (all Gopher menu items at all know locations). One of the two American sites (PSINet) is chosen. Moving the pointer to *8. Search gopherspace at PSINet <?>* and pressing the Enter key causes a search word prompt box to be displayed in the middle of the screen. In this case, all items with the word **business** in them will be searched. After the word **business** is typed in and the Enter key is pressed, the search is initiated.

Veronica Searches and Case

Veronica searches are case-insensitive—**Business, business,** and **BUSINESS** are all considered the same word.

```
             Internet Gopher Information Client v2.0.12
             Search titles in Gopherspace using veronica


        1.
        2.  FAQ:  Frequently-Asked Questions about veronica
            (1993/08/23)
        3.  How to compose  veronica queries (NEW June 24) READ ME!!
        4.  Search Gopher Directory Titles at PSINet <?>
        5.  Search Gopher Directory Titles at SUNET <?>
        6.  Search Gopher Directory Titles at U. of Manitoba <?>
        7.  Search Gopher Directory Titles at University of Cologne <?>
  -->   8.  Search gopherspace at PSINet <?>
        9.  Search gopherspace at SUNET <?>
        10. Search gopherspace at U. of Manitoba <?>
        11. Search gopherspace at University of Cologne <?>


   +------------------Search gopherspace at PSINet----------------+
   |                                                              |
   | Words to search for                                          |
   |                                                              |
   | business                                                     |
   |                                                              |
   | [Help: ^_]   [Cancel: ^G]                                    |
   +--------------------------------------------------------------+


   Press ? for Help, q to Quit, u to go up a menu        Connecting...
```

In anywhere from a few seconds to a couple minutes, the results of the Veronica search are displayed as a Gopher-style menu. This search yielded 13,008 items. By default, at this site only the first five pages (200 items) are initially sent, though that number can be changed. If, for instance, you wanted 500 sent, you would type **–m500** followed with no intervening spaces as shown in the following example:

```
+-----------------Search gopherspace at PSINet---------------+
|                                                            |
| Words to search for                                        |
|                                                            |
|   -m500 business                                           |
|                                                            |
| [Help: ^_]   [Cancel: ^G]                                  |
+------------------------------------------------------------+
```

Note that items found in this search include both documents and menus (ending with the forward slash /) that can be entered and searched in the usual Gopher manner. The following list is abbreviated.

```
          Internet Gopher Information Client v1.13
      Search gopherspace at University of Cologne: business
```

```
-->  1.  Alt.business.multi-level FAQ                       .
     2.  biz. ---------- business newsgroup listings   /
     3.     Business Assoc of Minorities.
     4.  INTERNATIONAL ASSOCIATION FOR BUSINESS AND SOCIETY (IABS).
     5.  1994 MIDWESTERN BUSINESS PLAN COMPETITION.
     6.  EMORY UNIVERSITY POSTDOCTORAL TEACHING-RESEARCH PROGRAM
         IN BUSINESS..
     7.  Internet Business Report - subscription info.
     8.  EUROPEAN BUSINESS ETHICS NETWORK INTERNATIONAL CONFERENCE.
     9.  International Academy of Business Disciplines (IABD).
    10.  Donahue, G.- Business and Society (MBA).
    11.  Donahue, G.- Business Ethics (UG).
    12.  Mazur, T.- Legal, Social, and Political Environment of
         Business.
    13.  Purdy, J.- BUSINESS, GOVERNMENT & SOCIETY: A
         PHILOSOPHICAL APPROAC...
    14.  Sodeman, W.- ENVIRONMENTAL INFLUENCES ON BUSINESS
         MANAGEMENT.
    15.  Sodeman, W.- BUSINESS AND ITS ENVIRONMENT.
    16.  Swinth, R.- Business, Ethics & Environment.
    17.  Int'l Assn for Business & Society (IABS) Discussion List/
```

```
18. Gopher Servers at Business Schools/
19. Restaurant-employees'-risky-business..
20. AgEd 3002    Experiential Learning: Agricultural Business.
21. AgEd 5072    Practicum: Agricultural Business and Industry.
22. BME 5305     Methods in Business and Marketing Education.
23. BME 5330     Spreadsheet Analysis Using Microcomputers
                 in Business ...
24. BME 5335     Teaching Microcomputer Business Graphics.
25. BME 5600     Field-Based Projects in Business and
                 Marketing Educati...
26. BME 5604     Clinical Experience in Business or
                 Marketing Education.
27. BME 5605     Clinical Experience in Business or
                 Marketing Education.
28. BME 5606     Clinical Experience in Business or
                 Marketing Education.
29. BME 5900     Directed Study in Business and Marketing
                 Education.
30. BME 8300     Seminar: Research in Business, Marketing,
                 and Economic...
```

```
Press ? for Help, q to Quit, u to go up a menu        Page: 1/5
```

Obviously, 13,008 items would be quite a list to browse through. Fortunately, Veronica can do complex searches, that is, those with **AND**, **OR**, **NOT**, and parentheses ( ). These are used as follows:

- **AND**—The words before and after **AND** must both be in the menu item for that item to be listed.

- **OR**—If either the word before **OR** or the word after appears in the menu item, it will be added to the list. Also, if both words appear in the menu item, that item will be added to the list.

- **NOT**—A menu item will be selected if the word preceding **NOT** appears in the menu item, but only if it doesn't also contain the word following **NOT**.

- Parentheses are used to contain groups of words separated by **AND**, **OR**, and so forth.

To make the list more manageable, several aspects of business can be searched for separately, such as business and environment.

Veronica searches look for exact whole-word matches, so using **environment** as a search term would not find Gopher menu items with

environmental, environmentalism, or **environments.** To find menu items with all of these, the asterisk wild card character can be used. A search for **environment*** will find **environment, environmental, environmentalism, environments,** or any other variation that has additional characters at the position of the *.

There may be times, however, when you don't want all of the variations on a word. In that case you can specify which specific variation you want by using parentheses to enclose word variations and **OR.** For instance, to find all Gopher menu items that have the word **business,** and either or both of the words **environment** and **environmental,** use this search command: **business and (environment or environmental).**

```
             Internet Gopher Information Client v1.13
             Search titles in Gopherspace using veronica


        1.
        2.  FAQ:  Frequently-Asked Questions about veronica
        3.  How to compose  veronica queries (NEW June 24) READ ME!!.
        4.  Search Gopher Directory Titles at PSINet <?>
        5.  Search Gopher Directory Titles at SUNET <?>
        6.  Search Gopher Directory Titles at U. of Manitoba <?>
        7.  Search Gopher Directory Titles at University of Cologne <?>
 -->    8.  Search gopherspace at PSINet <?>
        9.  Search gopherspace at SUNET <?>
       10.  Search gopherspace at U. of Manitoba <?>
       11.  Search gopherspace at University of Cologne <?>


 +----------------Search gopherspace at PSINet------------------+
 |                                                              |
 | Words to search for  business and (environment or environmental)|
 |                                                              |
 |                    [Cancel ^G] [Accept - Enter]      |
 |                                                              |
 +--------------------------------------------------------------+


 Press ? for Help, q to Quit, u to go up a menu          Page: 1/1
```

In the search results, some of the menu items have been truncated, so the words **business** and **environment** or **environmental** may not be displayed in all of the menu items, but they can be assumed to be there.

```
                    Internet Gopher Information Client v1.13

-->   1.  FIN 3056 LEGAL ENVIRONMENT OF BUSINESS.
      2.  464 The Business Environment in East/Central Europe and the Soviet.
      3.  100893:Small Business Size Standards; Environmental Services.
      4.  58 FR 44518:Disclosure of Confidential Business Information Obtain...
      5.  58 FR 32943:Disclosure of Confidential Business Information Obtain...
      6.  BE Business Environment/
      7.  badm200 the legal environment of business..
      8.  FIN 5004 : FUNDAMENTALS OF LEGAL ENVIRONMENT OF BUSINESS.
      9.  B LAW 243 - Legal Environment of Business.
     10.  badm200 the legal environment of business..
     11.  Environmental Education for Graduate Business Schools.
     12.  090993:Disclosure of Confidential Business Information Obtained Un...
     13.  59 FR 1485:Clean Air Act Approval and Promulgation of Title V, Sec...
     14.  58 FR 47446:Disclosure of Confidential Business Information Obtain...
     15.  011294:Approval and Promulgation of Title V, Section 507, Small Bu...
     16.  BE Business Environment/
     17.  082593:Clean Air Act Approval and Promulgation of Title V, Section...
     18.  082393:Disclosure of Confidential Business Information Obtained Un...
     19.  59 FR 1485:Clean Air Act Approval and Promulgation of Title V, Sec...
     20.  MGT 5304 SOCIAL, LEGAL AND ETHICAL ENVIRONMENT OF BUSINESS.
     21.  58 FR 44799:Clean Air Act Approval and Promulgation of Title V, Se...
     22.  B53 Management 301 LEGAL ENVIRONMENT OF BUSINESS..
     23.  112693:Clean Air Act Approval and Promulgation of Title V, Section...
     24.  011294:Approval and Promulgation of Air Quality Implementation Pla...
     25.  59 FR 1693:Approval and Promulgation of Air Quality Implementation...
     26.  BE Business Environment/
     27.  58 FR 44518:Disclosure of Confidential Business Information Obtain...
     28.  58 FR 42355:Small Business Size Standards; Environmental Services.
     29.  122193:Clean Air Act Approval and Promulgation of Title V, Section...
     30.  Mazur, T.- Legal, Social, and Political Environment of Business.


   Press ? for Help, q to Quit, u to go up a menu               Page: 1/3
```

This search provided 93 menu items ("matches" or "hits"), which will make it much easier to find the files of interest.

Searching for Menus

Another approach to dealing with the very large lists that some searches produce is to do a search just for menus (directories). The resulting list will be much smaller, and will provide the added benefit of finding

Gopher sites that customarily have the type of information you are interested in.

In the example below, PSINet is chosen for its proximity to my Internet access provider, but now the search will be for Gopher directory titles (menus). Item number 4 is selected, Enter pressed, and the search is conducted in the same manner as a gopherspace search.

```
              Internet Gopher Information Client v2.0.12
                Search titles in Gopherspace using veronica


      1.

      2.  FAQ: Frequently-Asked Questions about veronica  (1993/08/23)

      3.  How to compose  veronica queries (NEW June 24) READ ME!!
-->   4.  Search Gopher Directory Titles at PSINet <?>

      5.  Search Gopher Directory Titles at SUNET <?>

      6.  Search Gopher Directory Titles at U. of Manitoba <?>

      7.  Search Gopher Directory Titles at University of Cologne <?>

      8.  Search gopherspace at PSINet <?>

      9.  Search gopherspace at SUNET <?>

      10. Search gopherspace at U. of Manitoba <?>

      11. Search gopherspace at University of Cologne <?>


+-----------Search Gopher Directory Titles at PSINet------------+
|                                                               |
| Words to search for  forest                                   |
|                                                               |
|                                                               |
| [Help: ^_]   [Cancel: ^G]                                     |
+---------------------------------------------------------------+


Press ? for Help, q to Quit, u to go up a menu         Page: 1/1
```

The results of the search are now *all* Gopher menus, rather than gopherspace's mix of menus and files. This search yields 130 menus. Each of these Gopher menus can now be browsed and searched in the usual Gopher manner.

```
              Internet Gopher Information Client v2.0.12
                Search Gopher Directory Titles at PSINet: forest


-->   1.  FOREST PRODUCTS (ForP)/

      2.  FOREST RESOURCES (FR)/
```

```
3.  Department of Forest Products/

4.  Forest Products Course Info/

5.  Forest Product Class Materials/

6.  Forest Products Job Board/

7.  Department of Forest Resources/

8.  How To Reach Someone in the Dept of Forest Resources/

9.  Schoolhouse of Forest Resources Courses/

10. The Internet and Forest Resources/

11. 01:Forest Resources:Regional, National, International/

12. 17:Forest Management-General/

13. 37:Non-Industrial Forest Products/

14. Tropical Forest Conservation and Development Bibliography/

15. Forest Resources/

16. Nontimber Forest Products/

17. Recreation in the Urban Forest/

18. Wildlife in the Urban Forest/

19. Planning the Urban Forest/

20. Managing the Urban Forest/

21. Forest.Conference/

22. FWU...........Forest and Wood    /

23. FWU...........Forest and Wood    /

24. FOREST SERVICE FS   (36 entries)/

25. SOUTHERN FOREST EXP STATION   (2 entries)/

26. FOREST WILDLIFE FOUNDATION   (1 entries)/

27. FOREST SERVICE FS   (1 entries)/

28. FOREST SERVICE FS   (15 entries)/

29. FOREST SERVICE FS   (2 entries)/

30. WOOD WOOD SCIENCE AND FOREST PRODUCTS/
```

```
Press ? for Help, q to Quit, u to go up a menu          Page: 1/4
```

Limiting Your Search by Menu Type

Veronica allows even more control of the type of menu item that is returned with a search. Table 10.3 lists the types of Gopher menu items that you can selectively request. The instructions to Veronica to search for specific types of Gopher menu items are in the form of **-t** and the file type code preceding the search word or words. For example, if you

Table 10.3 Gopher Menu Items

File Type Code	Menu Item File Types
0	File
1	Directory
2	CSO (phonebook server)
7	Index search server
8	Telnet session
9	Binary file

wanted to just have binary file Gopher menu items returned from a search for **business**, the search instructions would look like this:

```
+-----------------Search gopherspace at PSINet-----------------+
|                                                              |
| Words to search for   -t9 business                          |
|                                                              |
|                              [Cancel ^G] [Accept - Enter]   |
|                                                              |
+--------------------------------------------------------------+
```

Using **-t9** to search for binary files is especially useful if you are looking for any type of software: CAD files, spreadsheet data files, graphics, and so on. You can also search for more than one file type in a single search. For example, if you are interested in index searches of databases and Telnet sessions (such as to bulletin boards and information server sites), these can be returned in one search in this way:

```
+-----------------Search gopherspace at PSINet-----------------+
|                                                              |
| Words to search for   -t78 business                         |
|                                                              |
|                              [Cancel ^G] [Accept - Enter]   |
|                                                              |
+--------------------------------------------------------------+
```

Finding Veronica

If you don't find Veronica on an easily accessible Gopher menu, you can Telnet to one of the sites listed in Table 10.4.

Table 10.4   Veronica Telnet Sites

Site Name	Login:
consultant.micro.umn.edu	gopher
ux1.cso.uiuc.edu	gopher
panda.uiowa.edu	(press Enter)

Or, if you have a Gopher client but can't find Veronica, point the Gopher to one of these (70 is the port number):

- gopher.micro.umn.edu 70
- veronica.scs.unr.edu 70
- wisteria.cnidr.org 70

ARCHIE

Some of the problems with FTP are knowing what files exist, which ones are worth tracking down, and where they are located. The Internet lacks a central record keeping system, so search programs like archie and Veronica were invented to assist in finding resources. archie was created for FTP site searches by McGill University in Montreal, Canada, and is now supported by Bunyip Information Systems.

archie is a search system used to scan a database containing information on all anonymous FTP sites in the world. The database contains the names and locations of files at those anonymous FTP sites. The database is automatically updated to include new listings. archie is used to obtain site, directory, and filename information by string (usually a single word) that can be either case-sensitive or case-insensititive.

To use archie, Telnet to an archie server (See Table 10.6), and log in as **archie**. Your system may also have an archie client; to determine this, type **archie** at your system prompt. If you have an archie client, you will get some form of the *archie>* prompt or help screen.

It is possible, through use of command line switches (options), to specify the kind of search you wish, as well as whether you want the listing that archie returns displayed on your screen only or displayed on your screen and put into a file for later searching and reference. In addition to finding files that may be of interest, archie will identify subdirectories with the search word as well. When you find subdirectories that look interesting, you can use FTP to examine the files stored there.

Usually, at the system prompt, you can obtain a listing of the command line options for archie, for example:

```
world% archie
Usage: archie [-acelorstvLV] [-m hits] [-N level] string
          -c : case sensitive substring search
          -e : exact string match (default)
          -r : regular expression search
          -s : case insensitive substring search
          -l : list one match per line
          -t : sort inverted by date
     -m hits : specifies maximum number of hits to return
               (default 95)
 -o filename : specifies file to store results in
     -h host : specifies server host
          -L : list known servers and current default
    -N level : specifies query niceness level (0-35765)


world%
```

The default setting is case-sensitive. With the **-s** option, which makes the search case-insensitive, **Next**, **next**, **NEXT**, and **NeXT** are all the same, while with the **-c** option all of those searches are different. If you are looking for a specific file, using the **-e** option will make the search very specific: A search for **hyteln65.zip** will find only that file.

The **-t** option gives you the information sorted by date, which will allow you to locate the most recent versions of files and programs. Niceness, the **-N** option, specifies the precedence your query should receive.

Different sites will have slightly different options, but most will contain options for case, the number of hits (matches) to return, a file storage option, sorting options, and the ability to choose which archie server to access. Typing **archie** after you have logged in at one of the archie sites will put you into interactive mode, with a prompt: *archie>*. (Some sites will automatically place you in interactive mode with the *archie>* prompt.) Table 10.5 shows some useful commands that can be typed in at the *archie>* prompt. Table 10.6 is a brief list of some archie sites and their locations.

Following are the abbreviated results of an archie search using the word **business**, with the list arranged by date. You can observe that some of these are directories, some are files, and some are software. These listings give you some starting places for further searching.

Table 10.5 Archie Commands

Command	Meaning
help	To get information on archie and currently available archie commands.
mailto	Lets you identify an e-mail address to which to send search results.
list	Lists the sites covered by the archie database.
set	Used to set up a number of parameters.
prog	Searches the archie database for a file.
bye	Exits the program.

Table 10.6 Archie Sites

Site	Location
archie.ans.net	New York
archie.rutgers.edu	New Jersey
archie.sura.net	Maryland
archie.unl.edu	Nebraska
archie.funet.fi	Finland
archie.au	Australia
archie.nz	New Zealand
archie.doc.ic.ac.uk	United Kingdom
cs.huji.ac.il	Israel
archie.ncu.edu.tw	Taiwan
archie.wide.ad.jp	Japan

```
world% archie -s -t business


Host freebsd.cdrom.com
 Location: /.1/cdrom/incoming
   DIRECTORY drwxrwxrwx  512  Jan 11 00:29  business


Host owl.nstn.ns.ca
 Location: /pub
   DIRECTORY drwxr-xr-x  512  Jan  4 14:17  internet- business-journal
```

```
Host sunsite.unc.edu
  Location: /pub/academic/business/.cap
    FILE -rw-r--r--        78  Jul 10 1993  internet-business-journal


Host calypso-2.oit.unc.edu
  Location: /pub/academic/business/.cap
    FILE -rw-r--r--        78  Jul  9 1993  internet-business-journal


Host sunsite.unc.edu
  Location: /pub/academic
  DIRECTORY drwxr-xr-x  512  Jul  1 1993  business


Host ftp.luth.se
  Location: /pub/mac/appl/filemaker
    FILE -rw-rw-r--     59326  May  4 1993  filemaker-pro-business-
                                           dir-302.hqx


Host ftp.uwp.edu
  Location: /pub/music/guitar/h/Hurt.Mississippi.John
    FILE -rw-rw-r--      1312  Feb 23 1993  NobodysBusiness.tab.Z


Host ftp.luth.se
  Location: /pub/misc/lyrics/m/men.at.work
    FILE -rw-r--r--      9668  Feb  8 1993  business.usual


Host ftp.sunet.se
  Location: /pub/mac/mirror-umich/util/organization
    FILE -r--r--r--    249933  Jan 15 1993  businessplanmaster.sit.hqx


Host ftp.luth.se
  Location: /pub/misc/lyrics/folk/b
    FILE -rw-r--r--      1413  Oct 22 1992  business_for_love
  Location: /pub/misc/lyrics/s/seeger.pete
    FILE -rw-r--r--      1680  Oct 22 1992  i_mind_my_own_business
```

archie netiquette calls for some basic rules:

- Use the closest server where possible—don't query Finland or Australia, unless the more local sources are not working.

- Query at off-peak hours for that archie site—be aware of time zone differences.
- Restrict searches to a reasonable number of hits—100 rather than, say 10,000.

Finding Archie

Some Gopher access to archie exists, and by doing a Veronica search as described in the previous section, you should be able to locate archie on Gopher. If you have an anonymous FTP site, or start one for your business in the future, the people who operate the archie system encourage you to send them the details about your public files so that the server tracking software can be configured to update the information. This is especially useful for creating a business presence, making it easier for others to locate your information. To register with archie, send electronic mail to **info-archie@bunyip.com**.

HYPERTEXT-BASED INFORMATION

There are a number of Internet programs that use a different approach to information searching, retrieval, and utilization—hypertext. World-WideWeb (WWW or W3), Lynx, Mosaic, and Cello are examples of these systems.

What Is Hypertext?

Hypertext offers a way of moving from one document to another through word links. Each marked word in a document has a link to another document or resource. This allows you to follow various paths within the system based on the contents of each document in a nonlinear fashion, according to subject. For example, when a word or concept is introduced in one document, you can move to another document that may simply be a definition or explanation of the term, or even a long document about that subject. The reader can open the second document, read it, and then return to the original, or move on to other documents based on the marked words in each new document.

Hypermedia works much like hypertext, but allows words in a document to be linked to nontext files of images, sounds, QuickTime movies, and so on.

Documents that use hypertext must be created using software that can create documents in the HyperText Markup Language—HTML format. The link information is embedded in the document, but is only visible as highlighted words or icons. On text displays, document links are sometimes marked by a number in brackets *[4]*, and image links usually appear as *[IMAGE]*, while graphical interfaces highlight items with color, and show small icons for images.

Creating Your Own HTML Documents

If you are interested in creating your own HTML documents, there is a source of information for HTML developers provided by OneWorld Information Service that can be found at **http:-//oneworld.wa.com/htmldev/devpage/dev-page.html**. Also, a hypertext editor for MS Windows called HTML Assistant is available via FTP to **ftp.cs.dal.ca** in the directory */htmlasst/* in the file **htmlasst.zip**. Another HTML document authoring tool is HTML Writer for Windows, which can be found via FTP to **ftp.byu.edu** in the */tmp* subdirectory as *htmlwrit.zip*.

There are a growing number of Internet tools that are using hypertext, among them WWW, Lynx, and Mosaic. The Internet has a suite of transfer protocols defining how to transfer e-mail, files, and other information. A new set of protocols has been developed for the Internet: the HyperText Transfer Protocol (HTTP).

Universal Resource Locators

Increasingly, when information is cited in documents, you are given what is called a universal resource locator (URL) address. Depending upon the configuration of your WWW or other server, you can directly enter these URLs to make connections. (This is a draft as opposed to a fully approved standard at this time.) Here are what some of these look like:

```
file://wuarchive.wustle.edu/mirrors/msdos/graphics/gifkit.zip

telnet://database.carl.org/

gopher://marvel.loc.gov/:70

news://alt.hypertext

http://nearnet.gnn.com/GNNhome.html
```

The first bit of information on each line tells you the access method or format of the item—a file, a Gopher, a Telnet site, a Usenet newsgroup, or a hypertext item. After the two slashes, the site name or machine is identified, and finally, information on the specific document or menu is given. URLs are useful because they give you all of the necessary information for locating resources in a common format.

To access WWW or hypertext information, you must either have a browser running locally (WWW, Lynx, MOSAIC, Cello, etc.), or Telnet out and use one of these browsers at another site.

WWW

The WWW project was started at CERN (the European Laboratory for Particle Physics), and it was the first Internet system to use hypertext. WWW uses hypertext over the network, connecting documents and resources at a variety of sites. WWW browsers can access files using FTP, Gopher, and other methods.

WWW uses the client-server model to provide access. To access WWW, you must use a client at your own site or via Telnet to another. WWW clients run on a variety of platforms, and information on those clients can be found at **http://info.cern.ch/hypertext/WWW/Clients.html**. (Use the **Go** command within WWW or Lynx.) Some of the browsers such as Mosaic and Cello require that you have a SLIP or TCP/IP connection on your PC, but others support plain vanilla text connections.

While Gopher and WAIS are also client-server systems, they differ in their capabilities. For Gopher, data is either a menu, a document, an index, or a Telnet connection. In WAIS, everything is an index, and everything returned from the index is a document. For WWW, everything is a hypertext/media document. Currently WWW does not have as large a user base as Gopher, but this is changing. At CERN, the use of the server is doubling about every four months.

To provide information to WWW, you must be running a WWW server on your local system. The software can be obtained from the FTP site at CERN or elsewhere, and then set up by your system administrators locally. Documents must be provided in HTML format.

When using a graphical interface, you access the WWW functions with a mouse by clicking on items; in line mode (text only), use the arrow keys to follow the links. The following is an example of WWW in action. This is the WWW Client at the New Jersey Institute of Technology (NJIT), and Figure 10.1 displays the NJIT opening screen showing a menu to select information about the university, and then WWW access by choosing item 2.

The items that can be accessed are shown in shaded text or numbers. The WWW opening screen appears, as seen in Figure 10.2, where you can choose from various menu options in brackets.

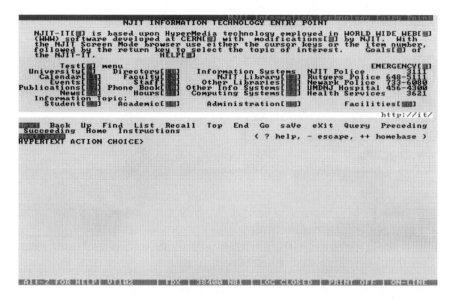

Figure 10.1 The NJIT Homepage.

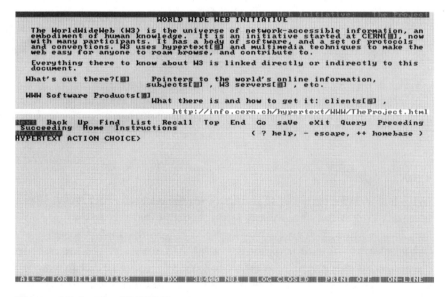

Figure 10.2 The WWW Homepage.

Table 10.7   WWW Browser Sites

Site	Location
vms.huji.ac.il	Israel (dual language)
info.cern.ch	Switzerland (CERN)
fatty.law.cornell.edu	USA
ukanaix.cc.ukans.edu	USA
www.njit.edu	USA

Table 10.7 lists sites that provide a WWW browser via Telnet (use the login of **www** for all of these addresses).

There are now several resources that provide a great deal of information about new and established servers and clients:

- An up-to-date list of browsers that are accessible by Telnet is maintained at **http://info.cern.ch/hypertext/WWW/FAQ/Bootstrap.html**.

- There is a new WWW resource locator called Nomad, put together by Rockwell Network. Reach it at **http://www.rns.com/**.

- There is an FAQ on WWW that can be obtained using anonymous FTP at **rtfm.mit.edu** in the */pub/usenet/news.answers/www* as the file **faq**. (When you are connected to MIT, don't do a **dir** or an **ls** to look at the subdirectory */usenet*—it is a huge listing, and you will sit through many, many screens.) This FAQ has the latest information about WWW at any given time.

- For a fun way to try out WWW, you can go to the WWW Sports Information Service, which covers many professional sports and includes an NBA server: **http://www.mit.edu:8001/services/sis/sports/-html**.

Lynx

Lynx is a WWW browser that allows low-end access to WWW. It is a text-only WWW browser for any terminal program that can emulate a VT 100. It uses full screen and arrow keys, with highlighting. Lynx grew out of the campus wide information server at the University of Kansas. Lynx clients give a user-friendly interface for WWW. Figure 10.3 is an example of a Lynx opening screen showing the Lynx default home page.

Arrow keys provide a way to navigate up and down on pages. The right arrow follows a link to a new page, while the left arrow returns you

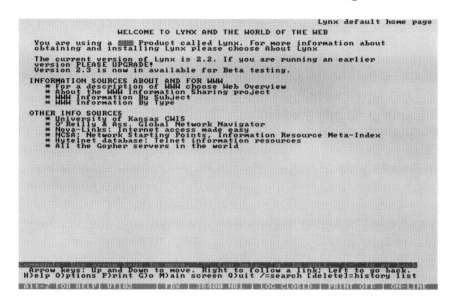

Figure 10.3 The Lynx Homepage.

to the previous page. By pressing the boldface letters, you can also get Help and set up your usage Options. The Print option will allow you to choose between an actual printout, saving to a file, or e-mailing the document to yourself or someone else. The Go command will let you enter an HTTP address for accessing a specific document. In this example, the HTTP address of the Washington and Lee Law Library has been entered: **http://honor/uc/wlu.edu:1020**. The result is shown in Figure 10.4.

Here you are presented with the home page of the Netlink server at Washington and Lee. I often use their menu by subject. Lynx can be obtained via FTP to **ftp2.cc.ukans.edu**, and versions for a variety of platforms can be found in the */pub/lynx* subdirectory. There are versions of Lynx for IBM, DEC Ultrix and Alpha, Sun, NeXT, and OpenVMS.

Mosaic

Mosaic is a graphical interface for WWW, developed by the National Center for Supercomputing Applications (NCSA), which is available currently without charge. Mosaic allows navigation by using a mouse to click on documents or images. It is available for several platforms, including Macintosh, MS Windows, and UNIX. Its features include:

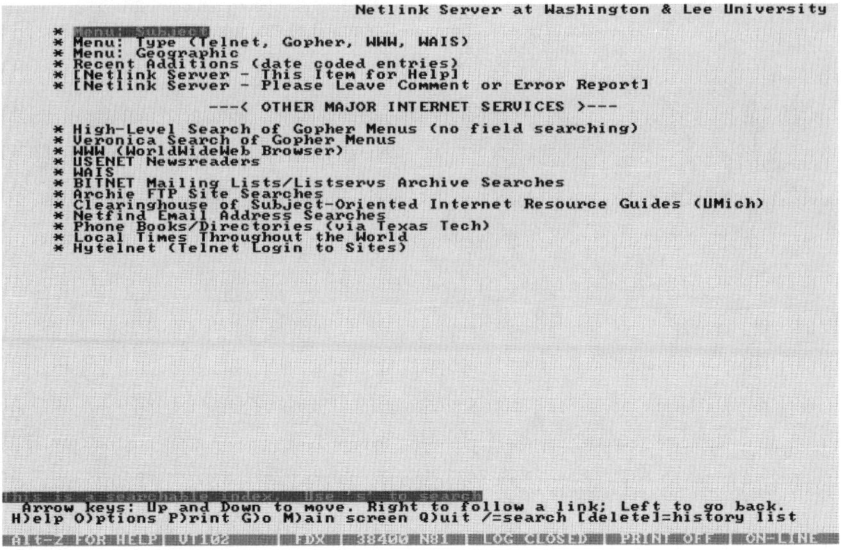

Figure 10.4 Using Lynx to access a specific document.

- a mouse-driven graphical interface
- the ability to display hypertext and hypermedia, in a variety of fonts, with boldfacing, and italics
- the ability to display complex layout elements such as numbered and bulleted lists, justified right and left margins, and newspaper columns
- support for sound, movies, and graphic images
- support for languages other than English, including French and German
- support for forms elements such as fields, check boxes, and radio buttons
- support for hypermedia links to Gopher, FTP, Telnet, and WAIS

This colorful interface lets you load any homepage (unique starting place) to begin, and then go to any HTTP document. It also lets you annotate documents, which can be shared, along with the original document, among a group of users.

Mosaic creates a list of the documents you have recently visited, called a "hotlist," for quicker access. As you browse a document, you can view the images directly, or for speed, choose to see them just as icons.

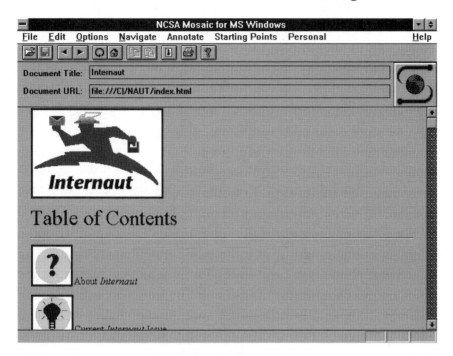

Figure 10.5 The Internaut via Mosaic.

The NCSA animated world logo moves during a retrieval of a document; if you click on it, the retrieval process will stop—this is especially useful when something is taking a long time and you have decided to move along, or you have clicked in haste and now wish to repent. Figure 10.5 shows Mosaic accessing *The Internaut*, a net newsletter. The table of contents contains icons for quick mouse navigation.

Mosaic is available via anonymous FTP from NCSA's FTP site: **ftp.ncsa.uiuc.edu**. The Windows version is in the directory */PC/Mosaic* in the file **wmos201a1.zip**. To run Mosaic for Windows, first install Win-Sock, available from **ftp.utas.edu.au** in the *pc/trumpet/winsock* directory as **winsock.zip**. Mosaic cannot be run by Telneting to another location. It has to be run directly using a SLIP or node connection with the Internet.

A stand-alone demonstration of Mosaic for Windows is now available via FTP from **ftp.cis.ufl.edu** in the *pub/sam* subdirectory as **disk_10.exe**. This version is designed for users who do not have a direct network connection, but wish to view HTML documents, and give Mosaic a test drive. Mosaic is inspiring all kinds of new activities, and will be a key tool in business use of the Internet.

The Future of HTML-based Information

WWW is growing rapidly, and the number of servers and WWW browsers is growing as well. Many feel that the future of advertising and marketing on the Internet lies with hypertext/hypermedia approaches to information. Businesses have the opportunity to create "slick" presentations, brochures, sounds, and images. Mosaic, with its full-image capability, may be the next step in Internet marketing, through online activity or offline browsing of files provided by a company.

WIDE AREA INFORMATION SERVER (WAIS)

When you have used archie, Gopher and Veronica, you can appreciate how time consuming sifting through listings can be—lists of several hundred items are common, and each item may need to be explored in order to find just what you are looking for.

Developed at Thinking Machines Corporation in 1990, WAIS (pronounced "ways") is a system designed to assist in Internet searches in cases where information is located in many different places. WAIS is a distributed information retrieval system that helps users search remote databases on a network, using a semi-friendly interface. (There is a variation of WAIS called SWAIS, which is a screen-oriented simplified version of WAIS. Increasingly SWAIS is becoming popular with the average Internet user.)

WAIS allows you to get information from a variety of hosts by means of "clients." The user tells the client program what to look for, and the program initiates the search. You can create queries and view the results locally. Each WAIS server indexes its collection of data, and lets other WAIS clients use those indexes to find information.

Access to WAIS can be through your own local WAIS client or through a variety of WAIS clients maintained by other sites. To see if your system is running a WAIS client, just type **wais** or **swais** at the system prompt. If your system is running WAIS, you will get a prompt. (On a UNIX system, try **xwais** and Enter.) If your site is not running a client, you will need to locate one by Telnet. There are two clients that will allow you to become familiar with WAIS. Telnet to:

- **quake.think.com and login as wais**
- **sunsite.unc.edu and login as swais**

Although clients differ, in general, a WAIS search works like this. After you Telnet to a WAIS server, then:

1. Select the set of databases to query by moving up and down the presented list with your arrow keys, and pressing the Spacebar to highlight or mark each item you wish to search.

2. Create a keyword query for the search: Press **w** and then enter your word or words at the prompt. In searching, note that WAIS does not use **AND, OR**, and **NOT** as logical operators, but treats them as ordinary keywords. Thus, **opus and bill** will find anything with **opus**, **and**, *or* **bill** in it. Newer versions of WAIS software treat searching differently, so be sure to follow the directions found with the client you are using. To search for all variations of your keywords, the list might look like this: **advertise advertisement advertisements advertising Advertise Advertisement Advertisements Advertising**. You might try **advertis*** to see if your client can use wild cards.

3. Run the query by hitting the Enter key.

4. Descriptors of the databases satisfying your query are displayed and ranked according to the number of matches to your search words.

5. You may then retrieve the document.

If you have located too much information, or have defined your search too broadly, you may need to narrow or refine your search to make it more accurate for your needs. Below is an example of a search for **business** and **marketing**:

```
Keywords: business marketing
Enter keywords with spaces between them; <return> to search;
   ^C to cancel


SWAIS                    Search Results
Items: 19
  #     Score    Source                    Title              Lines
001:  [1000]  (directory-of-se)  agricultural-market-news      23
002:  [ 750]  (directory-of-se)  Health-Security-Act          296
003:  [ 583]  (directory-of-se)  ersa                          55
004:  [ 500]  (directory-of-se)  ANU-Australian-Economics      99
005:  [ 500]  (directory-of-se)  ANU-CAUT-Academics            80
006:  [ 500]  (directory-of-se)  ANU-CAUT-Projects             84
007:  [ 500]  (directory-of-se)  ANU-SSDA-Australian-Census   106
008:  [ 500]  (directory-of-se)  ANU-SSDA-Australian-Opinion  114
009:  [ 500]  (directory-of-se)  ANU-SSDA-Australian-Studies  126
010:  [ 500]  (directory-of-se)  ASK-SISY-Software-Information  34
```

```
011:   [ 500] (directory-of-se)   IAT-Documents                33
012:   [ 500] (directory-of-se)   National-Performance-Review  62
013:   [ 500] (directory-of-se)   STAR-NIPO-Data               40
014:   [ 500] (directory-of-se)   academic_email_conf          61
015:   [ 500] (directory-of-se)   cerro-1                      23
016:   [ 500] (directory-of-se)   journalism.periodicals       58
017:   [ 500] (directory-of-se)   usda-csrs-pwd                47
018:   [ 500] (directory-of-se)   world-factbook               21


<space> selects, arrows move, w for keywords, s for sources,
   ? for help
```

This search revealed 18 items that contain the keywords. The items are ranked according to how many times the keywords appeared in each database. At this point, using the arrow keys to move up and down the listing, you can press the Spacebar to choose one or all of these for searching. In this case, I chose to look at the first of these:

```
SWAIS              Document Display                     Page:  1
(:source
   :version  3
   :ip-address "128.193.124.4"
   :ip-name "nostromo.oes.orst.edu"
   :tcp-port 210
   :database-name "agricultural-market-news"
   :cost 0.00
   :cost-unit :free
   :maintainer "wais@nostromo.oes.orst.edu"
   :subjects "business  marketing  commodities agriculture
              agricultural"
   :description "Server created with WAIS release 8 b3.1 on Oct 5
              22:48:47 1991 by wais@nostromo.oes.orst.edu


This server contains the agricultural commodity market reports
compiled by the Agricultural Market News Service of the United
States Department of Agriculture. There are approximately 1200
reports from all over the United States. Most of these reports
are updated daily. Try searching for 'Portland grain.'


For more information contact: wais@oes.orst.edu
```

At this point I could return to my resources menu, choose other databases to search, or finish my search. Table 10.8 shows some useful WAIS/SWAIS commands.

Table 10.8 WAIS/SWAIS Commands

Command	Meaning
Spacebar	Choose a database.
#*number*	Move to a source #.
s	Select new sources.
w	Select new keywords.
h	Display the help screen.
?	Display the help screen.
q	Quit the program.

WAIS/SWAIS can be a little slow to respond, so try to suppress your instincts to keep pressing keys—give it time. Also, remember to use it at off-peak times to lighten the network peak load and get faster responses. You can locate more information on WAIS using a bibliography of information maintained by Barbara Brooks at **ftp.wais.com**, in the directory */pub/wais-inc-doc*. There are three additional FTP sites that maintain WAIS information:

- **ftp.cnidr.org**
- **quake.think.com**
- **sunsite.unc.edu**

WAIS/SWAIS is a growing resource for Internet users, so look for it to expand in the near future. In addition, companies are using WAIS internally to manage their documents and information.

CAMPUS WIDE INFORMATION SYSTEMS

Many college and university campuses have installed a campus wide information system (CWIS—said "kwiss") for their own information management, and have connected their local sources to the Internet to make them available to others. A CWIS provides a wide range of information about a campus, usually including campus facts, course offerings, sports schedules, and more. Many times you can obtain student, faculty, and administrator phone numbers and e-mail addresses.

Other popular information is sometimes included, such as reference material, community information about restaurants, events, local weather, newsletters, access to counseling services, .GIF pictures of the campus, alumni contacts, and bookstore promotional items. Each CWIS is highly individualized. An example of a CWIS opening menu is this one from Michigan State University:

```
Internet Gopher Information Client 1.2VMS p10
              Michigan State University


1.   Gopher at Michigan State University.
2.   Help Using Gopher (More About Gopher)/
3.   Keyword Search of Titles in MSU's Gopher <?>
4.   About Michigan State University/
5.   MSU Campus Events/
6.   News & Weather/
7.   Phone Books & Other Directories/
8.   Information for the MSU Community/
9.   Computing & Technology/
10.  Libraries/
11.  MSU Services & Facilities/
12.  Outreach / Extension / Community Affairs/
13.  Network & Database Resources/
```

Under item 4, there is another menu giving access to information about the history of MSU, things to do on campus, addresses and phone numbers on campus, the MSU fight song, and an item called the Online Photo Gallery:

```
Michigan State University Online Photo Gallery


1.   About Online Photo Gallery.
2.   Photo credits.
3.   Administration Building in Spring (200 Kbytes) <Picture>
4.   Aerial view of Administration Building surroundings  <Picture>
5.   Another winter view of Red Cedar River (250 Kbytes)  '<Picture>
6.   Beaumont Tower (240 Kbytes) <Picture>
7.   Candidate Bill Clinton giving speech at M.S.U . <Picture>
8.   Canoes at Red Cedar Yacht Club (225 Kbytes) <Picture>
9.   Fall colors around Beaumont Tower (220 Kbytes) <Picture>
10.  Fall shot of a residence hall (245 Kbytes) <Picture>
11.  MSU's mascot at a football game (195 Kbytes) <Picture>
12.  Main Library in Spring (390 Kbytes) <Picture>
13.  Spartan Stadium on game day (170 Kbytes) <Picture>
14.  Statue of Sparty (330 Kbytes) <Picture>
15.  Students by Red Cedar in Spring (230 Kbytes) <Picture>
16.  Students juggling at M.S.U.(170 Kbytes) <Picture>
17.  Students work out (225 Kbytes) <Picture>
```

```
18. The Wharton Center for Performing Arts (230 Kbytes) <Picture>
19. View of Linton Hall (220 Kbytes) <Picture>
20. Winter scene on campus (225 Kbytes) <Picture>
21. Winter view of Beaumont Tower (230 Kbytes) <Picture>
22. Winter view of the Red Cedar River (225 Kbytes) <Picture>
```

As an MSU alumna, I found that the photos I downloaded and viewed on my PC were quite interesting to look at.

Some use of CWIS has started in support of distance learning activities. Colleges and universities are using the Internet for the delivery of remote courses, and have placed course materials on their local CWIS.

You can connect to most CWISs via Gopher or Telnet. Do a Veronica search for any campus of interest, and you will then be able to select that CWIS from a menu.

USEFUL GUIDES TO MORE INFORMATION

There are a number of guides available on the Internet for finding resources, and for using Internet tools. Those listed below are some of the most useful.

Special Internet Connections

Scott Yanoff maintains a list of Special Internet Connections that is very handy. He updates it twice a month, so it is always an up-to-date resource. The listing contains the following categories:

- Agriculture
- Aviation
- Computers
- Economics/Business
- Education/Teaching/Learning
- FTP
- Games/Recreational/Fun/Chat
- Geophysical/Geographical/Geological
- Gopher
- Law
- Libraries
- Medical/Health/Biology/Genetics
- Music
- News

- Religion/Bible
- Science/Math/Statistics
- Services
- Software
- Space/Astronomy
- Sports
- Travel
- User Lookup Services/Whois
- Weather/Atmospheric/Oceanic
- And more!

This listing is both useful and entertaining. Where else can you learn how to finger a coke machine to find out how many cold sodas it contains, or get information on contacting ham radio operators, playing chess online, the Billboard Charts Top 10, Nielson TV ratings, NFL scores, or subway routes of major cities in French or English?

This list is available via FTP from **csd4.csd.uwm.edu** in the */pub* subdirectory as **inet.services.txt**, or finger Yanoff at **yanoff@csd4.csd. uwm.edu**. The HTML version of this list for WWW and Mosaic is **http:- //www/uwm.edu/Mirror/inet.services.html**.

December's Guides

Compiled by John December, these two documents are rich resources of information. The *Internet and Computer-Mediated-Communication* document provides pointers to a wide range of information sources including the technical, social, cognitive, psychological, and communication aspects of the nets. The guide is broken into seven sections:

- How to Use This Document
- The Internet and Services
- Information Services/Electronic Publications
- Societies and Organizations
- Newsgroups
- Selected Bibliography
- Description of Items

This is a thorough, detailed, and well-designed guide to resources.

Another of December's guides called *Internet Tools* focuses on the tools of the Internet and how to access them. It outlines the tools for network information retrieval, computer-mediated communication, and other services, organized into six sections:

- Network Information Retrieval Tools
- Computer-Mediated Communication forums
- References
- Protocols/Standards
- Action Notation
- Description of Items

Both of these guides are available through many avenues:

Anonymous FTP

site:	**ftp.rpi.edu**
subdirectory:	*/pub/communications*
files:	**internet-cmc.txt**
	internet-tools.txt

HTML

http://ww.rpi.edu/Internet/Guides/decemj/internet-cmc.html

http://ww.rpi.edu/Internet/Guides/decemj/internet-tools.html

There are versions in LaTeX, PostScript, text .dvi, and .dat format.

Gopher Jewels

Created by David Riggins, *Gopher Jewels* is a list of interesting Gopher finds, organized by subject. It is very useful, and has many listings under economics, business, and government. The subject tree is organized this way:

- About Gopher Jewels.
- A List Of Gophers With Subject Trees/
- Agriculture and Forestry/
- Anthropology and Archaeology/
- Architecture/
- Arts and Humanities/
- Astronomy and Astrophysics/
- Biology and Biosciences/
- Books, Journals, Magazines, Newsletters, Technical Reports & Publications/

- Botany/
- Chemistry/
- Computer Related/
- Economics and Business/
- Education and Research (Includes K-12)/
- Employment Opportunities and Resume Postings/
- Engineering/
- Environment/
- Federal Agency and Related Gopher Sites/
- Fun Stuff & Multimedia/
- General Reference Resources/
- Geography/
- Geology and Oceanography/
- Grants/
- History/
- Internet Cyberspace Related/
- Language/
- Legal or Law Related/
- Library Information and Catalogs/
- List of Lists Resources Identified From A Veronica Search/
- Math Sciences/
- Medical Related/
- Military/
- Miscellaneous Items/
- Patents and Copy Rights/
- Photonics/
- Physics/
- Political and Government/
- Products and Services - Store Fronts/
- Religion and Philosophy/
- Search Internet Resources by Type (WAIS, Gopher, Phone, Other)/
- Social Science/
- Weather/

Gopher Jewels is available on the gopher at USC: **cwis.usc.edu** port-70 in the *Other_Gophers_and_Information_Resources* menu. A new source is **http://galaxy.einet.net/gopher/gopher.html** (searchable form), or **http://galaxy.einet.net/GJ/index.html** (traditional hypertext structure).

The Guide to Network Resource Tools (Nettools)

Produced by the staff at EARN, Nettools is a major guide to Internet resources. They have organized the guide into seven parts covering all of the primary tools of the Internet:

- Exploring the Network
- Searching Databases
- Finding Network Resources
- Finding People and Computers
- Getting Files
- Networked Interest Groups
- Other Tools of Interest

The guide also has an appendix with information on Gopher, WWW, and WAIS clients. This guide can be obtained via e-mail from **listserv-@earncc.bitnet** in both plain text and PostScript format. Send an e-mail message to the listserv with the following content:

GET NETOOLS PS   (PostScript format)

GET NETTOOLS TXT   (Plain text format)

In addition, it is available via FTP from **naic.nasa.gov** in the */files/ general_info* subdirectory as either **earn-resource-tool-guide.ps** or **earn-resource-tool-guide.txt**.

Clearinghouse for Subject-Oriented Internet Resource Guides

The Clearinghouse for Subject-Oriented Internet Resource Guides, at the University of Michigan, is a collection of subject-oriented resources lists. The guides are available via Gopher and FTP. The unique approach is that these guides are not organized by tool, like Gopher, or by FTP sites; rather, they each focus on a theme.

Currently all files are in ASCII format, but it is planned that the Clearinghouse will be able to accept lists in PostScript or other formats. Access to these guides is available via anonymous FTP, Gopher, and WorldWideWeb/Mosaic. From within Gopher, a WAIS index of the full text of these guides is searchable.

Anonymous FTP

site: **una.hh.lib.umich.edu**
subdirectory: */inetdirsstacks*

Gopher

site: **gopher.lib.umich.edu**
menu: *What's New and Featured Resources*
       Clearinghouse...

HTML

http://http2.sils.umich.edu/~lou/chhome.html or

http://www.lib.umich.edu/chhome.html

NYSERNet New User's Guide to Useful and Unique Resources on the Internet

NYSERNet is the New York Education and Research Network. Its *New User's Guide* is very useful, and is meant to help users learn about the Internet and its tools. While the guide is primarily for educators, it has information on a number of items of use to business users. To FTP the ASCII text version of the *Guide*, FTP to **nysernet.org**. The *Guide* is in the */pub/guides* directory. The guide is organized with sections on:

- Library Catalogs
- Databases
- Electronic Discussion Groups
- Directories
- Information Resources
- FTP
- Fee-based Information Services
- Software
- BBS
- Miscellaneous

The Online World—A Shareware Guide

By Odd de Presno, *The Online World* is an electronic shareware guide of some 280 pages. It explores selected applications and services, and information on a large number of specific resources. The guide is available in English, German, and Norwegian. It is organized into three parts:

- An Online World—the value of information, structure, and content of the Internet, using online services
- Applications—hobbies, home, health, education, work, using the networks to manage projects
- Working Smarter—practical tips

To get information on how to obtain the latest version of the guide, send e-mail to **listserv@vm1.nodak.edu** with the message **get tow master**. Because new guides appear frequently, use Gopher, Veronica, archie, and Hytelnet to search for and retrieve them.

WHERE FROM HERE . . .

Practice with these tools is critical to remembering how to use them and to gaining an understanding of the nature and scale of the Internet.

The next chapter will list specific Internet resources and sites of interest to anyone using the Internet.

Doing Business on the Internet

CHAPTER 11

Putting Together a Complete Internet Business Plan

GETTING DOWN TO BRASS TACKS

Now that we have discussed why businesses are using the Internet, discovered some techniques for creating a business presence, and learned how to use the tools of the Internet, it is time for you to review, take stock, and prepare to get on the Internet, if you are not already. There has been a lot information presented up to this point, but to make it valuable to your business it should be analyzed and assimilated into some concrete plans.

Businesses are using the Internet for many reasons and business functions, including communications, data transfer, logistics, cost containment, reaching new markets, collaboration, information retrieval, and direct marketing and sales. In each case, the Internet is useful in accomplishing these business functions.

STEP ONE: GET ON THE INTERNET!

If you are not already on the Internet, do it now—call one of the Internet providers, such as The World, Panix, or Netcom, and get an account. You are not wedded to your initial decision regarding an Internet service provider. Review Chapter 2 concerning access providers and use the chart in Figure 11.1 to help you further in deciding which provider has the services that you need. I remember my first session,

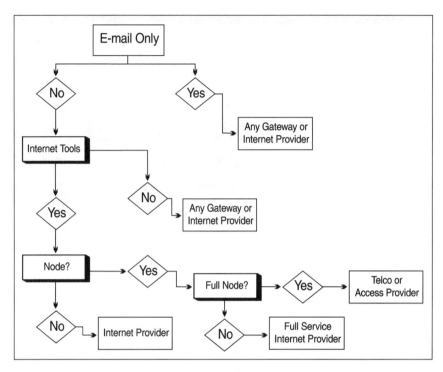

Figure 11.1 Flow Chart of Internet Provider Decisions.

and sending my first e-mail—it was a strange experience, and after I sent that first e-mail message, I called the recipient to be sure that it had arrived. Everyone has to start somewhere.

Now it is time to plan your business activities with the Internet.

STEP TWO: CHECK OUT THE COMPETITION

The next step is to join a few lists, read some newsgroups, and look around at the various Gophers and information sites while improving your Telnet, FTP, and Gopher search skills. Try out WWW using Lynx, WWW, or Mosaic. It is important to look around at what is going on to provide insight and ideas for planning.

What are your competitors doing? If they are not already using the Internet, you can beat them to the punch; if they are, you can learn from what they are doing, and do a better job. Here are some strategies for locating your competitors and seeing what they might be up to:

- *Use the lists*: Join several lists that are related to your industry or products. Review the membership list using the listserv commands outlined in Chapter 7. Look for company domains and names of familiar people. Read the archives, searching for particular products and company or individual names. What are they concerned or asking about? What information are they providing?

- *Use the Usenet newsgroups*: Begin regularly reading newsgroups of all kinds that touch upon your interests and industry. What are the hot topics, and who is talking about them? As with the lists, review the postings and .sig files of members. Finger the addresses of the individuals posting interesting information to look at their .plan files.

- *Use Gopher and Veronica*: Search for businesses, products, and subjects using Veronica. Be creative in your searching—use a broad range of keywords. Chapter 10 can help you in using Gopher and searching with Veronica.

- *Use WorldWideWeb*: Use WWW to locate business and product information. It is the fastest growing tool in the Internet right now, and many companies are creating home pages for searching. Chapter 10 can help you look for WWW/Lynx/Mosaic information.

- *Observe .sig and .plan files*: As you cruise the lists, newsgroups, and Gophers, look for clues about competitors, their activities, and their interests. Request information through their automated reply e-mail services, look at their Gophers, and cruise their FTP sites. Again, use *finger* to look at .plan files of interest.

- *Use archie*: Do some archie searches as outlined in Chapter 10 to hunt for files and directories containing keywords of interests such as names of companies and products.

- *Subscribe to Net-happenings*: *Net-happenings* is a list that sends update information on Internet-related items. It covers new Gophers, FTP sites, services, and more. It's like a home-town newspaper for the Internet. Use the normal majordomo subscription procedure to subscribe: send a message to **majordomo@is.internic.net** with the message **subscribe net-happenings** *yourfirstname yourlastname*.

- Finally, be an active citizen of the network. By "mixing it up" you will be able to keep tabs on your competitors.

STEP THREE: CREATE THE PLAN

Now is the time to begin your business plan using the Internet. How will you use the Internet? If you decide to use the Internet in direct marketing and sales, you will need to construct an Internet marketing plan. Which

Internet tools and resources will you use? Figure 11.2 shows which Internet tools are recommended to get things done.

Doing a business needs assessment can help clarify which Internet tools and resources to use, and which to emphasize. What are your particular business's needs? The form below outlines some of the key reasons that companies typically have for using the Internet.

Needs Assessment

__ 1. Communication

    __ Internal—networking

    __ External—vendors, customers, suppliers

__ 2. Data Transfer—between sites, to/from other companies, on-the-road staff

__ 3. Information Retrieval/Research/Utilization—marketing research, new materials, training, professional development

__ 4. Logistics—scheduling, planning, calendars, inventory

__ 5. Cost Containment—alternative communications

    __ Telephone

    __ Mail

    __ Personnel—efficiency of customer support, telecommuting, reduce the need for meetings

    __ Other—announcements, newsletters, etc.

__ 6. Collaboration/Product Development—workgroups

__ 7. Marketing Research—primary and secondary, surveys

__ 8. Direct Marketing/Advertising

__ 9. Sales—product support, distribution channels, information for vendors/customers, online sales

__10. Other _____

    _____

Using the results of this needs assessment, you can then turn to creating a plan for an Internet business presence. In creating a marketing plan, the first activity is to examine your company mission, goals and

	E-mail	.sig	.plan	Lists	Gopher	FTP	Newsletters	Usenet	W3 Mosaic	WAIS
Product Announcements	x	H	x	H			H	H		
Product Flyers	x		H	x	H	H	x	x	L	x
Product Specifications	x		x		x	H	x		L	L
Pricing Information	x		x		x	H	x	x	L	L
Catalogs	x		x		H	H	H		H	x
Events and Demos	x		x	x	H	H	x	x	x	x
Free Software					x	H			x	x
Customer Support	H			L	H	x	x			
Company Contracts	H		H	L	H	x	x		x	x
Promotional Notices	x	H	H	H	H	x	x	H	x	x
Documentation	x				H	H	x		x	x
Multimedia	L				L	x			H	
Surveys	H			x	x	x	x	L		x
Performance Data	x	L			x	x			x	x
Service Evaluation	x			x	x	H	x			x
Product Reviews				x	H	H	H	H	H	x
Customer Service Information	x		L	x	H	H	L		x	x
Job Placement/Recruitment	L			x	x	x	x	x		
Dialog	H			H	L			H		
L = Limited Usefulness or Access		x = useful			H = major source					

Figure 11.2   Analysis of Internet Tools.

objectives, and growth strategy. What is your underlying business philosophy, and your major business and marketing goals? What is your current position in the market? The following outline is intended to remind you of considerations important to any business plan.

Building an Internet Business Plan

I. Introduction

A. Business philosophy, mission
B. Business goals
C. Business objectives

II. Current Situation Analysis

A. Market situation
B. Customer situation
C. Company situation
D. Product situations
E. Competitive situation

III. Key Issues

A. Problems
B. Opportunities
C. Hurdles

IV. Marketing Strategies
  A. Product
  B. Price
  C. Promotion
  D. Place

V. Market Research—Analysis
  A. Primary sources
  B. Secondary sources

VI. Budget

VII. Plan

VIII. Evaluation

IX. Recycle/Reevaluate

If you are planning to use the Internet for marketing, you will have the same market concerns as you would conventionally:

Marketing Process	*New Product*
Identify opportunity	Un-met consumer need
Plan action	New product to meet needs
Execute plan	Simulate, test market
Evaluate results	Compare test market with plan
Review and revise plan	Look for improvements, recycle

Market Research

Focus groups, consumer problems, and complaints
Test alternatives
Track test results
Identify dissatisfactions
Test revised product

This analysis will yield strategies for marketing existing and/or new products, and suggest places where the Internet can assist. In developing Internet marketing strategies, use the usual indicators:

- market potential
- market forecast
- sales potential
- sales forecast
- market share
- market size
- customer and noncustomer needs

The Internet itself can be used for both primary and secondary market research. For primary research, use some of the resources noted in Chapters 12, 13, 14, and 15. Companies are also using the Internet to survey both current customers and potential customers.

For example, in order to gain specific demographic information and reading habits about Internet users, one company that provides access to newspapers and magazines ran a contest for those willing to fill out an online survey. They put out a news release to the *net-happenings* mailing list, announcing that the information was being made available on their Gopher. This is its Gopher entry:

```
Sweepstakes -- Win Two Round-trip Air Tickets to Europe!

1. Win Two Roundtrip Tickets to Europe -- READ THIS.
2. Enter the Sweepstakes Online <TEL>

-----------------------------------------
Win two round-trip air tickets to Europe!
-----------------------------------------

Imagine yourself sipping espresso on the Champs-Elysees
or strolling among the art masterpieces of the Uffizi
Gallery in Florence. Perhaps you have relatives you'd
like to visit in London, or Berlin, or Stockholm?

Here's your chance to win two round-trip air tickets to
any destination in Europe you choose. NO PURCHASE
NECESSARY. All you have to do to enter is send us the
following seven pieces of information about yourself by
email to: Sweepstakes@xxxxx.com -- or use the online
ordering form on our gopher (gopher.xxxxx.com)

1. Name and address
2. Gender
3. Age
4. Occupation/Profession
```

```
5. Level of Educational Attainment, i.e. High School
   Graduate, College Graduate, Graduate Degree, etc.
6. Favorite Magazine
7. Household Income Level (Use the corresponding number below.)
      Under $15,000         = 1
      $ 15,000 to $ 24,999 = 2
      $ 25,000 to $ 34,999 = 3
      $ 35,000 to $ 44,999 = 4
      $ 45,000 to $ 54,999 = 5
      $ 55,000 to $ 64,999 = 6
      $ 65,000 to $ 74,999 = 7
      $ 75,000 to $ 84,999 = 8
      $ 85,000 to $ 94,999 = 9
      $ 95,000 to $104,999 = 10
      $105,000 to $124,999 = 11
      $125,000 and over     = 12
```

This was followed by a disclaimer that it was only seeking composite data, and that names and addresses would not be used for solicitation or sold to another vendor.

This kind of survey can also be conducted by announcing it on appropriate lists and groups, and then, in response to a request, sending the survey out via e-mail.

As you build your own ideas, combine your responses to the preceding forms, and use the form below to identify the specific Internet tools that will fit your particular strategy and tactics. This will allow you to hone your specifications for creating your Internet presence.

Internet Tools Needed for Strategy #1

__ 1. E-mail

__ 2. Access to discussion lists

__ 3. Your own discussion/mailing lists

__ 4. Use of Telnet

__ 5. Use of file transfer protocol (FTP)

__ 6. Your own FTP archive area

__ 7. Use of Gopher

__ 8. Your own gopherspace

__ 9. Use of WorldWideWeb (WWW)/Lynx

__10. Your own WWW server

__11. Use of Mosaic

__12. Use of Usenet newsgroups

__13. Use of WAIS

Use copies of this form for each of your strategies, so you can develop a picture of your Internet needs and implementations.

If you are just using the Internet for market research, then you can probably use any Internet service provider. If you are going to use the Internet extensively for marketing *and* sales, you should consider a full-service, commercially oriented Internet provider, or consider establishing a node.

If you are installing your own node, or putting up your own Gopher or FTP site, you may need to hire additional personnel. Using one of the commercial providers with rental space will not usually require additional personnel, though it may mean some training costs and personnel time for maintaining and updating the files.

To have your own local Gopher client, FTP archive, and/or WWW server requires that you have your own node—through a full-time SLIP connection or leased lines. These are sophisticated software installations requiring considerable technical expertise, as well as the installation of TCP/IP connections. Most companies considering this level of Internet connectivity either hire personnel to install and maintain the equipment and software, or hire a consultant in the planning and training phases—sometimes both.

Many companies are arranging to "rent" gopherspace, FTP archiving, and WWW services through their Internet service provider. These are almost turnkey operations, which have numerous advantages—you do not need any special equipment or technical expertise, and do not need to worry if your node has technical difficulties. Many service providers will assist you in setting up these tools. Your involvement then becomes one of keeping up-to-date information on the server and responding to inquiries. Companies that are providing services to businesses wishing to rent space, advertise, and provide information are discussed in the next chapter.

In choosing your particular Internet configuration, consider the human resources implications of your decisions. If you are considering becoming a SLIP or full node, you will likely have to hire additional personnel or reassign someone to manage the network and Internet connection. This implementation will also require an investment in hardware and training.

To compare the prices of Internet service providers, you may want to use the following form to arrive at annual costs. Some providers, offer $5 a month shell accounts with a $2 an hour charge. Many providers have alternate usage plans such as "20/20" plans ($20 for 20 hours of use, and then an additional charge per hour above 20). Check with potential Internet access providers to see which of the items listed below incur charges and which are free with the account.

Base Cost of Account: _____

    Additional charges for e-mail messages

        in _____

        out _____

    Usage of account per hour _____

    Disk storage   _____

Use Charges Subtotal: _____ X 12 = _____

    or

Special pricing for 20/20 or other plans: _____ X 12 = _____

Additional Services:

  Corporate mailbox, or node: _____ X 12 = _____

  Special connections, SLIP other: _____ X 12 = _____

  (Discounts for multiple accounts: _____)

Special Services:

  Rental of Gopher and FTP space: _____ X 12 = _____

  Additional file storage costs: _____ X 12 = _____

  Subtotal for connection and services _____

Equipment Costs

  Purchase: _____

  Rental: _____ X 12 = _____

  Subtotal   _____

(Unless you are purchasing node or SLIP services, you may not need any new equipment, as regular Internet dial-up services can run on just about any computer with a modem.)

For SLIP, 56KB or better services:

  Installation of lines: _____

  Monthly usage and maintenance fees: _____ X 12 = _____

Personnel: _____

Training: _____

Grand Total: _____

STEP FOUR: CARRY OUT THE PLAN

Many businesses just beginning to use the Internet find that a staged approach to implementation is useful. The first few months, they simply experiment with using their .sig file and .plan file to begin a billboard type of presence. They use the vast resources of the Internet for market research and get a feel for what is going on.

Depending upon how that works out, they begin to put out useful announcements, and later add a Gopher and/or FTP presence. It is important to remember that caution is a virtue—breaching netiquette can gain you a bad name in minutes. Take the time to do it right the first time.

For most business users there is a phase-in of activities needed, similar to the strategies outlined earlier for learning about your competition:

1. Get on the Internet, scope out the competition as outlined earlier, and exercise your Internet skills. Subscribe to *net-happenings*, lists, newsgroups, and online newsletters. This usually is a one- or two-month undertaking, of 5–10 hours a week.

2. Consider hiring a consultant for advice on an Internet business plan—many Internet providers are offering this kind of assistance, and you can get some suggestions from Chapter 12.

3. Take some initial steps to create a business presence on the Internet by creating and updating a .sig and .plan file. Get your name out there. This is a one- or two-month undertaking, with no particular increase in your time investment from the 5–10 hours a week of #1 above.

4. Consider the next logical steps. For many businesses, the next step might be to register with some of the Internet advertiser services described in Chapter 12. They offer a broad range of online visibility from simple product announcements to full-blown storefronts. This is usually a one- or two-month activity, but may have a substantial time investment. The good news is that if you are successful, you will have an increase in business, but there will be an increase in the time commitment for Internet-related activities.

5. Finally, the last step, if appropriate, is to do a full-court press into doing business on the Internet through a Gopher, FTP, and WWW, either rented or on a node.

Start slowly and build upon your successes.

STEP FIVE: EVALUATE THE PLAN, ASSESSING SUCCESS AND YOUR POSITION

Once your plan is under way, you should evaluate its progress, checking on its effectiveness and profitability, but do not try to do a "bottom line" assessment too soon. Like all business strategies, Internet plans need to be fine tuned and to mature, and those on the Internet need to become aware of your presence.

Here are some indicators of success (depending upon your specific activities):

- An increase in e-mail traffic by 2–10 times (or more).
- Growth across 2–3 months in the number of requests for specific information, or general inquiries.
- Survey returns: If you do any kind of online surveys with customers or potential customers, Internet returns via e-mail usually exceed those through snail mail by 1.5 to 3 times, Gopher-based surveys are very popular.
- The receipt of flames: Yes, it means they are seeing what you are doing. Read these, and consider what they have to say, but remember that no matter what you do, there will be flames. (Resist the temptation to flame in return.) The usual ratio is 1:30 (bad to good) if you are using the correct approach; if this is worse, take these complaints very seriously.
- Good return on investment: Generally, Internet-related activities take from 6 to 24 months to gain profitability, depending upon the level and cost of the activity. A full-node installation can take two to three years to show profitability, depending upon your savings for telephone, delivery services, etc., and increases in business.
- Compare your results: Many Internet business users will share numerical and anecdotal data on discussion lists and in Usenet newsgroups.

One popular way to find out how you are doing is to have friends and/or employees monitor lists and groups, keeping an ear to the ground. You can also have them mention your business in discussion in a low-key way, and monitor the responses. Has anybody heard of you? What do they think?

Finally, consider what improvements need to be made. Track your results, review your effectiveness, and recycle your plan.

PLANNING HOW TO GIVE SOMETHING BACK TO THE INTERNET

A business's image on the network, as with any venue, is important. There are a couple of rules of thumb about maintaining a good network image: First, do no unsolicited advertising, and second, find a way to give something back to the Internet, both for good will and to attract customers.

If your plan for your business involves the use of the Internet, you should be exploring methods for returning something of value to the Internet. This could take the form of:

- providing free services of value
- distributing useful information
- giving opportunities for interaction
- participating in discussion lists or newsgroups

Here is one example of giving back to the network: Netcom maintains its own Gopher, with information about its services, but it also provides Internet information, the ability to do Veronica searches, access to other Gophers, access to directory services, and weather information.

```
NETCOM On-line Communications

1.    About this GOPHER server.
2.    Information about NETCOM/
3.    Internet information/
4.    Jughead - Search High-Level Gopher Menus (via
      Washington & Lee) <?>
5.    Search Gopherspace using Veronica/
6.    Other Internet Gopher Servers (via U.C. Santa Cruz)
7.    Weather (via U. Minnesota)/
8.    Worldwide Directory Services (via Notre Dame)/
9.    Interesting items/
10.   ATTENTION NETCOM users.
```

Selecting 2. *Information about NETCOM/* will display the following submenu:

```
Information about NETCOM

1.    Information about NETCOM
2.    About the Internet.
3.    Information about personal accounts.
4.    Information about business accounts.
5.    NETCOM local access numbers.
6.    Using the "guest" account to register.
```

Selecting 9 from the first menu will get you to a couple of universal items: Under 9. *Interesting items* they provide local times and a finger utility, which is especially useful for those who have no other access to it.

```
            Interesting items

  1. Today's Events in History.
  2. Local Times Around the World/
  3. Finger Lookup <?>
```

Another example is the Gopher maintained by fONOROLA. They provide access to their products, and extensive access to Canadian information, the *Internet Business Journal*, MAC Gopher servers, and a real bonus—Usenet newsgroups.

```
Welcome to fONOROLA's Gopher Space.

  1.   All the Gopher Servers in the Gopher Space/
  2.   Home of The Gopher (UofMN)/
  3.   Canadian Domain/
  4.   Internet Business Journal/
  5.   Internet Information/
  6.   Internet Registration Templates/
  7.   MAC Gopher Servers/
  8.   Phone Books/
  9.   Search WAIS Databases/
  10. Usenet News/
  11. Veronica and Jughead/
  12. fONOROLA's NIC Public Directory/
  13. fONOROLA's Software Archive/
  14. in.coming/
```

Choosing item 7, for example, will get you:

```
            MAC Gopher Servers

  1.     TBone MAC Gopher Server/
  2.     Test MAC Gopher Server/
```

Precisely what you provide is less important than making it your business to provide something of value. If you are just using the Internet for communication or for data transmission, you only need to be a good net citizen. If you are going "whole hog" and putting together a coordinated presence with a Gopher, FTP site, or other high-visibility activity, then the level of information and service provided needs to be higher.

What you provide is also related to the kind of business you are doing. Text-based services such as newspapers, magazines, and book publishers naturally provide some text and information for free. Software companies provide free working demos or small working utilities, while Internet providers give access to services such as Gophers and FTP sites, or support for activities such as the Online Book Initiative.

How much you contribute to the network depends upon your level of use, visibility, and type of product, but it is, in conjunction with your products, what will determine public opinion about your company, and the number of customers you will attract.

WHERE FROM HERE . . .

The next chapter can help you locate marketing, advertising, and consulting services for getting your business on the Internet.

CHAPTER 12

Resources for Doing Business on the Internet

There are numerous resources available via the Internet which can help you to create a business presence on the Internet. There are discussion lists, in-depth file archives, and extensive software collections and research tools. A new resource is the growing number of Internet access providers who are providing much more than just a connection—they are providing services and information on making use of the Internet for business purposes. Some have online catalogs and storefronts, and others offer corporate mailboxes and consulting.

Because the number, kind, and location of resources for doing business on the Internet changes frequently, there are a couple of useful resources for keeping up to date and locating new sources. MIT maintains a commercial services reference at **http://tns-www.lcs.mit.edu//commerce.html** that is extensive. This is an excerpt of that listing:

```
            LIST OF COMMERCIAL SERVICES ON THE WEB (AND NET)


    * Apollo Advertising, located in London UK
        * Branch Information Services located in Ann Arbor, MI.
            + Grant's Florist & Greenhouse
            + Health and Fitness
            + Promotional Items
            + Magazine Subscriptions
        * CTS Network Services, Internet Access provider located
          in San Diego area
```

* Cyberspace Development, Inc. located in Boulder, CO.
    + 3W Global Network Newsletter
    + Harmony Games
    + INFOMARK, international telecom information
    + Interactive Publishing Alert
    + On-line Bookstore
* Electric Press, Inc. located in Virginia. (2/25/94)
    + The International Electric Grand Prix Association
* Enterprise Integration Technologies is coordinating
  CommerceNet.
    + Amdahl
    + Apple
    + AVEX
    + Barrnet
    + Bank of America
    + CIT
    + DEC
    + Dun & Bradstreet
    + EIT
    + Financial Services Technology Consortium
    + HP
    + Internex
    + Inernet Shopping Network
    + Lawrence Livermore National Labs
    + National Semiconductor
    + Network Computing Devices
    + Pacific Bell
    + PartNet
    + RSA
    + Sun
    + Smart Valley, Inc.
    + Silicon Valley Public Access Link
    + Tandem
    + Trusted Information Systems
    + Xerox
* The Global Electronic Marketing Service located in
  Liverpool, NY.
    + Real Estate Guide
    + Missing Kids Index
* The Internet Business Directory
    + Too many to list
* The Internet Company gopher server, located in Cambridge, MA
    + Counterpoint Publishing
    + The Electronic Newstand (tm)
    + Dern's Internet Info, News and Views

```
* Internet Distribution Services located in Palo Alto, CA.
    + ANSWERS The Magazine For Adult Children of Aging
      Parents
    + The Center for Software Development
    + The Company Corporation
    + Country Fare
    + D3 Electric Catalogs for CD-ROM, Multimedia and more
    + The Directory, from the publishers of OutNOW!
    + Document Center
    + Gymboree
    + NetWorld+Interop 94
    + The Palo Alto Weekly
    + The Palo Alto Medical Foundation
    + N-Fusion Records
```

Another useful source of information is *The Internet Mall*, available via FTP at **ftp.netcom.com** in the */pub/Guides* subdirectory and on many Gophers as well.

Now for a look at some specific sites and services.

CommerceNet

CommerceNet is a new Internet service that started in Silicon Valley. They describe themselves as follows:

> CommerceNet is a consortium of Northern California technology-oriented companies and organizations whose goal is to create an electronic marketplace where companies transact business spontaneously over the Internet. CommerceNet will stimulate the growth of a communications infrastructure that will be easy to use, oriented for commercial use, and ready to expand rapidly. The net results for businesses in this region will be lower operating costs and a faster dissemination of technological advancements and their practical applications.
>
> CommerceNet first went online on April, 1994 and is specifically oriented to the commercial user. Potential customers can browse the directories and storefronts of members using WWW browsers such as WWW, Lynx and Mosaic. Their URL = **http://www.commerce.net/**. Customers may use the services for free to scan the information and products. CommerceNet offers two levels of membership for those who want to place their products in the electronic marketplace.
>
> CommerceNet is an Internet service provider, with a full range of Internet connectivity. To join CommerceNet as an information,

product, or service provider, register your interest by sending e-mail to **info@commerce.net**. You will receive a packet, an information questionnaire, and information on services and fees.

The developers of CommerceNet are among the first to use an updated version of Mosaic that includes public key encryption, and does not support the government's Clipper chip technology. What this means for your business is that Mosaic is now a tool that can be used to safely transfer extremely sensitive documents, such as credit card numbers, digital signatures, and time stamps.

The Internet Company

The Internet Company is a multifaceted business devoted to assisting other companies in bringing various projects to the Internet. The company has created the Internet Marketing Service, which maintains several mailing lists that are used to send out announcements of services, products, and publications.

Interested individuals subscribe to the lists in four areas: market, consumer, general computer, and the Internet. Each list is divided into four subcategories: information, products, services, and publications.

Subscribers receive product announcements, price lists, and other information. This is a classic example of solicited advertising—you subscribe to the lists in order to get the information (see Table 12.1).

Announcements must be kept short, and must contain worthwhile information about a new or existing service. The number of postings from each company is limited in order to increase variety. The goal is for the service to provide "real content"—something of genuine value to subscribers. This means that the announcement should have good, solid information about the product as opposed to hype.

Regular Internet and BITNET mailing lists make the identity of their subscribers available to members. The Internet Company does not. The Internet Company will not allow list members to be identified, so as to maintain privacy. To subscribe to a particular list, send an e-mail message to **maillist@internet.com**, with an empty *Subject* line, and the following in the body of the message:

subscribe *listname yourname* and *affiliation*

This procedure is a bit different from the normal mailing list subscription process. You will receive a welcoming message, and then start to receive the list postings. After reading the list for a while, you may want to post your own announcements. To do so, you must contact the Internet Company at **staff@internet.com** for a submission kit.

Table 12.1 Internet Marketing Service List Topics

List Name	List Topic
market.info	Information about the service and its development
market.discuss	Discussion about the service (OPEN)
computer.info	General information about computers
computer.products	Computer product announcements
computer.services	Computer services announcements
computer.publications	Computer publications announcements
internet.info	General information about the Internet
internet.products	Internet product announcements
internet.services	Internet services announcements
internet.publications	Internet publications announcements
consumer.info	General information about consumer products and services
consumer.products	Consumer product announcements
consumer.services	Consumer services announcements
consumer.publications	Consumer publications announcements

In addition, the Internet Company offers an electronic mail forwarding service, the Electronic Messenger. This service allows Internet users to receive mail sent to an Internet domain address, even though they might only have a single e-mail account on a commercial service. This is designed specifically to meet the e-mail needs of small companies or individuals who have e-mail accounts on services like CompuServe or MCIMail. The Electronic Messenger will allow you to have all mail sent to your own domain name—forwarded from one or more e-mail addresses, anywhere on the Internet. This allows a business presence with your own domain name, which is the same kind of identity usually affordable only to large companies. For information and pricing, send a mail message to **messenger@internet.com**.

The Internet Company offers a consulting service for businesses desiring to develop a business presence on the Internet. They will assist you in setting up Gophers, FTP sites, specialized mailing lists, storefronts, and more. They provide advice on how to develop a marketing identity for your business, how to build an information distribution service, how to manage your own Internet site, and information on how to form partnerships, and other topics. Send inquiries to **consulting@internet.com**.

MarketBase Online Catalog of Goods and Services

The MarketBase Online Catalog of Goods and Services is an online service designed to provide product marketers and sellers an electronic outlet for their goods. Access is free to purchasers, who can browse the catalog.

Vendors, who pay a small fee for registration and setup, are provided with an electronic storefront via a Gopher, Telnet, and FTP. MarketBase is a good example of the increasing number of Internet service providers that are appropriate for all kinds and sizes of businesses who want to create storefront on the Internet.

You can find the MarketBase Gopher by using a Gopher server and searching for **marketbase**. If you have your own Gopher, point it at **mb.com** port **70**. Access through Telnet is **mb.com** with a login of **mb**. MarketBase's opening Gopher menu covers terms and conditions, descriptions of products and services, and more about MarketBase. It looks like this:

```
Internet Gopher Information Client v1.1MarketBase Gopher


1.   Terms and Conditions of Use -- PLEASE READ!.

2.   Help.

3.   Classifications <?>

4.   Goods and Services Descriptions (can be long) <?>

5.   All Classifications (108 entries)/

6.   About MarketBase(tm), The - Catalog of Goods and Services/

7.   Register Product <TEL>
```

Choosing *5. All Classifications (108 entries)/* yields the following list (which has been abbreviated here):

```
1.   488 GPIB,  IEEE/

2.   Accelerators, Hardware/

3.   Access,  Internet/

4.   Accessories, Travel/

5.   Adapters,  Network/

6.   Automation Protocol,Manufacturing/

7.   Autonomous Underwater Vehicles/

8.   BBSs/

9.   Bicycles/

10. Bus,ISA/

11. C++ Class Libraries/

12. Catalogs/

13. CDROMs/

14. Class Libraries,  C++/
```

15. Codecs/
16. Collection Services/
17. Communications/
18. Computers, Parallel/
19. Computers, Pen-based/
20. Computing Environment, OSF's Distributed/
21. Consulting Services/
22. Coprocessors/
23. Data Networks/
24. Design, VLSI/
25. Distributed Computing Environment, OSF's/
26. Drives, Tape/
27. Education/
28. Electronic Mail, Wireless/
29. Emulators, Terminal/
30. Environment,OSF's Distributed Computing/
31. Equipment, Medical/
32. Ethernet/
33. File Servers/
34. Fonts/
35. Games, Software -/
36. GPIB, IEEE 488/
37. Hardware Accelerators/
38. Hypertext/
39. IEEE 488 GPIB/
40. Insurance/

Notice that while many of the categories are computer-related, there are a number of other interesting entries: Autonomous Underwater Vehicles, Collection Services, Communications, and Insurance, for example.

Under each category is a listing of goods and services, including prices. For example, under *27. Education/* the following currently appears:

Item	Price
===========	=====
1 VI Audio Course	$39.95
2 Introduction to Personal Computers Audio Cassettes	$19.95
3 SVR4 Training from Motorola	\<see item>
4 DCE Courses Offered	\<none>
5 Network Management/SNMP training seminars offered	\<none>
6 Sendmail Made Simple Seminar	$349
7 Fundamentals of C++ Programming Course	\<none>
8 Sendmail Made Simple Seminar	$349
9 PBS Videoconference Announcement	\<see item>

```
10   Debugging C++                                          $395.00

11   Standards as a Competitive Weapon                       <none>

12   Georgia Tech Continuing Education Short Courses      <see item>

13   "Programming with Kala" 2-day course                   <none>

14   Building OSF/Motif Interfaces with Ada                 <none>

Please enter an item number or hit the return key: 2
```

Choosing item 2, just as an example, you are presented with information on audio products called "Introduction to Personal Computers Audio Cassettes" put out by Specialized Systems Consultants, Inc. (SSC). The tapes are designed to assist businesses in the purchase of computer systems. Their two-cassette audio album is priced at $19.95. The ad then gives contact information via telephone, regular mail, and e-mail.

To register a product, get the registration form by way of e-mail to **register@mb.com**, requesting a product registration form. In addition, you can get a form through their Gopher, or you can Telnet to **mb.com** and log in as **register**.

MarketPlace from Cyberspace Development

MarketPlace.com is an Internet information mall created by Cyberspace Development, Inc. in Boulder, Colorado. They offer online shopping for information, entertainment, and tools. Many of their vendors take VISA or MasterCard. In addition, customers can set up an account allowing them to use a credit card for shopping with any of the vendors using an account name and password.

Cyberspace Development assists companies in creating Internet storefronts in their MarketPlace. They lease space to any business wanting to establish a commercial presence on the Internet, with several options:

- Brochure
- Information Center
- Storefront

In addition, they have a Commercial Internet Directory for listing any business on the Internet. The listing is free, but only provides a link to your information. For information on this service, contact them at **add-listing@marketplace.com**.

For general information, e-mail them at **info@marketplace.com** for an automated information reply. For a personal reply, e-mail them at **office@marketplace.com**.

MSEN and the Internet Business Pages

MSEN, as mentioned in Chapter 3, is an Internet service provider that sponsors the Online Career Center and the Internet Business Pages, among other services. Access to the Internet Business Pages is through the MSEN Gopher.

The Internet Business Pages are an Internet version of the telephone yellow pages; stated in their own words:

> When an Internet user needs the number of your sales dept . . .
> When an Internet user needs your e-mail address . . .
> When an Internet user wants a business that sells disk drives . . .
>   They will use the Internet Business Pages . . . .

Once you have invoked the MSEN Gopher and chosen Internet Business Pages, the main menu looks like this:

```
1. What are the Internet Business Pages?
2. Internet Business Pages Registration.
3. Internet Business Pages - INDEX.
4. Where Do I Get IBP Clients?.
5. Search The Internet Business Pages <CSO>
```

Item 3 will show the index of current listings, and item 5 will allow you to search various fields for companies. The following are two companies currently listed in the Business Pages:

```
        alias: acw
         name: Austin Code Works
        email: info@acw.com
 office_phone: +1 512 258 0785
support_phone: +1 512 258 0785
  sales_phone: +1 512 258 0785
    fax_phone: +1 512 258 1342
      address: 11100 Leafwood Lane
             : Austin, TX, USA, 78750-3487
  description: Austin Code Works markets C source code primarily
    for the PC.

        alias: apple
         name: Apple Computer, Inc.
        email: info@apple.com
 office_phone: (415) 974 7000
  sales_phone: (415) 974 7010
```

```
fax_phone: (415) 974 3209
  address: 25525 Marriani Ave
         : Mailstop MS-60
         : Cupertino, CA, USA, 93128
```
   description: Apple Computer is a computer manufacturer
as well as a computer software vendor. Their first
success was the Apple II computer which was an
educational hit! Today, the Apple Macintosh is one of
the most popular personal computers.

The Internet Business Pages can give interested browsers information about your business such as your street address, e-mail address, sales phone number, fax number, or whatever information you would like to have included in your listing.

The data entry form for the Internet Business Pages registration contains the following:

- Full name of company
- Address (may be multiple lines)
- City
- State
- Country
- Zip
- Voice phone
- Sales phone
- Support phone (technical support)
- Fax phone
- E-mail address for general queries and info
- General description (may be multiple lines)
- Keywords (e.g., software, hardware, vendor, UNIX, etc.)

The Internet Business Pages uses keywords for classifying your listing and as an aid in searching. They offer these as examples:

software	disks	dos
hardware	tapes	unix
vendor	monitors	windows
research	peripherals	xwindows
communications	support	TCP
mail-order	consulting	SLIP
marketing	macintosh	Internet

They encourage the use of lots of keywords with your listing.

The Internet Business Pages is a free service to the Internet community. Obtain the registration form online through the MSEN Gopher, or send e-mail to **ibp-info@msen.com** and put **send form** in the subject line or in the text of your message.

NetPages

NetPages is a project that attempts to make it easier for others to find you and your business by the use of their White Pages and Yellow Pages. NetPages are published twice a year in both hard copy and on the Internet. White Pages listings are free of charge, and contain your name, e-mail address, business e-mail address, company name, and "snail mail" address. If you need a longer listing, you can use their Yellow Pages. Contact them at **netpages@aldea.com**, or **info@aldea.com**.

Telerama Public Access UNIX

Telerama Public Access UNIX offers a wide range of services, including Internet access, domain name registration, tutorials, Gopher and FTP space rentals for businesses, and a Shopping Plaza for business services. Telerama has a Gopher menu that emulates a city:

```
Telerama Public Access

1.  Bus Stop/
2.  City Hall/
3.  Library/
4.  Post Office/
5.  Rec. Center/
6.  Shopping Plaza/
7.  Telerama Community College/
8.  Telerama Herald/
9.  Visitor Information
```

The Shopping Plaza is a repository of electronic catalogs. Item 6 provides a menu of commercial entities. Each of the catalogs maintains its own ordering arrangements. Potential vendors can contact **sysop@telerama.pgh.pa.us**.

Telerama offers Internet access to individuals and businesses, including intermittent dial-up SLIP. The Telerama School offers free classes on how to use Internet programs and services using Internet Relay chat (IRC), which allows real-time, interactive classes.

The World Software Tool & Die

The World, as mentioned in Chapter 5, offers many services to businesses: Internet access, Corporate Mailboxes including the registration of a domain name, the ability to create mailing lists, discounts for multiple accounts, and the "rental" of FTP and Gopher archive space. In addition, they provide on-site Internet training.

The Shops on The World is a Gopher offering vendors a virtual storefront for their products and services. This is its current Gopher menu:

```
Internet Gopher Information Client v1.1
Shops on The World

1.  Amzi! - Prolog & Expert Systems Software & More/
2.  Artech House - A Technical Book & Software Publisher/
3.  Electric Space Co. - Sound for real & virtual worlds/
4.  JP Software/
5.  JT Toys - An Adult Toy Store/
6.  Numerical Recipes Software/
7.  Quantum Books - A Technical And Professional Bookstore/
8.  Softpro Books - Computer Books and Software/
9.  Take Two - Digital Retouching and Restoration.
10. The Programmer's Shop - Online Resource Guide/
11. The Real-Time Intelligent Systems Corporation/
12. WORDNET - Language Translation Services/
```

The World also will assist you in setting up a business Gopher and FTP site on their system. This is a useful alternative for those businesses just starting to use the Internet, and for small and other businesses that do not want the hassle of creating and maintaining their own sites.

The World's Corporate Mailbox Service is for companies that want their own Internet domain name for the delivery of business e-mail to a World mailbox. This means that your business could have its own address without establishing a node through SLIP or leased lines. As with real nodes, the domain name must be unique.

The Corporate Mailbox application asks for the requested domain name, the names of the parties responsible for the account, any aliases that are requested, and some other billing information. The application can be obtained by requesting it from **office@world.std.com**.

Other Resources

The **Internet Ad Emporium**, from Multimedia Ink Design, is a server providing advertising for all kinds of business. It includes classifieds and business dossiers. The URL address is **http://mmink.cts.com/mmink-/mmi.html**.

From England, **Apollo Advertising** is supplying services to Europe and North America. They provide advertising and allow you to put your own WWW documents on the WorldWideWeb. Short advertisements are free; there is a small charge for HyperAdverts (Hypertext advertisements) or WWW documents. The URL address is **http://apollo.co-.uk/home.html**.

Branch Information Services sponsors the **Branch Mall**, "exit 1, just off the Information Highway." They provide online shopping services. Contact them at URL **http://Branch.com:1080**.

The Global Electronic Market Service (GEMS) in Liverpool, NY, likens itself to the special sections of your Sunday newspaper, where they provide guides to business, travel, real estate, and other subjects. They give assistance to companies in publishing their catalogs, and offer other corporate information. Contact them at URL **http://www.gems.com/index.html**.

Internet Distribution Services, Inc. provides electronic marketing, publishing, and distribution services on the Internet. Contact them at URL **http://www.service.com/**.

The Internex Information Services Company provides rental space on their Matrix Marketplace, connectivity services, and ISDN information. Contact them by URL **http://www.internex.com/** or use e-mail to contact them at **internex@internex.net**.

For something unusual, try the **UnderWorld Industries Shopping Maul** (UWI) at the University of Michigan. They offer a variety of online catalogs for what they call "weird/cool/fringe type HTML catalogs." This "maul" is quite unusual. Contact them at **uwi@pobox.pds.med-.umich.edu**.

Consultants and Other Resources

In addition to the companies just mentioned, there are some consultants who can assist you in connecting to the Internet, creating your Internet marketing plan, and more. EUnet can help you keep in touch with your Internet enterprises as you travel abroad.

Strangelove Internet Enterprises, Inc.

From Ottawa, Canada, Michael Strangelove has started a number of Internet business ventures, including several newsletters and the publication of a variety of business-related Internet books. In addition to publishing, his company also offers a wide range of Internet training programs. You can reach Strangelove Internet Enterprises at **mstrange@fonorola.net**.

Matrix Information and Directory Services

Located in Austin, Texas, Matrix (MIDS) is a company formed by Smoot Carl-Mitchell and John S. Quarterman. They publish the *Matrix News*, mentioned earlier. Their Gopher provides access to Matrix, other MIDS publications, maps of the networks, information about protocols, WHOIS, and more. They have particular expertise in assisting businesses in establishing physical Internet connections. You can contact them at **mids@tic.com**.

Oak Ridge Research

Oak Ridge Research provides Internet consulting and training. Their specialty is using the Internet for business and educational purposes, particularly for distance education and creating a business presence on the Internet. They publish the *Internet Demystifyer and Monthly Gazette*. Reach them at **oakridge@world.std.com**.

EUnet

When traveling, keeping in touch with your e-mail can be difficult, especially when you travel abroad. EUnet provides networking and Internet-related services in 27 countries in the greater European region, covering an area ranging from Iceland and above the Arctic Circle to Egypt—Eastern and Western Europe, North Africa, and the former Soviet Union. EUnet services include e-mail (RFC-822 and X.400), *Network News*, Archive Access, and connectivity via leased lines, ISDN, dial-up, and X.25. Based in Amsterdam, the Netherlands, they can provide local Internet access which makes it possible for you to connect, for the cost of a local phone call, to your account in North America. For more information, e-mail them at **info@EU.net**.

Required Reading

It is important, while creating an Internet marketing plan and creating a business presence on the Internet, that you look at what others are doing. It is also important to get out there and mix it up, taking the temperature of lists and newsgroups that might be a place for you to become more visible. One way to do that is to join discussion lists and newsgroups, and to subscribe to some of the important newsletters and magazines.

Useful Mailing Lists and Usenet Newsgroups

Table 12.2 contains a small sample of the discussion mailing lists and Usenet newsgroups that might be of interest to you as you begin to build a business presence on the Internet. Subscriptions to these lists are made through the listserv protocol outlined in Chapter 7.

Table 12.2   Discussion Mailing Lists

List Address/BITNET/Internet	List Name
AFA-ECOM@WSUVM1 AFA-ECOM@wsuvm1.csc.wsu.edu	AFA-ECOM Commerce on the Internet
AFA-EMKT@WSUVM1 AFA-EMKT@wsuvm1.csc.wsu.edu	AFA-EMKT Emerging Markets
AFA-MKTM@WSUVM1 AFA-MKTM@wsuvm1.csc.wsu.edu	AFA-MKTM Market Microstructure
AFA-GORE@WSUVM1 AFA-GORE@wsuvm1.csc.wsu.edu	AFA-GORE FinanceNet
AFA-PUB@WSUVM1 AFA-PUB@wsuvm1.csc.wsu.edu	AFA-PUB Public Finance
AFA-SBUS@WSUVM1 AFA-SBUS@wsuvm1.csc.wsu.edu	AFA-SBUS Small Business Finance
BIZLAW-L@UMAB	Law Regarding Business Associations and Securities
BPI@UTXVM BPI@utxvm.cc.utexas.edu	Business Process Improvement: Issues, opportunities
BUSETH-L@UBVM BUSETH-L@ubvm.cc.buffalo.edu	Business Ethics Computer Network
CNIDR-L@UNCCVM CNIDR-L@UNCCVM.UNCC.EDU	Networked Information Discovery and Retrieval
ESBDC-L@FERRIS ESBDC-L@MUSIC.FERRIS.EDU	Small Business Development Centers List
FEDTAX-L@shsu.edu	Federal Taxation and Accounting discussion
GISBUS-L@ECUVM1 GISBUS-L@ecuvm.cis.ecu.edu	Geographic Information Systems for Business
GLOBMKT@UKCC GLOBMKT@ukcc.uky.edu	Applied Global Marketing
HR-INFO@HARVARDA	Human Resources Information Discussion List
HRIS-L@UALTAVM HRIS-L@vm.ucs.ualberta.ca	Human Resources Information (Canada)
IL-ADS@TAUNIVM IL-ADS@vm.tau.ac.il taunivm.tau.ac.il	Israel Bulletin Board for Advertising

(continues)

Table 12.2 (Continued)

List Address/BITNET/Internet	List Name
JAPAN@PUCC JAPAN@PUCC.Princeton.EDU	Japanese Business and Economics Network
ORMS-L@UMSLVMA ORMS-L@UMSLVMA.UMSL.EDU	Operations Research
PROCUR-B@OSUVM1	Commerce Business Daily - Procure
QUALITY@PUCC QUALITY@PUCC.Princeton.EDU	TQM in Manufacturing and Service Industries
RITIM-L@URIACC RITIM-L@URIACC.URI.EDU	Telecommunications and Information Marketing
SPACE-INVESTORS@cs.cm u.edu	Investing in Space-Related companies
TBIRDS@ARIZVM1 TBIRDS@arizvm1.ccit.arizona.edu	Discussion of International Business

There are thousands of Usenet newsgroups, and many of these groups touch upon business issues (see Chapter 5 for some examples). The following Usenet newsgroups are probably the most useful for seeing how others have created a business presence on the Internet:

- biz.clarinet
- biz.comp...
- biz.control
- biz.digex...
- biz.misc
- biz.oreilly...
- biz.sco...
- biz.zeos

Useful Magazines and Newsletters

There are numerous paper-based and electronic periodicals, journals, newsletters, and magazines that can assist you in learning more about creating a business presence on the Internet. Many of the paper-based publications also maintain some online full-text versions of their materials. Here are a few of these resources:

- *The Global Network Navigator* is a WWW-based information service designed to give updates on network resources. It contains news, information, and feature articles. Included is the GNN Marketplace, which works with advertisers in providing information to potential customers of a business. Contact them at **info@gnn.com**.

- *The Internet Business Report*, a paper-based newsletter published by CMP Publications, focuses on the commercial opportunities of the network. It includes articles, opinion pieces, and occasionally a bit of satire. E-mail to **ibr@cmp.com** for more information.

- *The Internet Business Journal* is a newsletter that focuses on commercial opportunities of networking. Published in Canada by Strangelove Internet Enterprises, it has articles, resources, opinion pieces, and company profiles. They also publish *The Internet Advertising Review*, focusing on network advertising, and *ElectroPolis*, a newsletter about Internet-accessible government resources and public information, both in the United States and Canada. Contact them at **mstrange-@fonorola.net**.

- *The Internet Letter*, a paper-based Net Week publication, focuses on corporate users and information services. It covers networking issues of all kinds, including technical, regulatory, and governmental issues. It also includes tips and techniques, and information on upcoming events. Contact Net Week at **netweek@access.digex.net**.

- *Internet World* is a paper-based magazine published by the Meckler Corporation that covers the Internet broadly, including how-to articles, reviews, opinions, and issues. E-mail them at **meckler@jvnc.net**.

- *Matrix News* is a monthly newsletter about the global matrix of the Internet. It has a broad range of topics, such as networks and network growth, connectivity, the future of the network, reviews, and commentary. *Matrix News* can be reached at **mids@tic.com**.

- *Meta* is an electronic magazine covering a broad variety of networking issues. It is unusual in that it is a freely redistributable periodical, provided in Farallon's Replica for Windows format, and as PostScript files. *Meta* is an attempt to provide visually striking information by electronic means. It is available by FTP from **ftp.netcom.com** in the subdirectory */pub/mlinksva*. More information is available by e-mail to **mlinksva@netcom.com** with **sendinfo** as the subject line.

- *The Electronic Journal of Virtual Culture* is a multidisciplinary electronic journal devoted to issues of computer-mediated human behavior, thought, and interaction. Subscribe using the standard listserv commands, to **listserv@kentvm.bitnet** or **@kentvm.kent.edu**, with the message **subscribe ejvc-l** *yourfirstname yourlastname*.

Software Sources

As you proceed with creating your business presence, you will have need for software such as mail readers, TCP/IP, and Gopher. There are some excellent repositories of software readily available on the Internet. (See Chapter 9 for more information on how to use FTP to retrieve these software files.)

Table 12.3 shows mirror sites—they keep the same software in the same subdirectories at each site. They are huge repositories of thousands of pieces of software for PCs, Macintoshes, UNIX, OS/2, and others. Table 12.4 shows other software repositories. Get the **Read.me** files and the index files for lists of file descriptions.

FROM HERE . . .

From here, you should continue on to Chapters 13, 14, and 15 for more information on specific Internet information sources by categories. After reading these chapters, you might want to return to Chapter 11 for another look at your business plan for using the Internet.

Table 12.3   Mirror Sites

Address	Directory
oak.oakland.edu	*/pub*
wuarchive.wustl.edu	*/mirror*
archive.orst.edu	*/pub/mirrors*
ftp.uu.net	*/systems/simtel20*
nic.funet.fi	*/pub*
src.doc.ic.ac.uk	*/pub/computing/systems*
archie.au	*/micros*
nic.switch.ch	*/mirror*
micros.hensa.ac.uk	*/pub*

Table 12.4 Software Repositories

Address	Directory	Comments
garbo.uwasa.fi	*/pub*	Broad variety of software (garbo is mirrored at **wuarchive.wustl.edu** in */mirrors/garbo.uwasa.fi*; **archie.au** in */mcros/pc/ garbo*; **nctucca.edu.tw** in */PC-Ms- Dos/Garbo-pc.*)
ftp.cica.indiana.edu	*/pub/pc/win3*	Lots of Windows software
ftp-os2.nmsu.edu	*/pub/os2*	Lots of OS/2 software
rtfm.mit.edu,	*/pub/usenet/ news.answers*	Good source of FAQs
sumex-aim.stan- ford.edu	*/info/mac*	Lots of Macintosh software
mac.archive.umich.edu	*/info-mac*	All kinds of Macintosh software
prep.ai.mit.edu	*/pub/gnu*	UNIX software
sunsite.unc.edu	*/pub/micro/pc- stuff/ms-windows/*	Subdirectories for Winsock, Windows, applications
boombox.mi- cro.umn.edu	*/gopher*	PC, Mac, UNIX, NeXt, OS/2, VMS
info.cern.ch	*/pub/www*	WorldWideWeb software
ftp.ncsa.uliuc.edu	*/mosaic*	Mosaic software for several platforms

Professional and Business Resources on the Internet

CHAPTER 13

Online Resources, Databases, and Libraries of General Interest

The Internet is bristling with resources, databases, and information of all kinds and formats. Much of that information relates to specific subjects or fields, but there are some more general resources available for browsing:

- libraries
- electronic texts
- reference resources
- U.S. Government documents and information
- Canadian Government information
- images and sounds

LIBRARIES

Thousands of libraries worldwide are reachable online. In most cases, the catalog and some databases are available for remote searching using Telnet, Gopher, and WWW. There are public libraries, consortiums of libraries, and individual, technical, college, university, and organization libraries.

There are many guides to library resources found on the Internet. For example, *Internet Accessible Library Catalogs and Databases*, compiled by Art St. George and Ron Larsen, contains information on more than a hundred library catalogs. It can be retrieved by way of FTP at **ariel.unm-.edu**, in the directory */library*, as the file **internet.library**. Another interesting guide to libraries by Billy Barron is available by FTP from **ftp.unt.edu** in the */library* subdirectory as file **libraries.txt**.

Gaining Access

You can get access to libraries on the Internet in a variety of ways. Some libraries have Telnet addresses, some are connected using Gopher, and others are connected through alliances. To reach a particular library, it is usually easiest to use Hytelnet (see Chapter 10) or one of the large Telnet sites such as the Washington and Lee Law Library (mentioned in Chapter 8). Many Gophers have gateways to library catalogs as well, so that once you have reached one library, you can usually network out to others.

WorldWideWeb also provides library linkages; for example, Washington and Lee Law Library provides WWW and Mosaic access. In Lynx or WWW, type **G** for Go, then type **http://honor.uc.wlu.edu:1020** and then press Enter.

Consortiums of Libraries

Some libraries have created consortiums or alliances in order to extend and expand their services. In the 1970s and 1980s, they formed these consortiums in order to provide access to services and materials that were not on-site before the Internet really started to grow. Now, these alliances are providing their collective services on the Internet. The following is a sample of library alliances located using Hytelnet:

- Access Colorado Library and Information Network
- Boston Library Consortium
- Colorado Alliance of Research Libraries (CARL)
- C*O*N*N*E*C*T: Libraries in the Greater Hartford Area
- DALNET (Detroit Area Library Network)
- Fenway Libraries Online, Inc.
- Florida State University System
- HELIN (Higher Education Library Information Network)
- Houston Area Library Automated Network (HALAN)
- ILLINET On-line Catalog
- KELLY: Regional Online Catalog for WESTNET
- MARMOT Library Network

- Maryland Interlibrary Consortium
- Nevada Academic Libraries Information System (NALIS)
- OhioLink
- University of Maryland System
- Washington Research Library Consortium

A large library consortium, the Colorado Alliance of Research Libraries (CARL), provides a number of interesting services. CARL can be contacted by way of Telnet to **pac.carl.org** and log in as **PAC**. In addition, CARL is on the menu of numerous other libraries. Using CARL's UnCover database, you can search through and read thousands of magazine and journal abstracts, and using a credit card, order the full text for fax delivery within 24 hours.

University Libraries

There are hundreds of research organization, college, and university libraries that have online catalogs and other services including access to databases and special collections. This is just a sample (obtained through Hytelnet) of those libraries that are currently online:

- Air Force Institute of Technology
- Arizona State University
- Auburn University
- Bates College
- Boston University
- Bowdoin College
- Bowling Green State University
- Brandeis University
- Brookhaven National Laboratory
- Brown University
- Bucknell University
- Cal Poly State University
- California Institute of Technology
- California State University, Long Beach
- Carnegie Mellon University
- Case Western Reserve University
- Central Michigan University
- City University of New York

- Colby College
- Colgate University
- Colorado School of Mines
- Colorado State Department of Education
- Columbia University
- Connecticut State University
- Cornell University
- Museum of Fine Arts, Boston
- National Center for Atmospheric Research
- Nebraska State Colleges
- New England Conservatory
- New Mexico State University
- New York University
- North Carolina State University
- Rice University
- Rochester Institute of Technology
- Rockefeller University
- Roger Williams University
- Rutgers University
- University of Illinois at Urbana/Champaign
- University of Iowa
- University of Kansas
- University of Maine System

For example, you can reach the Michigan State University Library using Telnet (**merit-telnet-gw.msu.edu**), Hytelnet, or the WWW server at Washington and Lee Law Library (**http://honor.uc.wlu.edu:1010**). In this example, I was using Hytelnet:

```
Michigan State University


TELNET MERIT-TELNET-GW.MSU.EDU or 35.8.2.56
At the Which Host? prompt, enter MAGIC
At the terminal id, enter VT100


TELNET MERIT-TELNET-GW.MSU.EDUTELNET MERIT-TELNET-GW.MSU.EDUTELNET
MERIT-TELNET-GW.MSU.EDU Proceed (y/n)?Ok...
Trying...
```

```
Connected to MICHNET-TELNET-GW.MSU.EDU, a PDP-11/73 running MINOS.

%Merit:Hermes (EL052A:TN05:VT100:EDIT=MTS)
%You have reached MichNet, operated by Merit Network, Inc.
%Enter a destination, or enter HELP for assistance.

Which Host?magic

ENTER TERMINAL TYPE: vt100
VM/XA SP ONLINE

Michigan State University Computer Laboratory
          IBM 3090-200JVM/XA SP 2.1 slu 205+

                        / \
                --_____| |_
                |  /  |  \  |
                |  |  |  |  |
                |__|__|__|__|
          {  }} !      ___       !
       {        }!    / | \      !
         {{         !  ( / )  ! {{  }}
     { }}{ }}       !   \___/    !{        }}
     {{ {  } {      !_____!       } }
       {        }  }!           !       }}}
```

To reach the MSU Libraries, type **dial magic** on the COMMAND line

```
dial magic
```

The next screens present a fairly traditional library catalog, with the ability to search for books by title, author, and subject. Many libraries present menus of their regular catalogs, and various databases that they will allow guests to search, such as ERIC, dictionaries, and so on.

Canadian and European Libraries

Worldwide, there are a large number of libraries online, offering catalogs and databases in English and other languages. A sample of Canadian libraries as presented by Hytelnet includes:

- Acadia University
- Canada Centre for Mineral and Energy Technology
- Carleton University

- Concordia University
- Dalhousie University
- Ecole Polytechnique (Montreal)
- Laurentian University
- Laval University
- McGill University
- McMaster University
- Memorial University, Newfoundland
- Nova Scotia College of Art and Design
- Ontario Institute for Studies in Education
- Ottawa Public Library
- Saskatoon Public Library
- St. Boniface General Hospital Library
- University of British Columbia
- University of Calgary
- University of Guelph
- University of King's College
- University of Lethbridge
- University of Manitoba Libraries
- University of New Brunswick
- University of Ottawa
- University of Prince Edward Island
- University of Saskatchewan
- University of Toronto

A Hytelnet sample of libraries from the United Kingdom includes:

- Aberdeen University
- Cambridge University
- City of London Polytechnic
- City University
- Cranfield Institute of Technology
- Dundee Institute of Technology
- Durham University
- Edinburgh University
- Edinburgh University Online Information System

- Essex University
- Glasgow University
- London University Central Libertas Consortium
- London University, British Library of Political and Economic Science
- London University, Imperial College
- London University, Kings College
- London University, Queen Mary College
- Manchester University
- National Library of Scotland
- National Library of Wales
- Natural Enviroment Research Council (NERC)
- North East Wales Institute
- Nottingham University
- Open University
- Oxford Brookes University
- Oxford Polytechnic
- Oxford University
- Oxford Westminster College
- Queens University Belfast
- Reading University
- Royal Greenwich Observatory

Public Libraries

There are some public libraries currently accessible using the Internet, with more coming online. The following is a sampling:

- Abilene Public Library
- Atlanta-Fulton Public Library
- Bangor Public Library
- Beaumont Public Library
- Bemis Public Library
- Boulder, Colorado, Public Library System
- Carnegie Library of Pittsburgh
- Cedar Rapids Public Library
- Central and Western Massachusetts Public Libraries (via CARL)

- Cleveland Public Library
- Denver Public Library
- Detroit Public Library
- Estes Park Public Library
- Fort Morgan Public Library
- Harris County Public Library
- Houston Public Library
- Keene Public Library
- Lynchburg Public Library
- New York Public Library—Branch Libraries Catalog
- New York Public Library—Research Libraries
- Pasadena Public Library
- Port Arthur Public Library
- Port Neches Public Library
- Seattle Public Library
- Sonoma County Library
- Sterling Municipal Library
- Sterling Public Library

The venerable New York City Public Library (with the lions Patience and Fortitude now figuratively standing guard) has a database of all holdings in all branches, as well as in their special collections. Use Telnet to connect to **nyplgate.nypl.org**, and log in as **nypl**, with a password of **nypl**; or it can be found using Gopher or Hytelnet.

ELECTRONIC TEXTS

Full-length books and other large documents are often called electronic texts. There are several sources of electronic text; primary among them are Project Gutenberg and the Online Book Initiative at **world.std.com**. These can be found on Gopher and by way of Telnet.

The Online Book Initiative is available using FTP as well: **ftp.std.com**, user **anonymous**, in the /*obi* subdirectory. This archive is also accessible using the World Gopher. Project Gutenberg is seeking to put as many texts as possible on the Internet. Currently, it is working its way through books in the public domain. These texts can be accessed numerous ways, for example:

ftp mcrnext.cso.uiuc.edu   */pub/etext*
ftp quake.think.com   */pub/etxt*
ftp oes.orst.edu   */pub/almanac/guten*
E-mail to **almanac@oes.orst.edu**, and in body "send guide" *<filename>*

The following is a sample of the authors represented in The Online Book Initiative sponsored by The World Software Tool & Die:

- A.E. Housman
- Aesop
- Ambrose Bierce
- Arthur Conan Doyle
- Bram Stoker
- Charles Dickens
- Charles Hedrick
- Charles Lutwidge Dodgson
- Colin Higgins
- Edgar Allan Poe
- Edgar Rice Burroughs
- Edwin Abbott
- Eleanor H. Porter
- Emily Bronte
- Ezra Pound
- Francis Bacon
- Grimm
- H.H. Munro
- Henry David Thoreau
- Hippocrates
- J. W. Barrie
- James Matthew Barrie
- Jane Austen
- John Milton
- John Henry Newman
- Joseph Conrad
- Karl Marx
- Katherine Mansfield
- Lewis Carroll

- Lysander Spooner
- Mark Twain
- Martin Luther King
- Melville
- Nathaniel Hawthorne
- Percy Bysshe Shelley
- Philip Agee
- Plato
- Rudyard Kipling
- Saki
- Samuel Clemens
- Shakespeare
- Tennyson
- Thomas More
- Tommaso Campanella
- Tracy LaQuey
- Virgil
- Walter Scott
- Wilfred Owen
- William Blake
- William James

The Dartmouth University library offers a large collection of the works of Dante in electronic form, and provides a searchable database of the works of Shakespeare. Telnet to **library.dartmouth.edu**, and select *dante*, or *file s*.

The following is an example of a Telnet session to the University of Minnesota, to examine the electronic text section:

```
TELNET> consultant.micro.umn.edu
login: gopher
[Select the menu item Libraries, then select Electronic Books]

1990 USA Census Information
Aesop's Fables
Aladdin and the Wonderful Lamp
Alice's Adventures in Wonderland (Carroll)
CIA World Factbook 1991
Clinton's Inaugural Address
```

```
Complete Works of Shakespeare
Far From the Madding Crowd (Hardy)
Federalist Papers
Gift of the Magi (O. Henry)
Herland (Gilman)
Hunting of the Snark (Carroll)
Jargon File
King James Bible
Moby Dick (Melville)
Narrative of the life of Frederick Douglass
O Pioneers! (Cather)
Oedipus Trilogy (Sophocles)
PI to One Million Digits
Paradise Lost (Milton)
Peter Pan (Barrie)
Roget's Thesaurus
Scarlet Letter (Hawthorne)
Sleepy Hollow
Song of Hiawatha (Longfellow)
Square Root of 2
Strange Case of Dr. Jekyll and Mr. Hyde (Stevenson)
Through the Looking Glass (Carroll)
Time Machine (Wells)
United We Stand
War of the Worlds (Wells)
Zen and the Art of the Internet (Kehoe)
```

The Center for Text and Technology, in its CPET project, maintains a catalog of electronic text archives, which can be accessed by using Telnet to **guvax3.georgetown.edu**, user name **CPET**.

It is obvious from these listings that many of the current electronic books available online are not directly related to business. The number of e-texts is growing, so it is worth cruising listings like these from time to time to see what has been added.

REFERENCE RESOURCES

Reference materials are available online at many sites. These include phone books, dictionaries, the CIA Fact Book, news and weather, census information, zip code information, and more.

As an example, using Lynx, I connected to Washington and Lee Law Library, and looked at its reference section:

Go: **http://honor.uc.wlu.edu:1020**
Getting http://honor.uc.wlu.edu:1020
Making HTTP connection to honor.uc.wlu.edu:1020.

..Restrict by Subject
..Restrict by Type (Telnet, Gopher, WWW)
..Sort: Date (for date coded entries) [49 items]
..Sort: Alphabetic[49 items]
..Sort: Geographic [49 items]

Dictionaries (English Language)
U.S. Zipcode Search
Internet Reference Center from OECN/NWOCA (Ohio)
Phone Books Menu
Network & Database Resource Collection from Michigan State Univ.
Government Information
CIA World Fact Book 1992
Academic Resources
U.S. Zip Code Directory
U.S. State Department Travel Advisories
Geographic Names Database (U.S.)
CIA World FactBook
American English Dictionary
Subject Index to Concepts, Terms and Definitions
Roget's Thesaurus (pub. 1911) -- Browse
Australian Postcodes Database (WAIS db)
Grolier Academic American Encyclopedia
Virtual Reference Desk (U of Calif-Irvine)
Oxford English Dictionary .. (Login: oed)
News and Weather
Acronyms(from UK)
Electronic Addresses (Email) Directories
Electron Text Collections
Weather Forecasts
Time of Day and Time around the world
Serrate Titles of Documents & Menus in Gopherspace
International Information
Dictionaries
Webster's Dictionary (University of California, San Diego)
  (Login: expect "*login*";send "webster\r";)
Electronic Journal Collections
New Hacker's Dictionary (Computer Jargon)
U.S. Telephone Area Codes

```
U.S. Census Summary 1990
Reference Shelf
Reference calendars (P. Riddle, Rice U.)
Integrated Service for Information Resources (SIRI)
```

If you want to look up the word **computer**, select the menu item called *Dictionaries*. Then choose which of the two dictionaries that you want to use and, finally, enter **computer** at the prompt:

```
Dictionaries (English Language)

  Select one of:
(?) American English Dictionary (UK)
(?) Webster's Dictionary

  Webster's Dictionary selected

search: computer           .

computer (1646)
:one that computes; specif
:a programmable electronic device that can store, retrieve, and
process data
-- com-put-er-like \-,1[0xF5]^-k\ adj
```

A thesaurus service at this same site provided an in-depth response to a request for synonyms for "business":

```
Roget's Thesaurus
+||| Words to search for:|||| + business
Roget's Thesaurus: business

#625. Business.
 -- N. business, occupation, employment; pursuit &c.
622; what one is doing, what one is about; affair, concern,
matter, case. matter in hand, irons in the fire; thing to do,
agendum, task, work, job, chore [U.S.], errand, commission,
mission, charge, care; duty &c.
926.   part, role, cue; province, function, lookout, department
capacity, sphere, orb, field, line; walk of
life; beat, round, routine; race, career.
   office, place, post, chargeship, incumbency, living;
situation, berth, employ; service &c. (servitude)
749; engagement; undertaking &c.
```

676.

　　vocation, calling, profession, cloth, faculty; industry,
art;industrial arts; craft, mystery, handicraft; trade &c.
(commerce)

794.　　exercise; work &c. (action)

680; avocation; press of business &c.(activity)

#682. Business

　　V. pass one's time in, employ one's time in, spend one's time
in; employ oneself in, employ oneself upon; occupy oneself with,
concern oneself with; make it one's business &c. n.; undertake &c.
#676; enter a profession; betake oneself to, turn one's hand to;
have to do with &c.(do)

680.　　drive a trade; carry on a trade, do a trade, transact a
trade, carry on business, do business, transact business &c. n.;
keep a shop; ply one's task, ply one's trade; labor in one's
vocation; pursue the even tenor of one's way; attend to
business, attend to one's work.

　　officiate, serve, act; act one's part, play one's part; do
duty; serve the office, discharge the office, perform the
office, perform the duties, perform the functions of; hold an
office, fill an office, fill a place, fill a situation; hold a
portfolio.

　　be about, be doing, be engaged in, be employed in, be
occupied with, be at work on; have one's hands in, have in hand;
have on one's hands, have on one's shoulders; bear the burden;
have one's hands full &c. (activity)

682.　　be in the hands of, be on the stocks, be on the anvil;
pass through one's hands.

　　Adj. businesslike; workaday; professional; official,
functional; busy &c. (actively employed)682; on hand, in hand,
in one's hands; afoot; on foot, on the anvil; going on; acting.

　　Adv. in the course of business, all in one's day's work;
professionally, &c. adj.

　　Phr. "a business with an income at its heels" [Cowper]; amoto
quaeramus seria ludo [Horace]; par negotiis neque supra
[Tacitus].

　　Yes, that's the ticket—just the quote on business I was looking for—in
Latin by Horace!

　　A dictionary/spelling service of interest is located at **chem.ucsd.edu**
with a login of **webster,** or by Gopher to **wombat.doc.ic.ac.uk.**

　　One of the best collections of reference material in cyberspace is the
SOLINET Gopher. It has an acronym dictionary, Commerce Business
Daily, Copyright law, connections to desk reference tools, access to many
libraries, and access to several virtual reference desks. The SOLINET
Gopher address is **sol1.solinet.net port 70.**

GOVERNMENT DOCUMENTS AND INFORMATION

State and local government information varies greatly by location. Agencies at the federal level have been directed to provide more public information online. Because of this federal mandate, there are a growing number of government resources coming online.

The Library of Congress

The "card" catalog of that mother of all libraries, the Library of Congress, is maintained by Data Research Associates and is available using Telnet. The address is **dra.com** (or the alternative numeric address: **192.65.218-.43**), or you can reach them using Gopher at **marvel.loc.gov**, or Telnet to **marvel.loc.gov** and log in as **marvel**.

The Library of Congress also provides broader access through LO-CIS—the Library of Congress Information System. Following is a Telnet session to **locis.loc.gov**, which includes the LC catalog and access to other information. The opening menu screen is followed by search of business organization locations:

```
Telnet>locis.loc.gov
Trying 140.147.254.3...
Connected to locis.loc.gov.
Escape character is '^]'.


        L O C I S :  LIBRARY OF CONGRESS INFORMATION SYSTEM
           To make a choice: type a number, then press ENTER
    1  Library of Congress Catalog        4   Braille and Audio

    2  Federal Legislation                5   Organizations

    3  Copyright Information              6   Foreign Law

    *    *    *    *    *    *    *    *    *    *    *

    7  Searching Hours and Basics

    8  Documentation and Classes

    9  Library of Congress General Information

    10  Library of Congress Fast Facts

    11  * * Announcements * *

    12  Comments and Logoff


Choice: 5


ORGANIZATIONS
SCOR0003  Ready for new command
Search: business
```

```
To choose from list, see examples at bottom. FILE: NRCM
B06+BUSINESS ADMINISTRATION//(INDX=19)
B07 BUSINESS ADVISORY COUNCIL ON FEDERAL REPORT//(ORGN=1)
B08 BUSINESS AND ECONOMIC RESEARCH CENTER//(ORGN=1)
B09 BUSINESS AND ECONOMICS DEPARTMENT//(ORGN=1)
B10 BUSINESS AND INSTITUTIONAL FURNITURE MANUFA//(ORGN=1)
B11 BUSINESS AND LABOR DEPARTMENT//(ORGN=1)
B12 BUSINESS AND POLITICS//(INDX=1)
```

The following is a listing of the business organizations available on this LOCIS server:

```
Choose: B06+
ITEMS 1-4 OF 19          SET 1: BRIEF DISPLAY          FILE: NRCM
                          (ASCENDING ORDER)
1. PUB69-1705: Reference Library/Small Business Administration/
1441 L St. NW./Washington, DC 20416 LIMITATIONS:Free,
unrestricted; APPRV DATE: 87/07; INFO DATE: 87/07
2. PUB69-2608: Business, Economics, and Labor Department/
Cleveland Public Library/325 Superior Ave. NE./Cleveland, OH
44114-1271 LIMITATIONS:Free, unrestricted; APPRV DATE: 88/09;
INFO DATE: 88/09
3. PUB69-7262: Baker Library/Graduate School of Business
Administration/ Harvard University/Soldiers Field Rd./Boston, MA
02163 LIMITATIONS:Free, restricted; APPRV DATE: 87/06; INFO
DATE: 84/11
4. PUB69-9058: Library of the Schools of Business and Public and
Environmental Affairs (Business-SPEA)/Indiana University
Libraries/10th and Fee Lane/Bloomington, IN 47405 LIMITATIONS:
Free, restricted; APPRV DATE: 88/08; INFO DATE: 88/08
```

You could choose any of the listed items for further exploration or return to the main menu at any time. The anonymous FTP site for the Library of Congress is **ftp.loc.gov**.

FedWorld

The FedWorld National Technical Information Service Gateway offers access to numerous government computer BBSs, lots of government databases, publications, statistical files, job listings, satellite images, and libraries via Telnet to **fedworld.gov** (log in as **new**) and by way of their Gopher.

The Federal Register

The *Federal Register* is available through a commercially produced system (Counterpoint Publishing) that will allow you to browse or search the daily *Federal Register*. While the system limits the amount and type of information that nonsubscribers can retrieve, it is a useful resource. Reach the *Federal Register* by Gopher to **gopher.netsys.com**. Additionally, you may Telnet to **gopher.netsys.com** and log in as **fedreg** with a password of **register**.

Census Data

Census data are available from a variety of sites. For example, Telnet to **hermes.merit.edu (35.1.1.42)**, log in as **gopher**, and select *um-ulibrary*. Additionally, you can Gopher to **bigcat.missouri.edu** and look under the reference center menu for census data. Data are available as text and in Lotus 1-2-3 formats for U.S. cities, counties, metropolitan areas, states, and the nation, with comparisons from 1980.

Bureau of Justice Statistics

Bureau of Justice Statistics Documents maintains full text of some of their publications, and can be found using the Gopher at **uacsc2.albany.edu** under the item called *united nations-justice network*.

Other Sites with Government Information

The Gopher at **info.umd.edu** has a large collection of government information, including Supreme Court decisions, congressional information, text of the Constitution, and early confederation documents. It is also available using WWW or Mosaic as **URL://info.umd.edu:901/11/info/-Government/US/***file* where *file* could be **Constitution**, **Congress**, or **SupremeCt**. The full text of the 1993 and 1994 U.S. budget is available for searching at the **sunsite.unc.edu** Gopher.

Congress and Legislation

The U.S. House of Representatives Constituent Electronic Mail System is a pilot program to test the feasibility of establishing an e-mail system for constituents. Send a request for information to **congress@hr.house.gov**.

The United States Senate Bibliographies contains records from the 99th Congress to the present. These can be reached by FTP to either **ftp.ncsu.edu** or **ncsuvm.cc.ncsu.edu** in the */pub/ncsu/senate* subdirectory. This information is also available through the Gopher at **dewey.lib-.ncsu.edu** under *library without walls*.

Congressional information of all kinds such as congressional directories, biographies, agency directories, committee rosters, North American Free Trade Agreement documents, the Americans with Disabilities Act, the U.S. budget, and more, can be accessed through the Gopher to **gopher.lib.umich.edu** under *social science resources, government and politics, U.S. government*, and under the *educational resources, united states government* menu items.

The Library of Congress system allows users to search files that describe and track legislation introduced in the U.S. Congress from 1973 to the present. These files are updated daily, and can be reached using Telnet to **locis.loc.gov** under *federal legislation.*

Executive Branch Information

There are numerous executive branch resources available include executive branch directories, White House information, NAFTA documents, full text of the U.S. budget, and other documents, from the University of Michigan Gopher to **gopher.lib.umich.edu** in the *social sciences resources, government*, and *politics* menu items.

Also, you can reach the President and Vice President of the United States via e-mail:

```
president@whitehouse.gov
vice-president@whitehouse.gov
```

The Catalog of Federal Domestic Assistance

The Catalog of Federal Domestic Assistance provides information on more than 1,000 U.S. government assistance programs, from more than 50 federal agencies. It is keyword searchable at the Gopher at **marvel.loc.gov** under the heading *federal government information* and then using the menus to find information by agency.

The General Accounting Office (GAO)

The General Accounting Office Reports provides full text of GAO technical, transition, and other reports on the Gopher at **wiretap.spies.com** under *government docs*. These are also available via FTP to **ftp.cu.nih.gov** in the */gao-reports* directory.

State Department Travel Advisories

The State Department makes its Travel Advisories available through an archive of State Department travel information and advisories. The information is arranged by country. The files include information on medical facilities, crime, drug penalties, registration, current conditions, country descriptions, entry requirements, and embassy and consulate locations. Gopher to **gopher.stolaf.edu** and look under *internet resources*.

Guides to Other Sources of Government Information

The guide *Internet Sources of Government Information* by Blake Gumbrecht is available via Gopher or FTP. The Gopher is the University of Michigan Clearinghouse for Subject-Oriented Internet Resource Guides: **gopher-.lib.umich.edu** in the */clearinghouse* subdirectory. It is also available by FTP at NorthWestNet: **ftp.nwnet.net** in the */user-docs/government* subdirectory as **gumprecht-guide.txt**.

A guide called *Internet Resources: U.S. Federal Government Information*, by Maggie Parhamovich, is available via anonymous FTP at the University of Nevada (**ftp.nevada.edu**) in directory */liaison*.

Community/Civic/Rural/Local Info is a list of Internet/BITNET mailing lists that focus on community, civic, rural, or local issues, people, culture, and governments, compiled by Art McGee. It is an eclectic grouping, but provides a good guide to some interesting mailing lists related to community and government. It is available via anonymous FTP from **ftp.netcom.com** in the directory */pub/amcgee/community*. Table 13.1 shows a sample of those discussion mailing lists.

Table 13.1   Discussion Lists

Name	Address
ACE-MG Americans Communicating Electronically	almanac@esusda.gov
CAN-FREENET Canadian Free-Nets	listprocessor@cunews.carleton.ca
CET-NEWS Communities in Economic Transition News	almanac@esusda.gov
CNI-PUBINFO Access to Public Information Working Group	listproc@cni.org
COMMUNET Community and Civic Networks	listserv@uvmvm.uvm.edu
EFF-TALK Electronic Frontier Foundation Discuss	eff-talk-request@eff.org

(continues)

Table 13.1.   (Continued)

Name	Address
EPIN Electronic Public Info Newsletter Summary	**epin@access.digex.net**
GOVACCESS Access to Government Information in CA	**jwarren@well.sf.ca.us**
PACS-L Library & Public Access Computer Systems	**listserv@uhupvm1.uh.edu**
RURALDATA-INFO Rural Datafication Project	**ruraldata-info-request@cic.net**
TAP-INFO Taxpayer Assets Project	**listserver@essential.org**

CANADIAN GOVERNMENT DOCUMENTS

The full text of many Canadian government documents, including the Canadian Constitution Act, Meech Lake Accord, Charlottetown Constitutional Agreement, and other historic Canadian government documents, are available at the Gopher at **wiretap.spies.com** under the *government docs* listing. (Wiretap is an interesting site for all kinds of information.)

Statistics Canada makes the full text of its daily reports available, as well as various press releases, lists of publications, and other information, by way of Telnet to **info.carleton.ca**. Respond with terminal type **decvt100**, and then choose *statistics*.

IMAGES AND SOUNDS

The Internet offers a rich repository of images, pictures, clip-art, and sounds through a variety of formats. The Gopher at Texas Tech University has a menu called *Art and Images* that is quite interesting, shown here in an abbreviated list:

```
1.   ASCII Clipart Collection/
2.   DOS and Mac viewing software/
3.   TAEX Clip Art Collection (TIFF)/
4.   U.S. Weather Map <Picture>
```

```
5.  Entertainment Images from Texas A&M (GIF)/
6.  Entertainment Images from U Michigan (GIF)/
7.  WUARCHIVE Collection (GIF)/
8.  WUARCHIVE Collection (JPEG)/
    - - - - - - - - - - - - - - - -.
10. Search for Pictures/Images in all of GopherSpace <?>
.  - - - - - - - - - - - - - - - -.
12. Animals, Plants, Scenic Beauty from U of Indiana/
13. ArchiGopher: Images from U of Michigan/
14. Architectural Projects from Johns Hopkins U/
15. Art Gallery (from University of Vermont)/
16. Astronomical Images (from U of Arizona)/
17. Astronomical Images (from U of California at Irvine)/
18. Bicycling Pictures (from U of California, Irvine)/
19. Birds from U.S. Army/
20. Birds from U.S. Army (Individual descriptions)/
21. Bodleian Libraries Images (from Radcliffe Science
    Library)/
22. California Museum of Photography/
23. Campus Images from Michigan State University/
24. Campus Images from Texas A&M/
25. Campus Images from U of Texas at Austin/
26. Central American Images/
27. Centre for Innovative Computer Applications (Indiana
    Univ.)/
28. Craigdarroch Castle Images (from Victoria Freenet)/
29. Dallas Museum of Art - Information & Images/
30. Doctor Fun: The first daily cartoon of the Internet/
31. Endoscopic Test Images/
32. Global Satellite Images from NOAA and AMRC (collected by
    SSEC)/
33. Hubble Telescope Images/
```

Some Usenet groups—for example, alt.binaries, alt.fractal.pictures—maintain FTP sites with images. These are usually found in zipped files (.zip) or in .GIF or .JPEG formats.

The Smithsonian Institution maintains electronic images of many of its photographs dating from the last century. These can be found on various Gophers and via FTP to **photo1.si.edu**.

The Global Land Information System (GLIS) offers graphs and maps via Telnet to **glis.cr.usgs.gov**—log in as **guest**. Colored, shaded relief maps of the United States are available from the applied physics lab at Johns Hopkins University at the FTP site **fermi.jhupl.edu**.

Sound files are also available, as shown on the following Gopher menu from Texas Tech University:

```
                    Music and Sound

     1. About this section
     2. DOS and Mac listening software/
        - - - - - - - - - - - - - - - -.
     4. Search for Sounds in all of GopherSpace <?>
        - - - - - - - - - - - - - - - -.
     6. PC Sound Archives (SunSite UNC)/
     7. Sound Archiv (Oregon State Univ)/
     8. Sound Archives (SunSite UNC)/
     9. Animal Sounds
    10. CD Database of Hindustani and Carnatic music (Indian
        Classical)/
    11. COWPIE (Country and Western Guitar Music Archives)/
    12. Chinese Music (from Sunsite UNC)/
    13. Compact Disc Connection/
    14. Digitized Audio from the Presidential Debate/
    15. Internet Talk Radio/
    16. Lester S. Levy Sheet Music Collection (Under Construction)/
    17. MTV Gopher/
    18. Michigan State University Fight Song and Alma Mater/
    19. Music Archives (U of Wisconsin)/
    20. Music software (DOS)/
    21. Sound Archives (San Diego State U)/
    22. Sound Archives (from Texas A&M)/
    23. Techno Music (Rave Archives)/
    24. Vincent Voice Library (Michigan State U)/
    25. Whale Sounds/
```

Lyrics, chords, and pictures related to music are maintained at the FTP site **ftp.uwp.edu** in the */pub/music* subdirectory.

ELECTRONIC NEWSLETTERS

Now, for a few useful items for keeping up to date. Here are some newsletters of general interest:

- *Network-News* is available as a subscription to *nnews* from **LIST-SERV@NDSUVM1.BITNET** or **listserv@vm1.nodak.edu**. It is archived, and can be accessed via FTP from **vm1.nodak.edu** in the

/nnews directory. The newsletter is designed to provide updates on information resources and the Internet.

- E-D-U-P-A-G-E is a electronic information service, sponsored by Educom, regarding information technology. To subscribe to *edupage* send an e-mail request as usual to **listproc@educom.edu**. The archives are available by FTP from **educom.edu**.

- *Bits and Bytes Online* is an electronic newsletter about the intersection between technology and society. Subscribe to *bits-n-bytes* at **listserv@acad1.dana.edu**. It is archived and accessible via FTP to **dana.edu** in the */periodic* subdirectory, and available via Gopher at **gopher.law.cornell.edu**.

For keeping up to date, there is a very useful mailing list called *The InterNIC net-happenings* that issues notices, updates, announcements, and information on new Internet resources. The moderator, Gleason Sackman, provides daily (sometimes hourly) updates on what is new on the Internet. Subscribe to *net-happenings* at **majordomo@is.internic.net**. It is a great way to keep your ear to the ground.

FROM HERE . . .

For additional Internet resources in business and professional categories, continue on by reading Chapters 14 and 15.

CHAPTER 14

Business, Marketing, and Finance Resources on the Internet

Many people liken dealing with the amount of information available on the Internet to drinking from a fire hose. In the field of business, that fire hose is putting out a torrent of information. Finding business-related information, databases, and Gopher, Telnet, and FTP sites is an ongoing activity. New resources are coming online daily, and new online guides are being written. Addresses of resources change from time to time, so you will want to use the search tools discussed in Chapter 10. Following is an introduction to some of the most interesting and useful information resources for business.

DRINKING FROM THE FIRE HOSE

Brace yourself! To demonstrate how much information is available, here is the menu listing from Washington and Lee using Lynx (WWW or Mosaic would work just as well) to the address **http://honor.uc.wlu-.edu:1020**. The listing can also be accessed using Telnet and Gopher to **uc.wlu.edu** (for Telnet, log in as **lawlib**). This listing is under the menu item *Commerce, Business and Accounting*. There are over 225 categories; following is a small selection so you get an idea of the scope:

```
Business News (Southeast Asia)
Washington Univ-St. Louis, Economics Working Papers Archive
Federal Reserve Bank of Boston Data (SHSU mirror)
```

U.S. Dept. of Commerce, Office of Business Analysis (Budget &
    Econ. Conv.)

National Income and Products Accounts

Legal Information Resources

Federal Reserve Banks Publications

U.S. Industrial Outlook - 1994 (NTDB Version, From UM-St. Louis)

US Budget Information

Economic Bulletin Board, U.S. Dept. of Commerce (Login: expect
    "*connect*";exec sleep 2;send
"\r\r\r\r";expect "*user*";send "guest\r";)

National Bureau of Economic Research

U.S. Patent Database 1994- (WAIS db)

Agricultural Market News (search)

Trade News

Census Information (various)

Regional Economic Statistics

Economics and Business Journals

Price and Productivity Statistics

National Performance Review (Reinventing Government)

Employment Statistics

International Marketing Insights, Central & Eastern Europe

U.S. Zipcodes Directory (WAIS db)

CIA World Factbook (WAIS db)

Financial Times

Business and Commerce text database (Univ. of Victoria, CA)

Asia and Pacific Rim Agriculture and Trade Notes

Energy statistics

North American Free Trade Agreement (NAFTA) (Columbia Univ)(WAIS db)

Internet Business Journal

Overseas Business Reports (OBR) (UM-St.Louis)

Asia Pacific Business & Marketing Resources

U.S. Treasury Auction Results

General Agreement on Tariffs and Trade (GATT)

International Business Practices Guide (UM-St. Louis)

Japan Economic Newswire

Legal Information Institute - Cornell Law School

Guides to Census on CD-ROM

Current Business Statistics

Public Opinion Polls (Inst. for Research in Social Science)
    (Login: expect "*userid*";send "\r";expect
"*logon*";send "LOGON IRSS1\r";expect "*password*";send"IRSS\r";
send_user "For function keys try ESC n, e.g. ESC 3 for F3
\n";send "\032";exec sleep 7;send "\r";)

```
National Health Security Plan (from sunsite)
Economic Indicators
U.S. Department of Commerce
Security and Exchange Commission (SEC) filings (Edgar)
MarketBase: Online Catalog of Goods and Services (Login: expect
    "*login*";send "mb\r";)
Foreign Trade
Network Archive Tools
NETLIB - Mathematical, engineering and scientific software
Eastern Europe trade leads
USDA Agricultural leads
International Market Insight (IMI) reports
Commercial Services On The Web
Bureau of Labor Statistics (BLS), FTP Site
U.S. Dept. of Commerce, Information Infrastructure Task Force
```

And on for 200 more entries, many of which lead to yet other menus...

A CLOSER LOOK

Now let's have a closer look at some of the most useful Gopher, Telnet, and WWW sites. Where the site is a Gopher site, you will point your Gopher to the address listed (with a port of 70 unless otherwise noted). If you do not have your own Gopher, you may have to Telnet to a site, and use their on-site Gopher (see Chapter 10 for information on how to use Telnet, Gopher, WWW, and Lynx).

Economic Bulletin Board

This resource is reachable using Telnet, Gopher (log in as **gopher**), or FTP at **una.hh.lib.umich.edu**. The *ebb* subdirectory or menu item provides access to many other items. Maintained by the University of Michigan, this site provides data from the Department of State's Economic Bulletin Board. Data include daily foreign exchange rates for twelve countries, aggregate reserves of depository institutions, state and local government bond rates, daily U.S. Treasury statements, FRB selected interest rates, FRB bank credit and consumer rates, FRB money stock data, FRB foreign exchange rates, treasury savings bond sales, statistics on t-bill auction results, financial ratios for manufacturing corporations (FRMC), current business statistics, economic indicators, employment statistics, industry statistics, summaries of current economic conditions, durable goods shipments and orders, housing starts, monthly wholesale sales, business cycle indicators, revised composite indexes and indicators, summary text files for economic indicators, release dates for federal economic indicators, government bulletin boards, national trade data bank, telephone contacts for the Bureau of Labor Statistics, telephone directories for the Office of Business Analysis and the Office of Economic Affairs—and so on. Most of the data are presented in table format. Files can be accessed via FTP from **una.hh.lib.umich.edu** in the /*bin* subdirectory.

An example of one of the subdirectories is the Employment Cost Index, complete release, found under **ebb/employment/eci.bls**. This includes civilian labor force and unemployment by state, employees on nonagricultural payrolls by state, employment cost index, tables only (compressed DOS version), employment situation (compressed DOS version), employment-unemployment statistics by state, household employment statistics, local area employment and unemployment (complete release), major collective bargaining settlement, average wage and compensation, revised payroll survey employment estimates to 3/91, and unemployment rates by state and selected industry divisions.

Foreign exchange rates are also available at this site under the menu tree /*ebb/monetary/tenfx.frb*, where, for example, you can find the 10 A.M. and 12 noon EST foreign exchange rates, under /*ebb/monetary/noonfx.frb*.

Economic Information

The Economics Gopher at Sam Houston State University (point your Gopher to **niord.shsu.edu** and choose the /*economics menu*) contains a broad variety of material, and includes extensive connections to other business and economic Gophers. With close to a hundred entries under the /*economics* menu, there are items for Federal Reserve information, census, tariffs, and links to other business information sites.

The Gopher maintained by the Economics Department of Washington University (**econwpa.wustl.edu**, with a login as **gopher**) contains a large archive of business and economic data. A WWW server with information on the economics of the Internet can be reached at **http://gopher-.econ.lsa.umich.edu**.

Directory Information: Time, Telephone, and Postal Codes

Did you ever need to know what time it is in Ulan Bator or the postal codes in Germany? Check out:

- Local Times Around the World—Gopher to **gopher.austin.unimelb-.edu.au port 70**; select menu /*general information/local time around the world*.

- New German ZIP Codes—Gopher to **gopher.germany.eu.net**; menu selections: *Postieitzahlne-Konvertierung/manual (English)*.

- World Phone Books—Gopher to **gopher.nd.edu**; menu /*non-Notre Dame Information Sources/Phone Books--Other Institutions/All*.
- World Telephone Code Information—Gopher to **gopher.austin.uni-melb.edu.au**; menu /*general/phonecodes*.

International Information

Garbo, the Gopher at the University of Vaasa in Finland (**garbo.uwasa.fi port 70**), is a multifaceted site, containing information in accounting, finance, business economics, operations research, production economics, computer science, and more. In addition, Garbo contains a large software archive (described in Chapter 12). It has a Gopher interface as well as FTP. It is mirrored at **wuarchive.wustl.edu** (North America-Mirror), **archie.au** (Australia-Mirror), and **NCTUCCCA.edu.tw** (Asia-Mirror). Mirror sites contain the same files, stored regionally to lessen the communications and computing load at any one site.

In Great Britain, there is a useful site for Bank of England and government information. Telnet to **sun.nsf.ac.uk** (128.86.8.7) and log in as **janet** with a host name of **uk.ac.swurcc**. There is no password. When it asks for which service, type **?** and choose **PMAC** guest service. The files include the Central Statistical Office's macro-economic times series data, the World Bank socioeconomic data, and the Bank of England Quarterly Bulletin time series data.

The Gopher site at **info.lanic.utexas.edu 70** contains information on Latin America and the Caribbean, including economic, business, and trade information. Try the menus under /*USAID* and /*Latin America/Economic and Social Data*.

Canadian Information

There are a number of sources of Canadian information. Statistics Canada maintains its Internet service, Talon, through a Gopher, a listserv, and an anonymous FTP site. The site, **talon.statcan.ca (142.206.64.2)**, offers extensive access to all of their normal reports, and information on their paper publications.

The Canadian Broadcasting Company, in association with the Communications Development and Planning Branch of Industry Canada, is experimenting with the distribution of radio programming over the Internet. They provide lists of CBC radio programs, lists of transcripts, and sample radio programs in digital audio format (au). These are available via WWW at **http://debra.dgbt.doc.ca/cbc/cbc.html**; **//debra.doc.ca/-cbc/news.html** contains CBC newscasts.

In addition, there are other sites in Canada with useful information:

- Business and Commerce Resources (University of Victoria, CA)—Gopher to **malahat.library.uvic.ca 70**; menu /*Internet Resources*/*subj* from Waterloo/, and then choose from numerous entries such as /*accountancy*, /*economics*, and /*management*.

- Canadian Organizations—Gopher to **owl.nstn.ns.ca 70**; select menu /*White Pages*/*Canadian Organizations*.

- Business and Industry Statistics—Gopher to **freenet.victoria.bc.ca 70**; choose menus /*Government*/ and then look under several listings for the ministries of Health, Transportation, and Statistics.

The New England Electronic Economic Data Center

An interesting FTP site is the New England Electronic Economic Data Center (NEEED) containing New England banking data at **neeedc.umesbs.maine.edu** in the /*frbb*/*banking* subdirectory. The goal of NEEED is to provide economic data on the New England economy, including Federal Reserve Bank of Boston financial statements and performance measures for banks in the New England states from 1988 to the present, and unemployment, housing, and energy statistics for the Bureau of Economic Analysis. The focus is on New England, but many files also include some national data. Some of the data files can be used by spreadsheet programs such as Quattro and Lotus 1-2-3. The /*bea* subdirectory is for the Bureau of Economic Analysis data, and /*fbb* contains Federal Reserve Bank of Boston data. Look at the **read.me** file to get information on analyzing data using Lotus and Quattro.

Freenets and Public Access BBS

In most cases, the Freenets provide Internet services to urban areas. For the most part, access is through dial-up or via terminals in public libraries. Normally, the Freenets are open to guest logins, although sometimes they limit the services that guests are allowed to access. The menus are usually arranged with names for public services like the library and the courthouse. Table 14.1 shows some business-related resources that can be found on the Freenets. There is a central address that can be used to reach all of these sites, **uhura.neocom.edu** port **1070**, which has connections to most of the existing civic nets (see Chapter 8 for a list of Freenets and their addresses).

The National Capital Area Public Access Network—CapAccess—in cooperation with the Government Accounting Office (GAO), is providing access to the GAO Daybook, which lists current daily reports and testimony by the GAO. Telnet to **cap.gwu.edu** and log in as **guest** with a password of **visitor**. At the main prompt, type **go federal** and select the *Legislative Branch* menu.

Table 14.1 Business-Related Resources on Freenets

Topic	Freenet
Business & Industry Park	Youngstown Freenet
Buyer's Rights	Denver Freenet
Consumer Price Index	Buffalo Freenet
Entrepreneurship	Heartland Freenet
Foreign Missions	Singapore Citynet
Jobs	Triangle Freenet
Living & Working	Singapore Citynet
Major Companies	Singapore Citynet
National Health Care Reform	Denver Freenet
Planning & Zoning	Blacksburg Village
Professional Organizations	Triangle Freenet
Rules & Regulations	Triangle Freenet
Small Business Development Forum	Buffalo Freenet
Start-up Information	Buffalo Freenet
Supreme Court Decisions	Buffalo & Cleveland Freenet
Transit	Blacksburg Village
Yellow Pages	Triangle Freenet

Small Business Information

There are several sites that have information for small businesses. The Company Corporation offers information on incorporation through a Mosaic and WWW site **http://incorporate.com/tcc/home.html**.

Small Business documents are available using the Gopher at **um-slvma.umsl.edu**. Under menu items */library/subjects/business/US/SBA*, you can find Small Business Administration (SBA) State Profiles, and under */library/govdocs/*, you can find SBA Industry Profiles. SBA documents are also available through the Gopher at **gopher.mountain.net 70** in the */business resources and services/U.S. Small Business Administration* menu. The */business resources* menu has other entries as well.

There is a Small Business Bibliography on the Gopher at **gopher-.fsu.edu** under the *libraries/Strozier Library Research Guides/Topic* menu tree. This is a brief bibliography and "how-to-find" guide designed for small businesses. It tends to favor Florida sources.

Television and Radio

The Telnet site **pac.carl.org** contains access to television and radio transcripts prepared by Journal Graphics. Type **PAC** at the first prompt, and then choose the type of terminal you are working from or emulating—if in doubt, choose **vt100**, then choose the menu item *information databases/Journal Graphics*. This database provides recent information and access to over 75,000 transcripts from CNN, ABC, CBS, PBS, and National Public Radio from 1981 to the present. While printed transcripts can be ordered for a fee, often the abstract is sufficient to get the information needed. This site also gives you access to CARL and UnCover (mentioned in Chapter 11).

Magazines, Journals, and Serials

The Electronic Newsstand is maintained by the Internet Company on its Gopher (**internet.com**) under the menu *electronic/titles/arranged/current/business*. This is a collection of feature articles and editorials from a growing number of national and international magazines. Usually, there are tables of contents and editorial summaries for such magazines as the *Sloan Management Review* and *Inc. Magazine*. Check out the following for other online business-related journals:

- *Business News* (from Singapore) Gopher: **gopher.cic.net**; menu: */e-serials/alphabetic/b/business*.

- *Economics and Business Journals* Gopher: **s5.loc.gov**; menu: */global-/econ/journals*.

- Financial World Gopher: **una.hh.lib.umich.edu**; menu: */category/current/Business/financial_world_news*.

- The Harvard Business School Publishing Company—Gopher **johnny-mac.harvard.edu**; menu *search cases/search*. This provides access to the catalog of materials available from Harvard Business School Publishing. The Gopher menus serve as an index to the Harvard Business School catalog, *Harvard Business Review* reprints, Harvard Business School Press book titles, case studies, and MPG (business-related video materials). For most of these, the catalog begins with items from 1989, but classic cases and bestsellers date back to the 1960s. This site also includes access to an online order form.

WWW Virtual Library

The World-Wide Web Virtual Library at URL **http://web.doc.ic.ac.uk/by-Subject/Computing/Overview.html** offers a large collection of business and computing information, including algorithms, audio, graphics, human-computer interaction, hypertext and information, high performance, jargon, languages, networking, newsgroups, parallel supercomputing, products, software technology, telecommunications, text processing, UNIX, virtual reality, Windows, and more.

Internet Wiretap

There is a very useful, if offbeat, Gopher site called Internet Wiretap (**wiretap.spies.com**) that maintains a large collection of government documents, including GAO publications and other government information. It is a *avant-garde* site, offering alternative views of current events. If you are easily offended, use the menus with caution.

Tax Law Information

Villanova University maintains a large database of tax information through their Villanova Tax Law Compendium. Use Telnet or Gopher to reach it at **ming.law.vill.edu**, in the */taxlaw* menu. This contains a collection of student tax papers available through the Villanova Gopher. The Villanova Tax Law Society and the Villanova Center for Information Law and Policy jointly sponsor this compendium.

Social Security Administration

The U.S. Social Security Administration provides its Office of Research Services data files by way of anonymous FTP at **soaf1.ssa.gov**. (The site is echoed at the Cornell University Law School Gopher: **fatty.law.cornell.edu**.) This site maintains files of summary data of social security payments, including payment types and payment awards by state. Files are available in different formats, including Lotus. Get the **orsindex_txt** file for a description of the files and a table of contents, which is especially useful, since the filenames are cryptic at best.

Federal Labor Laws

The U.S. Department of Labor, Bureau of Labor Statistics has an FTP server called LABSTAT. FTP to **stats.bls.gov** and find information in the */pub/doc* subdirectory. Get the file **overview.doc** to give you the general lay of the land.

The *Federal Labor Laws—Report* and *Congressional Digest* are available by Gopher at **garnet.berkeley.edu 1250** in the menus */Labor Issues/History of Labor Law (Electronic Democracy Information Network - EDIN)*.

Cornell Law School

The Gopher at the Cornell University Law School is a gold mine of legal and federal statistical and economic information. Locate it using either Gopher or Telnet to **fatty.law.cornell.edu**; for Telnet, log in as **gopher**. There is also WWW access: **URL://gopher.law.cornell.edu/11/**. Under *Government Agencies* from the main menu, there are choices for *Economics Resources, FEDIX, Federal Register, FDA, FedWorld, GAO reports, Census*,

US Judges Database, and so on; and under the *Economics Resources* option there are choices for *EconData, Directory of Economists, Gross State Product Tables, Statistics and Econometrics Collections*, and more. The *Federal Register* has options for *Commerce Business Daily*, and a version of the *Code of Federal Regulations* that is "under construction." (Another source of the *Commerce Business Daily* is to Gopher to **cscns.com**, and select *Commerce Business Daily*.)

Riceinfo

Riceinfo at Rice University has a substantial amount of useful information. Reach it using the Gopher at **riceinfo.rice.edu**. This Gopher, called the Rice Subject Information Gopher, has one of the most extensive collections of information on almost any subject. From the main menu, under the *Government, Political Science, and Law* entry there are more than two hundred entries, including *CitizenUs Guide to Using FOIA, About the Iowa Political Stock Market, How to Use the Government Documents Database, Other US Government Gophers to Search, United States Government Programs,* and *Various US State Laws.*

Internet/BITNET Discussion Lists

The Financial Economics Network (FEN) is a large group of related Internet lists relating broadly to business and finance. FEN has become the largest electronic network in the world linking people with practical and academic interests in business and economics. They have distribution points in the United States, Canada, the United Kingdom, France, Germany, the Netherlands, Italy, Norway, Sweden, Australia, Finland, Russia, Estonia, Israel, South Africa, Zambia, New Zealand, Japan, Singapore, Malaysia, and Thailand, and estimate that they have more than 5,000 subscribers.

The Network consists of a master subscription, called AFA-FIN, with 40 channels or sublists. Currently 39 channels are available to AFA-FIN subscribers. Contact Wayne Marr at **marrm@clemson.clemson.edu** for subscription information. The total list is:

AFA-ACCT (Accounting and Finance)
AFA-ACTU (Actuarial Finance)
AFA-AGE (Gerontology Finance)
AFA-AGRI (Agricultural Finance)
AFA-AUDT (Auditing)
AFA-BANK (Banking)
AFA-CORP (Corporate Finance)
AFA-CFA (Financial Analysts)
AFA-DER (Derivative Securities)

AFA-DEF (Defense/Military Reconfiguration)
AFA-ECOM (Electronic Commerce)
AFA-ECMT (Econometrics and Finance)
AFA-EDU (Education Finance)
AFA-EMKT (Emerging Markets)
AFA-ENGR (Financial Engineering)
AFA-ENVI (Environmental Finance)
AFA-GORE (FinanceNet)—not ready
AFA-HEAL (Health Finance)
AFA-INST (Teaching/Instruction)
AFA-INT (International Finance)
AFA-INV (Investments)
AFA-JOB (Job Postings)
AFA-LDC (Bank/Finance LessDev C.)
AFA-LE   (Law and Economics)
AFA-MATH (Mathematical Finance)
AFA-MKTM (Market Microstructure)
AFA-PERS (Personal Finance)
AFA-PUB (Public Finance)
AFA-REAL (Real Estate)
AFA-REG (Regulation)
AFA-RES (Resumes)
AFA-RMI (Risk Management and Insurance)
AFA-S-IV (Small Investor)
AFA-SBUS (Small Business Finance)
AFA-SINV (Social Investing)
AFA-SOFT (Financial Software)
AFA-TECH (Technical Investment An.)
AFA-THRY (Financial Theory)
AFA-VCAP (Venture Capital)
AFA-WA-R (Re/Estate in Washington state)

Other lists of possible interest are given in Table 14.2.

Table 14.2 Additional Discussion Lists

BITNET Address	List Name	Internet Address
AISTFTBM@CUVMC	AIS Task Force Technology Business Management	
AWARDS-B@OSUVM1	Commerce Business Daily - Awards	
CARECON@YORKVM1	Caribbean Economy	@VM1.YorkU.CA

(continues)

Table 14.2 (Continued)

BITNET Address	List Name	Internet Address
COMMERCIAL-REALESTATE @syncomm.com	Commercial Real Estate	
CSEMLIST @HASARA11	Society of Computational Economics	
ECONOMY@TECMTYVM	Economic Problems in Less Developed Countries	@tecmtyvm.mty.itesm.mx
EDI-L%uccvma.bitnet @vm1.nodak.edu	Electronic Data Exchange Issues	
E-EUROPE@PUCC	Eastern Europe Business Network	@PUCC.Princeton.EDU
FINANCE@TEMPLEVM	The Electronic Journal of Finance	@VM.TEMPLE.EDU
GLED@UICVM	Great Lakes Econ Dev Research Group	@uicvm.uic.edu uicvm.cc-.uic.edu
GLOBALMC@TAMVM1	Global Marketing Consortium Discussion List	@tamvm1.tamu.edu
HRD-L@MIZZOU1	Human Resource Development Group List	@MIZZOU1.MISSOURI.EDU
IOOBF-L@UGA	Industrial Psychology Forum	@uga.cc.uga.edu
IDFORUM@YORKVM1	Industrial Design Forum	@VM1.YorkU.CA
INTLTRADE@world.std.com (This is a fee-based list; get information from **intltrade-@world.std.com**.)	International Trade Network	
MFN-STRATEGY@mailbase.ac.uk (subscribe to **mailbase@mail-base.ac.uk** with message **join mnf-strategy** *yourfirstname yourlastname*)	Manufacturing Strategy	
MEMSNET@UABDPO	Mineral Economics and Management Society	@uabdpo.dpo.uab.edu
NASIRN-L@UBVM	North American Service Industries Research	@ubvm.cc.buffalo.edu
OSF-BUS@UKACRL	Open Software Foundation Business and Marketing	
PCBR-L@UHCCVM	Pacific Business Researchers Forum	@UHCCVM.UHCC-.Hawaii.Edu
PEN-L@USCVM	Progressive Economists Network	@vm.usc.edu
PNWMARKT@WSUVM1	Agricultural Market News for WA and OR	@wsuvm1.csc.wsu.edu
RURALDEV@KSUVM	Community and Rural Economic Development	@ksuvm.ksu.edu
SBDC-L@VTVM1	Virginia's Small Business Development Centers	@vtvm1.cc.vt.edu
SNET-L@ARIZVM1.BITNET	Strategic Network System User Group	@arizvm1.ccit.arizona.edu

Some Additional Business Resources

These are a few more resources of interest:

- *ABI/Inform*: extensive database of business periodicals—**tn3270 gmuibm.gmu.edu**; select *xlibris, peri, abii*.

- *Agricultural Market News*: commodity reports—access via WAIS at **agricultural-market-news.src**.

- Asia Pacific Business and Marketing Resources; International Marketing Insights—Japan; East and Southeast Asian Business and Management; and Korean Business and Management: databases regarding cross-cultural management, government, and business relations in the Pacific Rim, and investment information—available by Gopher to **hoshi.cic.sfu.ca**.

- Centre for Labour Studies, University of Adelaide, Australia: Australian labor research data, labor briefings, international labor data— Gopher to **jarrah.itd.adelaide.edu.au**.

- CIA World Fact Book: demographic, geographic, social, and monetary information—Telnet **info.rutgers.edu** and choose *library/reference*, or by FTP to **nic.funet.fi** and look in the */pub/doc/Worldfacts* subdirectory.

- Dow Jones News Retrieval: investment, economic, and business article abstracts and full text—Telnet **djnr.dowjones.com** (this is a fee-based service).

- Israeli R&D Archive: information on R&D projects, information on high technology incubator projects—Telnet to **vms.huji.ac.il** and log in as **mop**.

- The Management Archive: management ideas and information, Academy of Management Archives, working papers—Gopher to **chimera.sph.umn.edu**.

- Patent Titles by E-mail: weekly mailings of all patents issued, information on ordering, information on specific patents—at **patents-request@world.std.com**.

- Research Results Database: summaries of agricultural and economic research—access via WAIS, at **usda-rrdb.src**.

- Science and Technology Information System: National Science Foundation information, grant material, and databases—Telnet to **stis.nsf.gov** and log in as **public**.

Usenet Newsgroups

There are a number of Usenet newsgroups that regularly distribute business-related information:

- sci.op-research—group for the entire operations research/management science community.
- sci.engr.manufacturing—newsgroup for manufacturing technology.
- clari.biz.economy—articles of general interest to the business community have included This Week in Business, Mortgage Rates, Farm-Price Report, Commerce Issues Gross Domestic Product, Jobless Rate, U.S. Consumer Price Index, etc.
- clari.biz.market.amex—American Exchange stock sales, indexes, active AMEX stocks, weekly report for ASE, AMEX market value index, etc.
- clari.biz.market.dow—Dow Jones closing stock and bond averages, Dow Jones closing stock and bond ranges, etc.
- clari.biz.market.ny —information on widely held NYSE stocks, the day's market activity, the most active NYSE stocks, NYSE stock sales, NYSE closing index, weekly report, etc.
- clari.biz.market.otc—most active OTC stocks, trends on OTC market, etc.
- clari.biz.report—selected mutual funds, volume and trends, Lipper mutual fund reports, stock market index report, Standard and Poors closing range, Standard and Poors daily history, etc.
- clari.news.gov.agency—information on various government agencies, grant awards, rules, etc.

FINDING EVEN MORE INFORMATION

There are references and tools for locating even more information on business-related resources on the Internet. Here are a few.

Government Sources of Business and Economic Information on the Internet, by Terese Austin and Kim Tsang, is available by anonymous FTP at **atuna.hh.lib.umich.edu** in the directory /*inetdiresstacks* as filename **govdocs:tsangaustin**. Many other Gophers also have these sources, and the URL for WorldWideWeb/Mosaic is **//una.hh.lib.umich.edu/00/inet-dirsstacks**.

Business Sources on the Net (BSN) is organized by subject. Each section is a separate file. It is available via anonymous FTP to **ksuvxa.kent.edu** in the /*library* subdirectory. BSN is also available at the Kent State University Gopher **refmac.kent.edu 70** under *business sources on the net*. The following are currently available:

- General business Internet sources
- Economics
- Foreign statistics, economic trends and international management
- Corporate finance and banking
- Human resources and personnel management
- Management science, statistical methods, and productions/operations management
- Accounting and taxation
- Management and the management of public and nonprofit organizations
- Computer science (as it relates to business)

Resources for Economists on the Internet by Bill Goffe is a thorough international listing, available through Usenet archives as **econ-resources-faq** in *sci-econ-research-archive*.

Also, don't forget to the search features contained in Gopher, Veronica, archie, and WWW to find other resources.

WHERE FROM HERE . . .

The next chapter provides more Internet resources, categorized by profession and subject area.

CHAPTER 15

Resources for the Professions

Here is a sampling of Internet resources, listed by profession, that provide good starting points for developing your own custom list. They are organized in the following categories:

- High Technology, Science, and Engineering
- Space, Satellites, and Astronomy
- Natural Resources and Environment
- Allied Health
- Biotechnology
- Journalism and Publishing
- Education
- Law
- Computers, Statistics, and Mathematics
- Agriculture
- Geography and Land Use
- Social Sciences
- International
- Miscellaneous

There are a number of subject-specific guides available from Clear-inghouse for Subject-Oriented Internet Resource Guides at the University of Michigan, on the library Gopher **una.hh.lib.umich.edu**, in the path */inetdirsstacks*. Also, there is a listing of useful Gopher sites called Gopher

Jewels that can be found on numerous Gophers, including **cwis.usc.edu 70**. The URL is: **gopher://cwis.usc.edu:70/11/Other_Gophers_and_Information_Resources/Gophers_by_Subject/Gopher_Jewels**.

It is important to remember that Internet resources can change locations, contents, login procedures, and addresses in the twinkling of an eye. If one of these resources is unavailable, use one of the search tools mentioned in Chapter 10 to find it. Also, one of the subject-specific guides that are available may give you an updated address or access information.

HIGH TECHNOLOGY, SCIENCE, AND ENGINEERING

The following sections describe resources for science, high technology, engineering, and related fields.

Science and Technology Information System (STIS)

This a full-text database of National Science Foundation (NSF) publications, open to the public. Searches for files can be done by keyword or phrase. The publications available include: *NSF Bulletin, Guide to Programs*, grants booklet with forms, program announcements, press releases, NSF telephone book, reports of the National Science Board, abstracts and descriptions of research projects funded by NSF, and analytical reports and news from the International Programs Division.

Telnet: **stis.nsf.gov**

Login: Type **public** and press Enter; then select **VT100nes**, or your terminal type if different.

National Nuclear Data Center (NNDC) Online Data Service

NNDC, which is located at the Brookhaven National Laboratory in Upton, NY, provides the following databases: NSR, ENSDF, NUDAT, CINDA, CSISRS, ENDF, and XRAY. There is no charge for having an account.

Telnet: **bnlnd2.dne.bnl.gov**

Login: **nndc**; follow the sign-up prompts.

Physics Information Network (PINET)

This fee-based database of the American Institute of Physics has information in the fields of physics and astronomy. Areas covered include jobs in industry and academia, searchable calendar of meetings and symposia, prepublication advance abstracts of member society journals, abstracts of more than 120 journals going back more than five years, news, newsletters, and electronic mail. For information on fees and getting an account, send a request for information to **admin@pinet.aip.org**.

The Scientist

A biweekly newspaper for scientists, this is published in both paper and electronic form by The Scientist, Inc., Philadelphia, PA, for researchers, policy makers, and administrators in industry, government, and academic positions. Subjects covered include trends in research, funding, legislation, grants, ethics, career advancement, and salary trends.

FTP: **ds.internic.net**

pub/the-scientist

Gopher: **internic.net 70**

InterNIC Directory and Database Services (AT&T)/

Publicly Accessible Databases/

The Scientist-Newsletter/

Chemical Engineering Digest

The *Chemical Engineering Digest* is available via Gopher.

Gopher: **ucsbuxa.ucsb.edu 3000**

.Journals/

.C/

.chemeng

Business Gold, National Technology Transfer Center

NTTC's online system provides information on business opportunities that have resulted from federally funded research and development projects.

Telnet: **iron.nttc.edu**
Login: **visitor**

SPACE, SATELLITES, AND ASTRONOMY

There are many useful resources in the fields related to space, because of their early use of the network.

NASA Archives

This is an FTP site with many directories of NASA files including files concerning Apollo, contracts, Galileo, headline news, launch advisory, Magellan, Mars Rover, Pioneer, software, weather, press releases, shuttle and payload status reports, and pictures in the .GIF format.

FTP: **ames.arc.nasa.gov**

/pub

Following is a list of other NASA databases that you can explore.

Space science data

Telnet: **nssdc.gsfc.nasa.gov**

Login: **nodis**

Extragalactic database

Telnet: **ned.ipac.caltech.edu**

Login: **ned**

NASA news

Finger: **nasanews@space.mit.edu**

Astronomy, geology, and geophysics information

Telnet: **lpi.jsc.nasa.gov**

Login: **lpi**

NASA news, satellite updates, and shuttle schedules

Telnet: **spacelink.msfc.nasa.gov**

National Radio Astronomy Observatory (NRAO)

This NRAO/Socorro information system includes the following top menu selections: *Official VLA, VLBA and VLBI NUG Schedules, VLA Specific Information,* and *VLBA Specific Information.*

Telnet: **zia.aoc.nrao.edu**

Login: **vlais**

AXAF Science Center Information Service

The Smithsonian Astrophysical Observatory maintains this site with news, mail, and documents concerning information relating to the Advanced X-Ray Astrophysics Facility and the ASAF Science Center.

Telnet: **asc.harvard.edu**

Data Dissemination Network of the European Space Agency

The welcome screen contains the following choices: *Information Retrieval Service - EMITS - DODIS, Prototype International Directory, European Space Information System, Columbus Users Information System,* and *Ers-1 European Central Facility.*

Telnet: **esrin.esa.it**

NASDA

The National Space Development Agency of Japan's Earth Observation Center provides a BBS and information about SINFONIA, JERS-1, and ERS-1.

Telnet: **nsaeoc.eoc.nasda.go.jp**; respond to the *Username:* prompt with **nasdadir**.

NOAA Space Environment Services Center

This site provides current data on upper atmosphere and space conditions. The welcome menu includes *Solar Forecast, Region Report, Activity Report, Coronal Report, Daily Flare Listing,* and *GOES plots.*

Telnet: **132.163.224.10**; respond to the *Username:* prompt with **sel**.

Hubble Space Telescope Daily Status Reports

This site provides an itemized list of the Hubble telescope's "activities scheduled and accomplished" for each 24-hour period.

Telnet: **stinfo.hq.eso.org**
Login: **stinfo**

NATURAL RESOURCES AND ENVIRONMENT

One of the most popular topics on the Internet is the environment; the following are some of the sources of information.

Quakeline

This is the National Center for Earthquake Engineering Research (NCEER) database of bibliographic information relating to earthquakes, earthquake engineering, and natural hazards mitigation. They have available citations, abstracts, and information on acquiring monographs, journal articles, maps, videotapes, technical reports, and conference papers.

> Telnet: **bison.cc.buffalo.edu**; respond to terminal type prompt with **VT100**; choose *INDX*.

Technology Transfer Network (TTN)

TTN is a network of bulletin boards operated by the EPA Office of Air Quality Planning and Standards. To get to the following bulletin boards, Telnet to **ttnbbs.rtpnc.epa. gov**.

AIRS—Aerometric Information Retrieval System

AMTIC—Ambient Monitoring Technology Information Center

ATPI—Air Pollution Training Institute

BLIS—RACT/BACT/LAER Information Systems

CAAA—Clean Air Act Amendments

CHIEF—Clearinghouse for Inventories/Emission Factors

COMPLI—Stationary Source Compliance

CTC—Control Technology Center

EMTIC—Emission Measurement Technical Information Center

NATICH—National Air Toxics Information Clearinghouse

NSR—New Source Review

SCRAM—Support Center for Regulatory Air Models

Oceanic—The Ocean Information Center

This is an in-depth service for researchers in the fields of oceanography and marine studies provided by the University of Delaware's College of Marine Studies. Information is available on current worldwide research, oceanic research observations, many research sites, programs and projects, drifters, sea level data, hydrography, time series, and databases of algorithms and standards. Also, there are schedules of research vessel cruises and a directory of active oceanographers and marine studies researchers.

> Telnet: **delocn.udel.edu**; respond to *Username* prompt with **info** and then press the Enter key; then type in your full name.

Earth Images Catalog

An ESA/Earthnet database of space-borne earth observation imagery, this includes catalogs of images from Landsat, AVHRR/SHARP, MOS-1, and NIMBUS CZCS.

Telnet: **glis.cr.usgs.gov**

At the first prompt, enter **guest**.

Select *vt100* as the terminal type.

Select *REMOTE* from the first menu.

Select *REMOTE* from the next menu.

Respond to the *Username:* prompt by typing in **CATALOGUE** and then press Enter.

Earth Observation Satellite Data Inventory Service

Search for data from these satellite systems: MOS -1/1b MESSER/VTIR-/MSR, LANDSAT 1,2,3 MSS/RBV, LANDSAT 4,5 MSS/TM, SPOT HRV-XS/HRV-P, JERS SAR/OPS/OVN, EERS AMI, and NOAA HRP/AVH.

Telnet: **glis.cr.usgs.gov**

At the first prompt, enter **guest**.

Select *vt100* as the terminal type.

Select *REMOTE* from the first menu.

Select *REMOTE* from the next menu.

Respond to the *Username:* prompt by typing in **NASDASIN** and then press Enter.

World Paleomagnetic Database

This site uses a special search program that provides ASCII data files of paleomagnetic databases. Before using this site, get instructions via FTP:

FTP: **earth.eps.pitt.edu**, filename **Search.doc**

The World Paleomagnetic Database itself is located:

Telnet: **earth.eps.pitt.edu**
Login: **Search**

Weather Underground—North Carolina State University

The Weather Underground's welcome menu includes the following choices:

U.S. forecasts and climate data

Canadian forecasts

Current weather observations

Ski conditions

Long-range forecasts

Latest earthquake reports

Severe weather

Hurricane advisories

National weather summary

International data

Marine forecasts and observations

Telnet: **measun.nrrc.ncsu.edu 3000**

Meeman Archive of Environmental Journalism

This site provides a database of articles about the environment from 1980 to the present.

Telnet: **hermes.merit.edu**

Respond to the *Which Host?* prompt with **mirlyn** and press Enter.

Press Enter again to accept *vt100* as the terminal type.

Respond to the database selection prompt with **meem** and press Enter.

Global Land Information System (GLIS)

GLIS is a bulletin board with data sets, news, access to remote systems, and ordering information.

Telnet: **glis.cr.usgs.gov**

Login: **guest**; respond to terminal type prompt with **VT100**.

Sierra Club National News Report

Environmental news can be found in:

Gopher: **envirolink.hss.cmu.edu 70**

EnviroOrgs/
Sierra Club

World Watch Institute Paper

Environmental information is available under *EnviroOrgs/World Watch*.

Gopher: **envirolink.hss.cmu.edu 70**

> *EnviroOrgs/*
> *World Watch*

Advanced Technology Information Network

This California Technology Information Network database provides supporting databases for agricultural marketing, international exporting, and the educational community of California.

Telnet: **caticsuf.cati.csufresno.edu**

Login: **public**

Classroom Earth!

NASA funds this source of environmental education materials. Menu items include files, programs, message area, search international environmental treaties, and connection to other resources.

Telnet: **classroom_earth.ciesin.org**; when connected, just press Enter.

ALLIED HEALTH

Allied health resources on the Internet abound. Some of the most interesting are listed here.

White House Health List Online

This is a mailing list of White House health reform announcements for health professionals.

Subscribe to the list by sending an e-mail message to **sfreedkin@igc.apc.org** using the following format:

Topic: **SUBSCRIBE LIST.HEALTHPLAN**

Body: **ADD**: *your-electronic-address-here* (your real name in parentheses)

> *Your real name here*
> *Your postal address* (optional)
> *City, State*

Profession

Professional interest in health care (if any)

Institutional affiliation (if relevant)

Healthline

The University of Montana Student Health Services provides information on drug and alcohol addiction, mental health, sexuality, disabilities, and general health and medical information.

Gopher: **selway.umt.edu 70**

Telnet: **consultant.micro.umn.edu**

Login: **gopher**

Food and Drug Administration Electronic Bulletin Board

Topics covered include Drug and Device Product Approvals list, Centers for Devices and Radiological Health Bulletins, Current Information on AIDS, Enforcement Report, FDA consumer magazine index and selected articles, FDA Federal Register summaries by subject, summaries of FDA information, index of news releases and answers, text of testimony at FDA congressional hearings, veterinary medicine news, and import alerts.

Telnet: **fdabbs.fda.gov**

Login: **bbs**

The Health Sciences Libraries Consortium Computer-Based Learning Software Database

This database contains listings of PC-compatible and Macintosh programs used in health sciences education.

Telnet: **shrsys.hslc.org**; *username* **CBL**

Health Info-Com Network

Medical and health articles are available in */info/ReadingRoom/NewsLetters/HealthInfoCom*.

FTP: **info.umd.edu**

National Institutes of Health Guide

The National Institutes of Health maintain back issues of its Guide via FTP.

FTP: **sunsite.unc.edu**

/pub/docs/nih-nsf/nih

Update in Health Services Research

An update of health services research is maintained in:

FTP: **ftp.u.washington.edu**

/public/larssondir/up

Mednews

Mednews is a weekly electronic newsletter with information from the Center for Disease Control, medical news in *USA Today*, AIDS statistics, and more.

Mailing List: **listserv@asuacad.bitnet**

To subscribe, type **sub mednews** *yourfirstname yourlastname*.

World Health Organization (WHO)

WHO offers access to full-text files of WHO publications, world health statistics, press releases, and so on.

Gopher: **gopher.who.ch**

Health Sciences Libraries Consortium CBL Software Database

A database of computer software uses in computer-based health sciences education, its listings contain both PC and Macintosh programs.

Telnet: **shrsys.hslc.org**

Login: **cbl**

Medline

Some health and medical databases and services provided by the National Library Service include MEDLINE and MEDLARS library services, toxic chemical release inventory, registry of toxic effects of chemical substances, hazardous substances data bank, chemical carcinogenesis research information system, toxicology literature, serials online, health planning and administration, AIDS information and clinical trials, Bioethicsline, chemical identification, and clinical alerts.

An account is needed to access Medline. For information on getting an account, send an e-mail message to **gmhelp@gmedserv.nlm.hih.gov** or connect to the dial-up BBS: the Grateful Med BBS, 800/525-5756.

NIH Grant Line

The Public Health Service distributes information to the biomedical research community through this site (also know as DRGLINE Bulletin Board).

Telnet: **wylbur.cu.nih.gov**

Respond to the first prompt with **,gen1**.

Respond to *INITIALS?* with **bb5**.

Respond to *ACCOUNT?* with **ccs2**.

The National Library of Medicine's E.T. Net

E.T. Net is a topical messages and files system. Current topics include general discussion of computers in health science education, computer-assisted instruction, the AVLINE database, hardware and peripherals, exchanging health sciences shareware, digital images/radiology, an E.T. Net archive, and research in nursing care.

Telnet: **etnet.nlm.nih.gov**

Login: **etnet**

Health Information List and Guide

PANET-L is a useful list regarding medical information and education:

-L **panet-l@yalevm.bitnet**

A useful guide to resources in allied health is one written by Lee Hancock called *Internet/Bitnet Health Sciences Resources*. It is available via FTP from **ftp/sura.net** in the directory */pub/nic* as the file **medical.resources**.*XX-XX*, where *XX-XX* represents the date. It is also available on the University of Kansas gopher **ukanaix.cc.ukans.edu**, and via e-mail: **listserv@templevm.bitnet**, with **GET MEDICAL RSCRS** in the body of the message.

BIOTECHNOLOGY

In addition to the allied health and environmental resources outlined, there are many sources of biotechnology information on the Internet.

Sequence Retrieval System

This is a menu-based access to sequence and literature databases. Databases are available on nucleic acid (and daily updates), protein sequence, international protein sequence, protein motif, restriction enzyme, PDB sequence subset, eukaryotic promoter, e. coli, enzyme name/reaction/-EC number, and biocomputing literature.

Telnet: **biomed.uio.no**; respond to *Username:* prompt with **srs** and press Enter.

Genomic Database of the Mouse (GBASE)

Main menu items include GENETIC MAPS of the mouse, LOCUSBASE—locusdata and references, MATRIX - mouse strains vs locus data, MOUSE LOCUS CATALOG, and INTEGRATED OMIM/MOUSE LOCUS CATALOG.

Telnet: **morgan.jax.org**

Login: **guest**

Biotechnet Electronic Buyer's Guide

There are five databases at this site covering these categories of products: chromatography, electrophoresis, instruments and apparatus, liquid handling, and molecular biology. Within these categories, products can be searched for by name or application. The names and addresses of the manufacturers of the products are available.

Telnet: **biotechnet.com**

Respond to the *Username:* prompt with **biotech**.

Respond to the password prompt with **bguide**.

NSF Center for Biological Timing

The National Science Foundation's Science and Technology Center for Biological Timing provides this as a source of information for the study of various aspects of biological timing. "The Center studies the internal timing mechanisms which control cycles of sleep and waking, hormone pulsatility, neuronal excitability, and reproductive rhythmicity." Investigators are involved with research from behavior testing to molecular genetics.

Telnet: **minerva.acc.virginia.edu**

Login: **biotiming**

Biological Mailing Lists

A useful mailing list is Biomch-L maintained at **Biomch-L@nic.surfnet.nl**.

JOURNALISM AND PUBLISHING

Journalists are heavy Internet users, and some of the most interesting resources in journalism and publishing are given here.

Newsletter of the Visual Communication Division of the Association for Education in Journalism and Mass Communication

A very useful newsletter on journalism and mass communication called *Viewpoints* is maintained at FTP: **borg.lib.vt.edu** in the */pub/VIEW-POINTS* subdirectory.

National Publisher's Newsletter

The National Publisher's Newsletter is maintained in electronic version in the */pub/msdos/ventura/npenw-13.arc* in the subdirectory at FTP: **oak.oakland.edu**.

Book Reviews

A broad variety of book reviews are maintained through the CARL system via Telnet under the *Book Reviews* item.

Telnet: **pac.carl.org**

Select the *Book Reviews* item from the CARL system menu.

Book Stacks Unlimited, Inc.

Book Stacks is an online book store with more than 240,000 titles which can be searched by author, title, or subject. Books can also be ordered online and shipped directly to you. In addition, they offer a message area where books and other topics can be discussed.

Telnet: **books.com**; press the Enter key once after the connection is established.

Useful Lists for Journalists

Two mailing lists of use to journalists are CARR-L and NIT.

Name	*Address*	*Topics*
CARR-L	**carr-l@ulkyvm.bitnet**	Computer-assisted Reporting & Research
NIT	**nit@chron.com** subscribe: **nit-request-@chron.com**	Discussion list for current and former working journalists

Guides to Resources for Journalists

The Journalism List by John S. Makulowich was a useful guide that is available through the Clearinghouse for Subject-Oriented Internet Resource Guides at the University of Michigan, on the library Gopher **una.hh.lib.umich.edu**, in the path *inetdirsstacks/Journalism.*

EDUCATION

One of the earliest users of the Internet was the education community. There are resources for all levels of education on the Internet, and some of the most useful are given here.

Academe This Week

The venerable *Chronicle of Higher Education* provides access to information via its Gopher.

   Gopher: **chronicle.merit.edu**

Academic Exchange Information Center (AEIC) News Releases

News releases from the AEIC provided by way of FTP.

   FTP: **ifcss.org**

   /org/cal-aeic

CATALYST

From the National Council on Community Service and Continuing Education, an electronic version of their journal called *Catalyst* is available via FTP.

   FTP: **red.css.itd.umich.edu**

   /zines/Catalyst

CoSN News

From the Consortium for School Networking, CoSN News is available via FTP. CoSN News provides timely information on schools and networking.

FTP: **cosn.educom.edu**

Daily Report Card

Access to the Daily Report Card is provided by the University of Maryland through its Gopher.

FTP: **info.umd.edu**

/info/ReadingRoom/Newsletters/DailyReportCard

Gopher   **nysernet.org 70**

Special Collections/

K-12/

Daily Report Card News Service

DECNEWS for EDU

Digital Equipment Corporation's education announcements are maintained at FTP: **gatekeeper.dec.com** in the subdirectory */.b/DEC/DECinfo-/DECnews-EDU.*

DEOSNEWS

The Distance Education Online Symposium News mailing list provides a lively discussion of all facets of Distance Education.

Mailing List: **listserv@psuvm.psu.edu**

New Horizons in Adult Education

New Horizons in Education is an electronic journal regarding adult and distance education.

FTP: **ftp.acs.ohio-state.edu**

/pub/oasis/journals/horizon

Online Chronicle of Distance Education and Communication (DISTED)

DISTED is a journal with topics in distance education, communication, and other topics related to education.

FTP: **ftp.acs.ohio-state.edu**

/pub/oasis/journals/disted

NASA Spacelink

A space-related information database specifically designed for teachers, but open to the public. Information available includes NASA projects history, current news, classroom material, educational services, and space program spinoffs, and technology transfer.

Telnet: **spacelink.nsfc.nasa.gov** (Welcome screen contains login information.)

Usenet Newsgroups

Newsgroups of interest to educators include **comp.ai.edu** on using artificial intelligence for education; **comp.edu** computer science education; and **sci.edu** scientific approaches to education.

Software and Courseware On-Line Reviews (SCOR)

SCOR's database includes information about, and reviews of, educational software and courseware. It also provides the Schools Computing On-Line Resources database, which is concerned with all aspects of the use of computer in schools, including professional development for school teachers and curriculums.

Telnet: **cc.curtin.edu.au**

Respond to the *Username* prompt with **guest** and press Enter.

For terminal emulation, select *vt100.*

From the first menu, select SCOR database.

From the next menu, select SOFTWARE & COURSEWARE ON-LINE REFVIEWS.

International Education Bulletin Board

This BBS provides support information for faculty and administrators of international education programs. Areas covered include U.S. government programs and information, international education grants and resources, international education bibliographies, contact individuals, statistics, study abroad programming, insurance, travel services, State Department travel advisories, visa information, and other materials relating to international education.

Telnet: **nis.calstate.edu**

Login: **intl**

Mind Extension University Bulletin Board System

This BBS provides a newsletter, files area, and messaging system in support of the Mind Extension University programs that operate at various places throughout the country.

Telnet: **bbs.meu.edu**

Guides of Use to Educators

A useful guide to further information is *An Educator's Guide to E-Mail Lists* by Prescott Smith. It is available by FTP from **nic.umass.edu** in the directory */pub/ednet* in the file **educatrs.lst**. Another useful list for adult and distance education is *Dr. E's Eclectic Compendium of Electronic Resources in Adult/Distance Education*. It can be obtained via FTP from **ftp.std.com** in the subdirectory */pub/oakridge* as file **dre-list.txt**. Both of these are also available in the Clearinghouse for Subject-Oriented Internet Resource Guides at the University of Michigan, on the library Gopher **una.hh.lib.umich.edu**, in the path *inetdirsstacks/*.

LAW

Many law libraries and other locations are maintaining resources related to the law and legal issues.

Washington and Lee Law Library

This site has one of the largest menus, covering all aspects of Internet resources in addition to its law resources. It has a user-friendly menu system and overall is highly recommended.

Telnet: **liberty.uc.wlu.edu**

Login: **lawlib**

MOSAIC, WWW, Lynx: **http://honor.uc.wlu.edu:1020**

Project Hermes—U.S. Supreme Court Opinions

U.S. Supreme Court opinions, concurring opinions, and dissenting opinions are made available immediately through a Supreme Court program called Project Hermes, which also supplies a syllabus summarizing each ruling. At Case Western Reserve University the files are originally received in the Atex8000 format and are stored in the *atex* directory, but are then converted to standard ASCII format and are stored in the *ascii* directory.

FTP: **ftp.cwru.edu**

/hermes

Telnet: **freenet-in-a.cwru.edu** (select *2. A Visitor*)

Computer Underground Digest

This journal concerned with computer law and crime.

FTP: **ftp.eff.org**

/pub/cud/cud

Gopher Law Server at Cornell University

This is a good collection of resources for law, jurisprudence, and government information.

Telnet: **fatty.law.cornell.edu**

Privacy Rights Clearinghouse Bulletin Board Service

The University of San Diego Center for Public Interest Law administers this BBS, which is funded by the Telecommunications Education Trust. It provides fact sheets, legislative information, and other material related to telecommunications privacy.

Telnet: **teetot.acusd.edu**

Login: **privacy**

Other Useful Law Resources

COMLAW is an Internet list discussing computers and legal education:

COMLAW-L   **comlaw-l@ualtavm.bitnet**

A useful guide to law-related information is *The Legal List, Law-Related Resources on the Internet and Elsewhere* by Erik J. Heels, available through **legal-list@justice.eliot.me.us**, FTP at **ftp.midnight.com**, and through the University of Maine Gopher, **gopher.usmacs.maine.edu**.

COMPUTERS, STATISTICS, AND MATH

In the areas of computer science, math, and statistics, there are some very interesting sources of information.

Journal of Statistics Education (JSE)

JSE is a journal with content in all phases of the teaching of statistics.

> FTP: **jse.stat.ncsu.edu**
> */jcs*

The International Journal of Analytical and Experimental Modal Analysis

MODAL is the electronic version of the International Journal of Analytical and Experimental Modal Analyses. It is available via FTP.

> FTP: **borg.lib.vt.edu**
> */pub/MODAL*

NetLib-News

This is a NetLib newsletter concerning mathematical subroutine libraries.

> FTP: **aun.uninett.no**
> */uninettinfo/mathematik*

Math Algorithm Bibliography

A large bibliography of items related to math algorithms is available from AT&T via Telnet.

> Telnet: **research.att.com**
> Login: **walk**

American Mathematical Society

E-math is a BBS that provides software, documents, a messaging system, the Bulletin of the AMS, math reviews, and access to e-math Gopher and e-math WAIS in support of the American Mathematical Society.

> Telnet: **e-math.ams.org**

Login: **e-math**

Password: **e-math**

Select terminal type **vt100**

Hewlett-Packard Calculator Bulletin Board

This BBS is for the exchange of software and information between Hewlett-Packard calculator users, software developers, and distributors.

Telnet: **hpcvbbs.cv.hp.com**

Login: **new**

Asset Source for Software Engineering Technology (ASSET)

"ASSET is a United States Department of Defense project to promote the reuse of computer software and software-related products. . . ASSET strives to be the national clearinghouse for software reuse sources and information." It is concerned with government, commercial, and public domain software, and provides a newsletter, brokerage services, consulting, a message board, a library of reusable components, training, and workshops.

Telnet: **source.asset.com**

Login: **starsbbs**

Cornell National Supercomputer Facility

CNSFinfo provides online information on the Theory Center's Cornell National Supercomputing Facility. The welcome screen contains these menu choices: *About.cnsfinfo, Copyright.Notice, Events, Forms, Hot-Tips.and.News, IBM.3090.Information, Languages.and.Libraries, Mass.Storage, Tapes.and.File.Transfer, Migration.Guide, NQS.Batch.Processing, Networks.and.Access.Information, Policies, RS6000.Information, Software, Technical Reports, Tutor, Visualization.*

Telnet: **info.tc.cornell.edu**

Login: **info**

RISC System/6000 Hardware and Software Information

Information at this site is made available through InfoExplorer, which links articles in a hypertext system.

Telnet: **jumbo.hrz.uni-giessen.de**

HPCwire

HPCwire is provided for the high-performance computing industry. Topics covered include news, stories, Internet info, software, calendar, help and employment wanted, newsletters from supercomputer centers and industry experts, discussion forums, partnership and joint research opportunities, research project profiles, information on products and services, and user surveys.

Telnet: **hpcwire.ans.net**

Login: **hpcwire**

NIST Guide to Available Mathematical Software (GAMS)

This site provides information about software that has been made available from the Computing and Applied Mathematics Laboratory of the National Institute of Standards and Technology.

Telnet: **gams.nist.gov**

Login: **gams**

StatLib Server

An e-mail server in support of StatLib products is available. Get the index document to explore the system.

E-mail: **statlib@stat.cvmu.edu**, message **send index**

Further Information

See Chapter 12 for online sources of software.

AGRICULTURE

There are many resources related to agriculture on the Internet. Some of the most interesting are given here.

Advanced Technology Information Network

This California Technology Information Network database provides supporting databases for agricultural marketing, international exporting, and the educational community of California.

Telnet: **caticsuf.cati.csufresno.edu**

Login: **public**

Cornell Extension Network (CENET)

The Extension Electronic Technology Group of Cornell Cooperative Extension developed this site. Its main menu includes the following choices:

Information on various agricultural topics

Community education and resources

Field crops and agronomy information

Food and nutrition information

Fruit and vegetable information

Global awareness

Information from the College of Human Ecology

Forestry, wildlife, water, and marine science

News bulletins, new releases, and media information

Ornamental horticulture, floriculture, home/grounds

Integrated pest management and pesticide information

Weather information

Information about youth programming

Telnet: **empire.cce.cornell.edu**

Login: **guest**

PENpages

This is a major agricultural market database from the Pennsylvania State University College of Agriculture. Some of the information is Pennsylvania-oriented—for example, market reports for Pennsylvanian livestock, feeder pigs and cattle, hay and grain, and timber. Most of the information is concerned with national agricultural markets: grain futures (Chicago Board of Trade), meat futures (Chicago Mercantile Exchange), poultry market news, national grain market summary, fruit and vegetable market news, flower market news, dairy market news, New York auctions, and food market news.

Telnet: **psupen.psu.edu**

Login: **pnotpa**

Illinois Flood Information Service

This service is part of the Illinois Dial-up Extension Access System (IDEA). It lists disaster relief organizations and government agencies and provides information on how to cope with floods for individuals, small businesses, communities, farms, and other agricultural businesses. It also provides flood help bulletin boards, disaster handbook updates, health and safety information, and recommendations on how to care for flood-damaged housing, furnishings, and equipment.

Telnet: **idea.ag.uiuc.edu**; respond to the *Username* prompt with **flood**.

Iowa State University Extension Flood Information

This site contains a collection of documents primarily concerned with flood cleanup for homes and farms. Topics covered include saving flood-damaged hay and grain, cleaning flooded wells, reconditioning flood-damaged farm implements, motors, appliances, heating equipment, electrical systems, and how to sanitize food utensils.

Telnet: **exnet.iastate.edu**

Login: **flood**

Additional Information

A useful guide of resources, *NOT JUST COWS, A Guide to Internet/Bitnet Resources in Agriculture and Related Sciences*, written and compiled by Wilfred Drew, is available on the Gopher at SUNY Morrisville Agricultural and Technical College, **snymorvb.cs.snymor.edu.**

GEOGRAPHY AND LAND USE

Geographical and land use information is readily available on the Internet.

Geographic Name Server

In response to a city name or a zip code, the server provides city, county, state, nation, telephone area code, elevation, feature code, latitude/longitude, and population. Information is primarily from the U.S. Geodetic Survey and U.S. Postal Service.

Telnet: **141.212.99.9 3000**

Online Retrieval of Cartographic Data (ORCID)

ORCID provides large data files of boundary data which can be processed and used in mapping packages.

Telnet: **sun.nsf.ac.uk**

Login: **janet**

Respond to *hostname:* prompt with **uk.ac.swurcc** and press Enter.

Respond to *Username:* prompt by pressing Enter.

Respond to *Which Service:* prompt with **pmac**.

Select **4** from the menu.

U.S. Naval Observatory Automated Data Service

This Washington, DC, site provides frequently updated information on the Global Positioning System, LORAN, OMEGA, USNO time service publications, the TRANSIT satellite, astronomical data, and navigational information.

Telnet: **tycho.usno.navy.mil**

Login: **ads**

USGS Branch of Global Seismology and Geomagnetism

The United States Geologic Survey provides this online data concerning epicenter determinations, earthquake lists, and geomagnetic field values.

Telnet: **neis.cr.usgs.gov**

Respond to the *Username:* prompt with **qed**.

SOCIAL SCIENCES

There is a lot of information on the Internet relating broadly to the social sciences, as shown here.

Inter-University Consortium for Political and Social Research (ICPSR)

ICPSR is said to be the world's largest database of computer-based research and instructional data for the social sciences. Areas covered include criminal justice, economics, history, gerontology, political science, public health, law, public health, and sociology. ICPSR is a not-for-profit consortium of universities and colleges, but nonaffiliated individuals can get accounts. For access, login, and fee information, contact Member Services, ICPSR, P.O. Box 1248, Ann Arbor, MI 48106-1428, phone 301/763-5010.

Social Sciences Data Archive

This database from Hebrew University, Mount Scopus Libraries can be accessed in either English or Hebrew. It can search for data sets by file number, title, author, or subject. The welcome screen has further information on how to order the data sets.

Telnet: **har1.huji.ac.il**

Respond to the *Username:* prompt with **ssda.**

Select 2 from the Function selection menu.

ESRC's Archive Online Catalogue and Subject Index

There are more than 3,000 research project data sets at this site, including large-scale and continuous longitudinal studies. A special word-matching search tool allows for finding a data set in several different ways.

Telnet: **155.245.10.133**

Login: **biron**

Password: **norib**

Other Social Science Resources

A list useful to social scientists is CUSSNET:

cussnet-request@stat.com, a list for Computer Users in the Social Sciences

A useful guide to information in the social sciences is *INTERNET VOYAGER: SOCIAL SCIENTIST'S GUIDEBOOK to AARNET/INTERNET Online Information Services,* by Dr. T. Matthew Ciolek, available by FTP from **COOMBS.ANU.EDU.AU**, as */coombspapers/coombsarchives/coombs-computing/internet-voyager-inf/internet-voyager-2-2.txt.*

INTERNATIONAL

Because of the international nature of the Internet, there are some useful resources with an international flavor.

EX-USSR Data Files

These are data files concerning the 15 republics that made up the former Soviet Union.

Telnet: **ukanaix.cc.ukans.edu**

Login: **ex-ussr**

RUSSGUS

This site has a database of literature citations for anything having to do with the USSR, Russia, and the Commonwealth of Independent States (CIS). There are currently more than 100,000 citations to newspapers, periodicals, essays, monographs, reviews, and dissertations.

Telnet: **fub05.zedat.fu-berlin.de**

Respond to *PLEASE LOGON* with **LOGON FU72L4PB, FU72L**.

Respond to *CONTINUE* with **NO**.

Use **GAST** as the password.

Friends and Partners

This information service is concerned with issues affecting relations between Russia and the United States. "It is hoped that it will, at least in some small way, promote better understanding between our countries."

Telnet: **solar.rtd.utk.edu**

Login: **friends**

MATIMOP

The Israeli Industry Center for R&D provides this site with a database of Israeli R&D projects and information on high technology incubator projects.

Telnet: **vms.huji.ac.il**

Respond to the *Username:* prompt with **mop**.

MISCELLANEOUS

One final interesting resource is Career Connection's Human Resources Electronic Advertising and Recruiting Tool (HEART), which provides a menu-oriented interface for listing job openings. This service is free for job seekers. All positions are posted and updated by the companies themselves. HEART is intended to provide an inexpensive way for companies to advertise and recruit worldwide.

Telnet: **career.com**

FROM HERE . . .

At this point, after reviewing the many resources available on the Internet, you may wish to return to Chapter 11 in order to refine your business plan for using the Internet; or you can finish up with the next chapter.

Epilogue: The Future of Business on the Internet

The Internet has grown explosively, doubling in recent months, and is poised for more. The government is about to fund the Information Superhighway, providing higher speed and greater capacity. The commercial sector itself is ripe for more growth, with estimates that there will be more than 100 million users on the Internet by the end of this decade.

- The Internet is constantly changing, and so too will the methods for marketing on the Internet. The best way to keep abreast of those changes is to stay plugged into the lists and Usenet, and to observe what others are doing.

- Acceptable use policies are under revision now, and you can expect changes in these as the network matures, as projects like Commerce Net expand, and as the Information Superhighway gets underway.

- New protocols will be coming, and businesses will be making increased use of existing protocols such as MIME and interactive virtual reality programs such as MOOs and MUDs. It is likely that the audio and video capacity of the Internet will grow, creating many marketing opportunities.

- Hypermedia-based applications such as WorldWideWeb and Mosaic are growing rapidly, offering many diverse opportunities for business use. Mosaic, with its full sound and video capabilities, may just be the "killer app" of the Internet. Certainly, it opens up a much wider range of business possibilities.

- New products and services are coming online quickly which will themselves offer opportunities for businesses. For example, O'Reilly and Associates, along with SPRY, have created "Internet in a Box," which will provide Internet access through cable television systems. This kind of product will provide opportunities for other businesses to reach much larger and demographically different audiences.

- The Internet Engineering Task Force (IETF) is discussing the creation of an Internet Mercantile Protocol (IMP), which will include plans to adapt current protocols to create ways to automate and complete business transactions using Multipurpose Internet Mail Extensions (MIME) and Privacy Enhanced Mail (PEM). A mailing list has been set up to discuss IMP: **imp-interest@thumper.bellcore.com**. You can subscribe by way of **imp-interest-request@thumper.bellcore.com**. And, in another initiative, The American Bankers Association is also studying electronic commerce.

- Encryption, a hot topic on the Internet, will likely make the Internet more secure. In addition to enhancing privacy and security of e-mail, this would facilitate the use of the Internet for commerce, banking, and sales. Electronically verifiable signatures will allow the verification of messages and transactions.

This is an excellent time to be learning about this whole new way of doing business. The Internet provides unexpected new opportunities for businesses to change directions and excel. It is not an uncharted sea, but the value of the Internet is only beginning to be recognized and explored. This is the network that is changing the world.

Bon voyage!

Finding, Configuring, and Installing Hardware and Software

This appendix is for those who have not previously used communication software and modems to connect to a BBS or other dial-up service. It should give you an idea of what hardware, software, and information you need to get online.

If you have already used communication software, even if you aren't an advanced user, you are probably ready to contact an Internet access provider and go online.

HARDWARE

Despite the tremendous size and high-tech nature of the Internet, the minimum required hardware is quite simple and inexpensive. Of course, specifications can be written for a $250,000 hardware package, but a few hundred dollars can get you started even if you don't have any equipment now.

Computers

The basic requirements for the computer are that communications software available for it, and that there is some means of connecting a modem. This describes almost any computer built in the last ten years—from the Commodore 64 to the present. For e-mail, FTP, and Gopher, even an old IBM XT will work (though any file processing thereafter would be considered tedious by today's standards). If you plan to do any real work with graphics and sound files, a faster machine is necessary.

Because you will be downloading large files, lists, and software, you will find that the more disk space you have, the better. It is quite amazing how fast another 10MB of data can come onto your hard drive when you are harvesting the Internet. Files can of course be stored on floppy disk, but that takes extra time, and the data becomes less accessible for searching or using—another cost/time trade-off. Do get the fastest and largest machine that is reasonably affordable, because it will save a lot of time; but don't let anyone tell you that you can't use the Internet if you're not running one of the new Pentium machines.

Modems

This is the one place to spend the money and get the best. A near-state-of-the-art modem for use on standard phone lines runs at the speed of 14,400 baud and has, under the correct conditions of data compression, the ability to send and receive data with the equivalent of 57,600 baud. Such modems are available in the ballpark of $150 from mail order houses.

There are slower modems available—a 2,400 baud modem can be found for around $50. Consider this if you are thinking of the cheaper modem: If a file is being downloaded from your Internet access provider using a 14,400 baud modem and that (rather large) file takes 4 minutes, it will take 1 hour and 36 minutes with the 2,400 baud modem. And even if time is not a consideration for you, imagine the difference in long distance charges and the access provider's connect time charges between 4 minutes and 1 hour, 36 minutes!

Don't even think of using that old 300 baud modem that someone will give you for free: The same 4-minute download would take 12 hours and 48 minutes on that snail.

A much less important consideration in buying a modem is whether to get an "internal" or "external" modem. Many computers have a "bus" or other connection system inside, which will allow you to install the modem inside the computer. The advantages are that the modem sold in this form is usually a bit cheaper, and that you have fewer external wires to worry about. The external modem, however, can be moved from computer to computer more easily and is not made to work with just one type and model of computer. It also usually has a set of indicator lights on the front that allow you to keep track of the data transfer (especially helpful for when things aren't working correctly).

The internal modem is installed according to the manufacturer's instructions; you then connect a phone line between it and the phone jack in the wall of your house or office. The manufacturers usually supply an extra jack on the modem so that you can use it to reconnect the phone that was formerly connected to that wall jack.

External modems require three connections: (1) the phone wiring, which is done in the same way as for the internal modem; (2) the power connection, usually a small transformer that plugs into an electrical outlet in the wall with a thin wire with a connector that goes to the matching connector on the back of the modem; (3) the data connection, usually a 9-pin or 25-pin connector. If a data cable didn't come with the modem, one will need to be purchased. This cable is connected between the data jack on the back of the modem and one of the COM connectors on the back of the computer.

Other Hardware Considerations

A standard monochrome monitor can be used for most Internet activities, except with some of the graphics programs, but a VGA or better monitor increases readability and ease of use of the Internet a great deal. The VGA monitor allows more lines on the screen and therefore improves your ability to scan long menus and documents. Also, the variations in color on a VGA screen make the status indicators in various programs much easier to see. A VGA or better monitor allows for the use of graphics-oriented programs and systems such as Windows, and will be increasingly helpful for use with the Internet hypertext tools. And finally, to view the increasing number of photo and graphics images, a graphics-compatible monitor such as VGA is needed.

SOFTWARE

There are a variety of new graphics-oriented and Internet-oriented communication software packages that are becoming available, but to get started using the Internet you only need one of the many hundreds of communications programs that can provide some basic types of terminal emulation. Terminal emulators are programs that follow a standardized way of carrying on transfers of data between computers, and of displaying that data.

In the early years of computing, people communicated with computers using terminals that were hard wired (physically connected) to the computer and that sent and received information using well-defined sets of protocols. These protocols defined what types of signals would be sent, how fast, and so forth. Also, they defined what each particular signal meant. That is, if a particular group of eight on/off signals were sent to the terminal, the terminal would "know" that, for example, the screen was to clear, or the cursor was to drop down a line, or the letter z should be displayed on the screen.

As computers developed, a number of different and incompatible types of terminals evolved. Later, however, as the power and complexity of both large and personal computers improved, programs were written that allowed a computer to emulate a particular kind of terminal. In other words, to the another computer, your computer could "look like" one of the standard hard-wired terminals. Some programs available for use on personal computers today can emulate dozens of types of terminals, and therefore allow you to communicate with most other computer makes, models, and operating systems.

Here are some common emulation protocols:

VT100: This terminal was made by Digital Equipment Corporation. It varies from ANSI in only minor ways.

ANSI: This is a protocol designed by the American National Standards Institute (ANSI). It allows for color and graphics characters.

VT52: This is an earlier and simpler terminal made by Digital Equipment Corporation.

Dumb terminal: Its features are primarily limited to carriage returns, line feeds, and form feeds—no fancy cursor control, colors, or other capabilities.

The most commonly used protocol on the Internet is VT100. If your communication software can do VT100 emulation, set it for that before connecting with your Internet access provider. If it can't, use the protocol that you have available that is the highest on the list above.

There are hundreds of commercial and shareware communications programs available that are suitable for the Internet. They vary in the numbers of emulations they handle, the downloading protocols available, availability of scripts, and dozens of convenience factors. The following sections will examine several communications programs that work well with the Internet.

Procomm Plus

Communications programs vary greatly not only in features, but in the methods or keys they use to accomplish even the most common communications procedures. The following example is a popular and sophisticated program called Procomm Plus. Check your communications program manual or on-disk documentation for directions in accomplish-

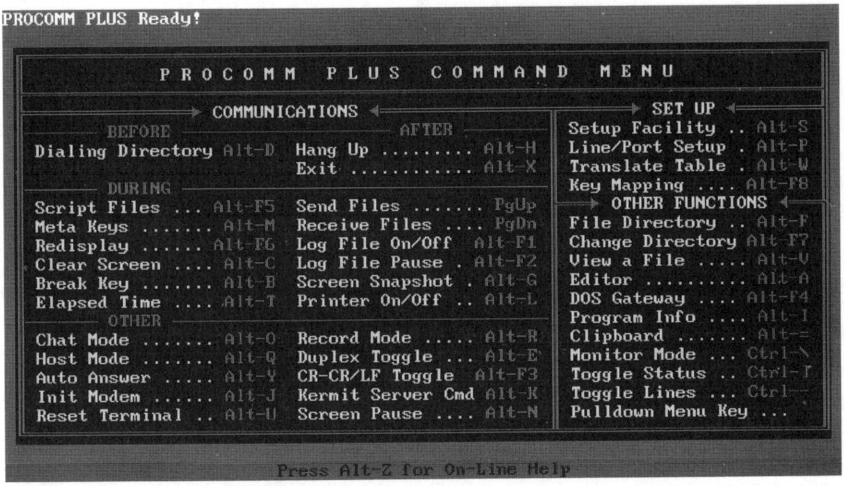

```
PROCOMM PLUS Ready!

┌────────────────────────────────────────────────────────────────────┐
│          P R O C O M M   P L U S   C O M M A N D   M E N U          │
│  ──────▶ COMMUNICATIONS ◀──────           ─────▶ SET UP ◀─────      │
│  ──── BEFORE ────        ──── AFTER ────   Setup Facility .. Alt-S   │
│  Dialing Directory Alt-D  Hang Up ........ Alt-H  Line/Port Setup . Alt-P │
│                           Exit ........... Alt-X  Translate Table . Alt-W │
│  ──── DURING ────                                 Key Mapping .... Alt-F8  │
│  Script Files ... Alt-F5  Send Files ...... PgUp  ──▶ OTHER FUNCTIONS ◀── │
│  Meta Keys ....... Alt-M  Receive Files .... PgDn  File Directory .. Alt-F │
│  Redisplay ...... Alt-FG  Log File On/Off  Alt-F1  Change Directory Alt-F7 │
│  Clear Screen .... Alt-C  Log File Pause . Alt-F2  View a File ..... Alt-V │
│  Break Key ....... Alt-B  Screen Snapshot . Alt-G  Editor .......... Alt-A │
│  Elapsed Time .... Alt-T  Printer On/Off .. Alt-L  DOS Gateway .... Alt-F4 │
│  ──── OTHER ────                                   Program Info .... Alt-I │
│  Chat Mode ....... Alt-O  Record Mode ..... Alt-R  Clipboard ....... Alt-= │
│  Host Mode ....... Alt-Q  Duplex Toggle ... Alt-E  Monitor Mode ... Ctrl-\ │
│  Auto Answer ..... Alt-Y  CR-CR/LF Toggle  Alt-F3  Toggle Status .. Ctrl-T │
│  Init Modem ...... Alt-J  Kermit Server Cmd Alt-K  Toggle Lines ... Ctrl-  │
│  Reset Terminal .. Alt-U  Screen Pause .... Alt-N  Pulldown Menu Key ...   │
│  ────────────────────────────────────────────────────────────────  │
│              Press Alt-Z for On-Line Help                          │
└────────────────────────────────────────────────────────────────────┘
```

Figure A.1 Procomm's Main Help Screen.

ing the following steps using your communications software. Refer to Figure A.1 for a summary of Procomm commands.

Procomm provides the help screen shown in Figure A.1 to show which key combinations to use to access menus or to send immediate commands to the program.

1. Hold down the Alt key and press the **D** key. The Procomm dialing directory will be displayed.

2. Press the **A** key. A window will open which will allow you to add a new phone number, name, and communications protocols. See Figure A.2.

3. Type in the name you want for this phone entry, press Enter, enter the phone number, then press the Enter key again. Now enter the maximum baud rate of your modem and press Enter. Continue in a similar manner with parity (none), data bits (8), stop bits (1), and duplex (full). (Some access suppliers and networks use 7 data bits, even parity, and 1 stop bit—try these settings if you see random characters on the screen when you first connect with an access provider.) The port you select will depend on how your internal modem was configured (check your modem manual for the default setting) or into which serial port you plugged your external modem (check the back of the computer and look for a label next to the connector that says COM 1, COM 2, etc.). On all other items, just press Enter to accept the default value.

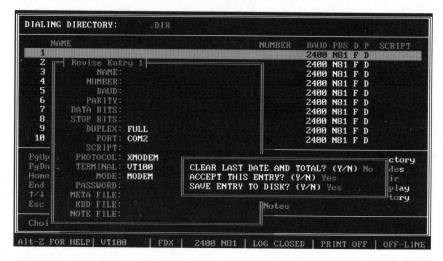

Figure A.2 Procomm's Dialog Box for Entering Dialing and Communications Protocols. It allows you to use different modem settings, speeds, and scripts for each phone number in the dialing directory.

Determining Which Port Your Modem Uses

If you have trouble determining which port your modem is using, set your program's port to COM2, then at the terminal screen type in **ATZ** and press Enter. If you don't see "OK," change the port number and try again.

4. With this phone number highlighted, press Enter to dial the number.

A status box will appear showing which number is being dialed, how long your computer has waited for a response, and other information. Through your modem, you will probably also hear a dial tone, the sounds of dialing and ringing, and then a raucous sound of the other computer's modem. When the second modem sound joins in, your modem will go quiet and you will soon see a "connect" notice on your screen. Now you should see your Internet access provider's login screen and its prompts for your login name and password.

Windows 3.1 Terminal

Windows comes with a terminal program that is not as full-featured as many communications programs, but it will work for communicating

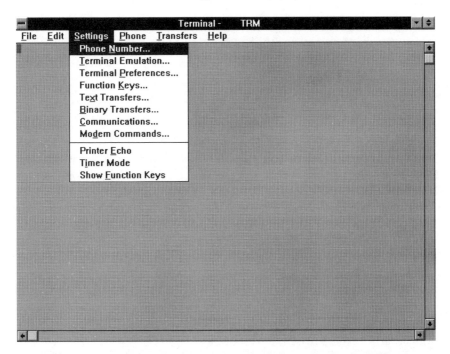

Figure A.3 Windows Terminal Screen Showing the Settings Pull-down Menu.

with the Internet, and it does some things very well. Also, if you have Windows, you won't have to find and buy another terminal program right away, and learning time should be short, since it operates in the familiar Windows fashion.

Key to using the Windows terminal program is to look through each of the items in the *Settings* pull-down menu (see Figure A.3) and make changes as appropriate. Here are a few things to keep in mind:

- *Phone Number*—Since this terminal program sends dialing and other commands directly to the modem, the phone number entered is just as you would dial it.

- *Terminal Emulation*—Select the VT100 option to get the most out of the Internet.

- *Function Keys*—This feature will allow you to set up four sets of eight function keys, which will help you avoid having to retype common commands or look up hard-to-remember names and numbers. Be sure to select Show Function Keys while in the Function Keys dialog box. Then you will have labeled buttons at the bottom of the terminal screen that you can use the mouse to activate.

- *Binary Transfers*—The Zmodem transfer method works well with most sites on the Internet.
- *Communications*—These settings (described below) are critical to communicating properly with your modem, and to making any connection.

If you dial direct to most Internet access providers, you will probably set your communications software to "8-bit," "No parity," and "1 stop bit." However, if you reach your access provider through one of the telecommunications networks such as TYMNET or CompuServe's network, you may use "7-bit," "Even parity," and "1 stop bit." Check with your access provider both for information on which telecommunications networks you can use to access them (to save long distance charges) and on which communications settings will be needed for those networks.

After making all of the appropriate changes to the settings, click on the *File* menu and select *Save As*. Now select a name for this file, which will save all of these settings. This will be the file that you open each time you want to use the Windows terminal program to communicate with your Internet access provider's computer.

Other Internet Software

There are hundreds of other freestanding communications programs. In addition, there are communications programs that are part of integrated packages such as Geoworks Pro and Microsoft Works. These integrated packages include applications such as word processors, spreadsheets, databases, and file-handling utilities, along with the communications program. They all use one common structure and appearance. If you are just getting started in computing, one of these integrated packages may save learning time and therefore make the computer a productive tool more quickly.

Internet software is available from a variety of sources including Internet service providers, mail order, and on the Internet itself. Sources of software were discussed in Chapters 10 and 12.

Briefly, here are some sources of specifically Internet-related software:

Electronic Mail-Related Programs

Eudora for the Mac

FTP to **sumex-aim.stanford.edu**   */info-mac/mac/comm*
FTP to **ftp.qualcomm.com**   */mac/eudora*

Eudora for the PC

FTP to **sunsite.unc.edu** */pub/micro/pc-stuff/ms-windows/winsock/apps*

FTP-Related Programs

Fetch for the Mac

FTP to **sumex-aim.stanford.edu** */info-mac/comm*

Telnet-Related Programs

WinQVT for Windows

FTP to **biochemistry.bioc.cwru.edu** */pub/qvtnet*

NCSA Telnet and FTP for Mac

FTP to **sumex-aim.stanford.edu** */info-mac/comm*

FTP to **ftp.ncsa.uiuc.edu** */mac/telnet*

NCSA Telnet and FTP for DOS

FTP to **merit.edu** */pub/ppp*

FTP to **ftp.ncsa.uiuc.edu** */pc/telnet*

Gopher-Related Programs

Gopher client for the Mac—TurboGopher

FTP to **sumex-aim.stanford.edu** */pub/info-mac/comm*

Gopher client for DOS—Hgopher for Windows

FTP to **lister.cc.ic.ac.uk** */pub/wingopher*

A range of Gopher clients for a variety of platforms are available.

FTP to **boombox.micro.umn.edu** */pub/gopher*

Gopher servers are also available for DOS, UNIX, X-Windows, Macintosh, and VMS at the boombox site above.

TCP/IP and SLIP

SLIP routers and support software are available from several commercial companies—for example, Cogwheel, Inc (303/444-1338, e-mail **info@cogwheel.com**) and Livingston Enterprises (510/426-0770, e-mail **sales@livingston.com**).

To get information on TCP/IP software, FTP to **netcom1.netcom.com** and get the file *|pub|mailcom|IBMTCP|ibmtcp.zip*. This is an up-to-date listing of TCP/IP applications.

(Mosaic can be located at the **ftp.ncsa.uiuc.edu** site as well—see Chapter 10 for details.)

OBTAINING HARDWARE AND SOFTWARE—HINTS AND TIPS

While there are many good deals on computers, software and peripherals at local stores and at national retail chains, in some cases purchasing directly through mail order can provide some extra options and price breaks.

The computer equipment market is volatile, and so getting up-to-date price and supplies information is important. This information can be found through a variety of magazines and periodicals, such as *Computer Shopper*, *PC Magazine*, *Home Office Computing*, *Byte*, and *Windows Magazine*, which have large sections of mail-order advertisements. There are magazines and guides specifically for laptops, mobile computing, wireless technology, Macintosh, Amiga, and other areas. These magazines and guides offer direct mail-order shopping from some of the major computer vendors, including IBM, Dell, CompuAdd, Gateway, and Compaq. A variety of Macintosh products are available too. There are numerous catalogs of supplies, hardware, and software offered through these magazines as well.

Increasingly, software vendors are offering free disks with demonstrations and working versions of their software. These are useful for trying out software before you buy.

Many people who buy directly, order via the telephone. When placing a telephone order, be sure to state your understanding of the terms of the sale, such as price, tax, shipping data, return policies, and warranties. Be sure to state all of the specifications such as make and model, size, and included components. Don't assume that a computer shown with a monitor in the advertisement will necessarily come with a monitor. Be sure to find out if a substitute will be sent if your model is unavailable, and let the dealer know if that is acceptable.

Keep notes of your conversation, and always ask for the salesperson's name and phone number. Using your credit card to pay will give you some additional options if things do not go well with your purchase.

ONLINE SOFTWARE

There is a great deal of software available online, as mentioned in Chapter 12. Software specifically related to communications can be found at a variety of sites. For example, the following are mirror sites containing the same software in the same subdirectories worldwide:

St. Louis, MO: **wuarchive.wustl.edu** (128.252.135.4)
/systems/ibmpc/msdos

Corvallis, OR: **archive.orst.edu** (128.193.2.13)
/pub/mirrors/oak.oakland.edu/simtel20/msdos

Falls Church, VA: **ftp.uu.net** (192.48.96.9)
/systems/ibmpc/msdos/simtel20

Australia: **archie.au** (139.130.4.6)
/micros/pc/oak

England: **src.doc.ic.ac.uk** (146.169.2.1)
/pub/packages/simtel20

Finland: **ftp.funet.fi** (128.214.6.100)
/pub/msdos/SimTel

Germany: **ftp.uni-paderborn.de** (131.234.2.32)
/pcsoft/msdos

Israel: **ftp.technion.ac.il** (132.68.1.10)
/pub/unsupported/dos/simtel

Poland: **ftp.cyf-kr.edu.pl** (149.156.1.8)
/pub/mirror/msdos

Switzerland: **ftp.switch.ch** (130.59.1.40)
/mirror/msdos

Taiwan: **nctuccca.edu.tw** (140.111.1.10)
/PC/simtel

Thailand: **ftp.nectec.or.th** (192.150.251.32)
/pub/mirrors/msdos

A quick Internet search, using the archie program, of files with the word *communication* in their description reveals several hundred entries—for example:

```
String to locate?          ? communication


## Filename    Type  Date          Description


 1 privacy2.zip  B   890717   Electronic Communications Privacy Act

 2 asynlib2.zip  B   910324   ASYNC communications library callable from '

 3 pcl4c34.zip   B   930322   Asynchronous communications library for C

 4 dmetd4fp.zip  B   910622   Communications lib for dBASE 4 and FoxPro

 5 desqcomm.zip  B   920518   QOS Technote: Communications under DESQview

 6 ft4a-ibm.zip  B   901021   Jennings' FidoTerm V4a telecommunications pg

 7 asctdd11.zip  B   920122   Simple free communications pgm for ASCII TDD

 8 rock114.zip   B   911026   Speech friendly basic communications pgm

 9 rstutor.zip   B   881106   Tutor for communications, serial interface

10 async.zip     B   870307   Asynchronous communications routines

11 comhex42.zip  B   890124   Serial communications display program

12 abmdemo.zip   B   920406   ABM vers. of HDLC communications protocol de

13 boyan52a.zip  B   940221   Boyan 5.2 full-featured communications, 1 of

14 boyan52b.zip  B   940221   Boyan 5.3 full-featured communications, 2 of

15 commodsz.zip  B   900403   Zmodem for COMMO communications package

16 depty309.zip  B   940114   Communication program with MNP5 support

17 emma22.zip    B   910428   Communications utility for MCI mail users

18 mc105doc.zip  B   880126   Multi-Com v1.05 communication pgm, 2of2, doc

19 mc105prg.zip  B   880126   Multi-Com v1.05 communication pgm, 1of2, exe

20 mxlit195.zip  B   940114   MxLight telecommunication program by J.Field

21 panther2.zip  B   930821   Panther 2.0: Freeware communications program

22 pccp019.zip   B   920516   Communications package. Terminal emulator

23 qtalk541.zip  B   910603   Q-Talk 5.41, Small Communications Program

24 rcomm-v2.zip  B   880224   TSR background communications program

25 robo42-a.zip  B   921031   RoboCom, automated communications program, 1

26 robo42-b.zip  B   921031   RoboCom, automated communications program, 2

27 rus_comm.zip  B   930622   Cyrillic editor with modem communication

28 suncom.zip    B   910329   Turbo Pascal v5.5 communications program

29 tmlink.zip    B   900503   The Missing Link v1.0, communications program

30 tphone.zip    B   890226   TSR terminal communications program

31 tt105.zip     B   881128   Tiny Terminal v1.05, communications program

32 viscom.zip    B   911126   Communication program, browse manual

33 xpc401.zip    B   920312   X.PC v4.00+ communications driver, with sour

34 prcm243.zip   B   890122   ProComm 2.43 Communications utility - 1 of 3

35 asylib11.zip  B   921107   AsyLIB, communications functions for QB 4.x
```

```
36 qbser320.zip  B  940111  QBasic serial communications library v3.20

37 tlx322-1.zip  B  940209  Telix v3.22 communications program, 1 of 4

38 tlx322-2.zip  B  940209  Telix v3.22 communications program, 2 of 4

39 tlx322-3.zip  B  940209  Telix v3.22 communications program, 3 of 4

40 tlx322-4.zip  B  940209  Telix v3.22 communications program, 4 of 4
```

An incredible variety of software is available on the Internet; for example, here is a quick reference list of SimTel Software Repository's /pub/msdos/ subdirectories.

4dos	cpluspls	food	litratur	pctech
ada	cron	formgen	logo	pctecniq
ai	crossasm	forth	lotus123	pcvrmag
animate	database	fortran	mac	perl
archiver	dbase	fossil	mapping	pgmutil
arcutil	dbms_mag	freemacs	math	pibterm
asm_mag	ddjmag	genealgy	mathcopr	pktdrvr
asmutil	decode	geogrphy	memutil	plot
astrnomy	demacs	geology	menu	postscrp
at	deskaccs	geos1x	microsft	printer
autocad	deskjet	geos2x	misclang	procomm
awk	deskpub	geosnews	modem	prodigy
bakernws	desqview	gif	modula2	projmgr
basic	dirutil	gnuish	mormon	qbasic
batutil	disasm	graph	mouse	qedit
bbs	diskutil	graphics	msjournl	qemm
bbsdoor	djgpp	gtsmusic	music	qmodem
bbslist	dv_x	hamradio	naplps	qtrdeck
bible	editor	handicap	ncsatlnt	ramdisk
binedit	educatin	hebrew	network	rbbs_pc
biology	eel	hypertxt	neurlnet	rip
bootutil	ega	iconlang	nfs	satelite
borland	electric	info	notabene	science
c	emulator	io_util	novell	screen
cad	engineer	irit	oberon	security
calculat	envutil	ka9q	oemacs	simulatn
catalog	execomp	kermit	offline	sound
cdrom	ezycom	keyboard	opus	spredsht
chemstry	fido	lan	packet	sprint
citadel	filedocs	langtutr	pascal	starter
clipper	fileutil	laser	pathutil	statstic
clock	finance	legal	pcboard	stunnpc
compress	flowchrt	linguist	pcmag	surfmodl

swap	tex	ubasic	voice	wpj_mag
sysinfo	textutil	uemacs	voicmail	wwiv
sysutil	tiff	uucp	waffle	x_10
tagbbs	tsrutil	ventura	weather	xlisp
taxes	turbo_c	vga	wildcat	xwindows
teaching	turbobas	virus	windows3	zip
telegard	turbopas	visbasic	wordperf	zmodem
telix	turbovis	viscii	worldmap	zoo

Sending and Receiving Files

This is a quick overview of uploading (sending) and downloading (receiving) files. This is not the all-you-ever-need-to-know, just a short guide to get you started. Uploading and downloading is an activity common among dial-up users. SLIP or TCP/IP users usually use FTP to move files up and down.

Some useful definitions:

- *Upload*—the process of sending a copy of a file that is stored on your local personal PC to a remote computer
- *Download*—the process of getting a copy of a file from a remote computer on the Internet to your own PC

Let's suppose that you have used FTP to get a file called **foobar.txt** from Washington and Lee. The file is now located in your account's directory on your Internet service provider's computer, and you want to bring it home to your own personal computer.

The details for downloading a file vary with your communications software, your Internet access provider, the provider's software, and the downloading protocol selected, but here are some fairly standard procedures:

1. Boot up your computer, and use your communications program to contact your dial-up Internet provider.
2. Log on to your service as usual.

3. Choose your download protocol—this could be Zmodem, Xmodem, Kermit, or others, depending upon the protocols supported by your service provider and your communications software. Zmodem is quicker than most. Check with your user services to get more information, or type **help** and look for information on file transfer.

4. Type **ls** to look at a list of your files to be sure of the correct spelling of the filename.

5. Invoke the transfer protocol through the command line or running the software. For example, to send an ASCII text file called **foobar.txt** using Zmodem, type this at the system prompt:

   ```
   sz -a foobar.txt
   ```

6. After you have given the send instructions to the remote computer, you will need to tell your personal computer's communications software to receive the file. Using Procomm, for example, you would press the Page Down key and choose **Z** for Zmodem to initiate the download. In some cases with Zmodem, this process is automatic.

7. To download a binary file called **foobar.zip**, type:

   ```
   sz -b foobar.zip
   ```

   and, as before, give the receive command to your local computer.

To use Kermit to download an ASCII text file called **foobar.txt**, type **kermit** at the system prompt to bring up the Kermit program, and then give it a command to send the file:

```
kermit
Kermit>send foobar.txt
```

As before, you will need to tell your local communications software to receive the file. In Procomm, this means pressing the Page Down key, followed by choosing **K** for Kermit.

To send a *binary* file called **foobar.zip** using Kermit, there is an extra step involved:

```
kermit
Kermit>set file type binary
Kermit>send foobar.zip
```

Then, as above, use your communications program to receive the file.

The file is now located on your home machine, ready for use. There are numerous variations on this, but in essence, the steps are similar.

Uploading a file to your account works in a similar way—it is the flip side of downloading.

1. You must tell the remote computer to expect an upload, by typing **rz -a** *filename*, or for a binary file, **rz -b** *filename*; or invoke Kermit and type **receive** *filename*; or, for a binary file, set the file type to binary as above, then type **receive** *filename*.

2. You then must have your communications software upload the file using whatever command that it uses. In the case of Procomm, press the Page Up key and identify the protocol with a **Z** or a **K** as appropriate to match the remote computer's protocol and then enter the filename when prompted.

After a few seconds (or minutes, depending on the size of the file and modem speed), the process will end. You can then list your account's directory at the remote computer to confirm that the transfer was successful.

Each piece of communications software will differ in the specific keys to press, but they all have some method for carrying out these functions.

Some Useful UNIX Commands

UNIX is ubiquitous on the Internet. Most of the dial-up Internet providers use the UNIX operating system, and most of the machines that carry the FTP archives run on UNIX. You will encounter UNIX on the Internet, and it is sometimes quite cryptic.

The following is by no means an exhaustive listing of shortcuts, files, or commands; rather it is a list of those particularly helpful to Internet users. UNIX commands are case-sensitive—that means that **LS** is not the same as **Ls** or **ls**.

Some useful files:

.login   A file that contains configuration information that is used by the computer when you first log in to customize your account.

.plan   A file that is sent out when your account is fingered. It can contain information about you and your business.

.signature   A file that contains personal and business information that can be appended to e-mail and Usenet postings.

Useful key combinations:

^C   Interrupts the current process.
^S   Suspends the screen scroll.
^Q   Resumes the screen scroll.

(Note that the ^ character represents the Ctrl (Control key), which is held down while the letter key is pressed. Although it is common practice to show the letter key in uppercase, it is actually typed in as a lowercase, unshifted letter.)

Useful commands (press the Enter key after each command):

cat	Displays file contents continuously. syntax: **cat** *filename*
more	Displays file contents one page at a time (use the Space-bar to advance to the next screen, the **b** key to go back a screen). syntax: **more** *filename*
cd	Changes directory. syntax: **cd** *directoryname* or **cd** *directoryname/subdirectoryname/* etc.
pwd	Displays the name of the directory you are currently in. syntax: **pwd**
mkdir	Creates a new directory. syntax: **mkdir** *directoryname*
rmdir	Removes or deletes a directory. syntax: **rmdir** *directoryname*

ls	Lists the files and subdirectories in the current directory.
	 ls -l lists them in long form, with file size, date, etc.
	 ls -a lists all files, including hidden files.
	 syntax: **ls**
	      ls -l
	      ls -a
	      ls -a -l

cp	Copies a file to a new location. syntax: **cp** *filename copyname* for example, **cp foobar.txt myfoo.txt**
rm	Removes or deletes a file. syntax: **rm** *filename*
mv	Moves or renames a file. syntax: **mv** *oldfilename newdirectory/newfilename* or to rename a file: **mv** *oldfilename newfilename*
help	On some systems, will get you the help files and/or a list of available commands.
man	Gets specific help from the online manual. syntax: **man** *command*
clear	Clears the screen.
logout	Logs you out of the system, exit.

chfn   Changes your finger name—the name that you are known by to the system.
        syntax: **chfn**
        (You will then be prompted for the new name.)

passwd   Changes your password.

whoami   Shows your current finger name information.

kermit   Invokes the Kermit file transfer program.

sz   Sends a file by way of the Zmodem file-transfer protocol.
      sz -b sends a binary file
      sz -a sends an ASCII file
      syntax: **sz** *filename*
              sz -a *filename*
              sz -b *filename*

Glossary

Address (network address)—(1) Internet site addresses come in two forms: as a set of numbers such as **128.999.29.81**, and as alphanumerics such as **kite.binford.com** (these can represent the same address, and either could be used, for example, with Telnet). (2) An individual's e-mail address—for example, at this site, Ben Franklin's might look like this: **bfranklin@kite.binford.com**. (See Chapter 6.)

Anonymous FTP—The use of the FTP protocol with Internet-connected sites that offer public access to their files without requiring your ID or a password. Usually, after making a connection with the FTP site, the user responds to the login prompt with the word **anonymous** and then to the password prompt with his or her full Internet address. (See Chapter 9.)

archie—A service that can be used to search network-wide for FTP-accessible files and directories that have user-specified words in their names. (See Chapter 10.)

ASCII (American Standard Code for Information Interchange)—Now a world-wide standard in which the numbers, uppercase letters, lowercase letters, some punctuation marks, some symbols, and some control codes have been assigned numbers from 0 to 127. The ASCII numbers, in digital form, can be stored as 7-bit binary numbers. For instance, using ASCII, the letter "a" is always stored as binary number 1000001. Documents created using only the ASCII characters are very easy to transfer over the Internet. Most e-mail systems use only ASCII.

Binary—Broadly speaking, binary has to do with any data stored or transferred in digital form. In more common usage, binary refers to data stored with 8 bits (which provides 256 numbers). Unlike 7-bit ASCII files, binary files have no standard way of being interpreted. Instead, they are used for software and for data files that are only meaningful when used with a compatible program (for example, a word processing data file from WordPerfect is not readable on all other word processor programs).

BITNET—An acronym for "Because It's Time Network," it is a global academic and research network started in 1981 and operated by EDUCOM.

BBS (bulletin board system)—Usually menu-oriented, this is a remote computer user interface offering a variety of services such as e-mail, ways to post public messages in various topical discussion groups, ways to offer files to and receive files from the public, and increasingly, access to other remote computers and services. Access may be via the Internet and/or through direct dial-up. BBS software for PCs is readily available on the Internet.

Bounce—When e-mail is undeliverable, it is sent back to you (bounced) so that you will know it was not delivered, and will be able to determine what the problem was.

Campus Wide Information System (CWIS)—A navigation and information retrieval tool that provides data from a variety of campus sources available through one user interface.

Client/Server—A way of distributing information on a network that involves using a small number of server programs to provide data to client programs installed on many computers throughout the network. The server program maintains a database and provides information to the client programs, through the network, when requested. Some of the server programs also have the ability to collect data and update their database files. The client programs provide a user-friendly and consistent interface. Examples of Internet client/server systems include Gopher, archie, and Veronica.

Command Line—On your PC and on your Internet access provider's computer, when you are at the system's main prompt, you are on its command line (prompts often end in symbols such as $ or % or >). More broadly, any time that you can type in commands to the computer, whether you are at the operating system's prompt or within a program, you are on the command line.

Communicon (communication + icon)—Combinations of letters and symbols used in Internet e-mail and public postings to provide emphasis, perspective, or clarification. These include very loosely standardized "smileys," "emoticons," abbreviated phrases, underlining methods, and parenthetical phrases. (See Chapter 4 for details.)

Communications Software—Usually used in reference to programs that run on a personal computer which allow the computer to communicate with a modem, and thus through the phone lines. These programs also allow the personal computer to "look like" a particular type of terminal to the computer it is connected to through the phone lines. (See Appendix A.)

Cross-Posting—Sending the same message to more than one mailing list or discussion group. It is usually discouraged unless the posting is specifically appropriate for each list it is on, and there is reasonable expectation that each mailing list that the message is posted on has a substantially different audience.

CSO—A widely used system for retrieving data from simple database files such as phone books. Named after the University of Illinois's Computing Services Organization.

Daemon—A UNIX program that will report errors in delivering e-mail messages.

Domain Name System (DNS)—An Internet addressing system that involves a group of names that are listed with dots (.) between them in the order of most specific to most general. In the United States, the top (most general) domains are network categories such as **edu** (education), **com** (commercial), and **gov** (government). In other countries, a two-letter abbreviation for each country is used, such as **ca** (Canada) or **au** (Australia). (For more about Internet addresses, see Chapter 6.)

Download—To receive on your local computer a copy of a file that currently exists on some remote computer. Many protocols for doing this have been devised, such as Zmodem, Xmodem, Ymodem, and Kermit, each with its own commands and syntax. (See Appendix B.)

E-Journal (electronic journal)—A publication distributed on the Internet at regular intervals. Distribution may be by active means such as e-mail mailing lists, or by placing the publication at an FTP site or other public location for people to retrieve. Most e-journals are distributed in standard ASCII text, though some are offered as formatted text with graphics and pictures in specific formats such as PostScript. Some are off-shoots of paper-based publications, but most are purely electronic and are distributed free.

Electronic Mail (e-mail)—Private messages delivered via networks to an individual's e-mail account. Used with automatic group mailing list software, e-mail is the basic for discussion groups and many other Internet services. "E-mail" is used both as a noun and verb ("I received his e-mail three days after I e-mailed him"). (See Chapter 6.)

Emoticons (*emotion* + *icon*)—One group of communicons that includes both "smileys" and expressions of surprise, annoyance, sarcasm, and so on. (See Chapter 4.)

Finger—An Internet system that allows you, if you have someone else's e-mail address, to find out what that person's name is, when he or she last checked for mail, and several other items. If the person has written a .plan file, that will also be displayed. To see the account information and .plan file for the address **oakridge@world.std.com**, just type **finger oakridge@world.std.com** at your access provider's main prompt.

Freeware—Software available from many locations on the Internet (often via FTP) which is totally free.

FTP (File Transfer Protocol)—A system used to transfer copies of files from one computer to another on the Internet. It includes several features to make this process easier. (See Chapter 9, see also *Anonymous FTP*.)

Flame—To send e-mail or make public postings with harsh, provocative tirades. This can result in flame wars and other negative consequences. (See Chapter 4 for cautions and guidelines concerning flaming.)

FAQs (Frequency Asked Questions)—Because newcomers are always arriving at Usenet newsgroups and on topical mailing lists, the same questions can be asked repeatedly (to the dismay of more advanced, long-time members of the group). Therefore, volunteers will often assemble a document that presents, in question-and-answer format, the basic facts about the topic and group. This FAQ is revised and posted at regular intervals to the group and is also stored, for access at any time, at a public location such as an FTP site. (See Chapter 7 for listings of some useful FAQs about the Internet.)

Gateway—A computer that connects two or more networks. Especially in the past, before TCP/IP protocols were so widely used, these computers often had to pass data between incompatible network systems.

GIF (Graphics Interchange Format)—A type of picture storage file developed by CompuServe, and now widely used on the Internet. Files in this format have an extension of **.gif** as in **mars.gif**. GIF files vary greatly in size and number of colors. (See Chapter 13 for some GIF picture archives on the Internet.)

Gopher—A widely used Internet tool for finding and retrieving files of all kinds throughout the Internet. It is menu-oriented, with the top menu at each Gopher site leading to many submenus and files. (See Chapter 10.)

Host—Your Internet access provider's computer. You may use one of its hard-wired terminals, if you are at an institution with a mainframe computer connected directly to the Internet, or you may dial up and use a modem to connect with the Internet access provider's host computer. (As computer systems have changed, the term "host" has changed in meaning, so do expect some confusing references to "host" at times.)

Hypertext—Used by several Internet search-and-retrieval tools such as Lynx, Mosaic, and WWW. Documents are presented in which some of the words are highlighted. These highlighted words represent links to other documents that allow you to view, with just a few keystrokes or clicks of a mouse, these other documents. The documents accessed through these links may have links to still other documents.

Hytelnet—Frequently updated database, available for many computer systems, that provides information about specific Telnet sites and aids in connecting to them. It is also available via Telnet at some Internet sites. (See Chapter 8.)

IRC (Internet Relay Chat)—An Internet system that allows Internet users to "chat" (via keyboard) in real time. Separate channels are available with various options for privacy, filtering out unwanted messages, and one-to-one messages.

Internet—A digital communications network connecting over 25,000 smaller networks from most countries of the world. Started in the United States, and still heavily reliant on the National Science Foundation's backbone network system, it transfers data using a standardized protocol called TCP/IP.

JPG—The filename extension used on JPEG (Joint Photographic Experts Group) graphics/pictures files (e.g., **moon.jpg**). This file format can be much more compressed than, for example, GIF, but high compression causes some loss of detail. JPG is among the three most popular picture file formats on the Internet, along with GIF and PCX.

Listserv—A program that provides automatic processing of many functions involved with mailing lists (discussion groups). E-mailing appropriate messages to it will automatically subscribe you (or unsubscribe you) to a discussion list. Listserv will also answer requests for indexes, FAQs, archives of the previous discussions, and other files. (See Chapter 7.)

Log File—In PC communications programs, a feature that allows you to save in a file everything that is displayed to the screen, thus providing a record of the activity for a full or partial online session.

Login—When one computer seeks to establish a connection to another computer, there will be a login process on the remote computer which usually involves some user steps beyond those things taken care of by the computer software. This may be as simple as pressing Enter, or may require a specific login word and a password to be entered. (Usually used interchangeably with "logon.") (See Chapter 8.)

Logoff—To leave, or disconnect from, a computer system. Often accomplished by selecting a menu item for disconnecting, or typing **exit, bye,** or **logout**, at the command line prompt.

Lurk—To read messages from discussion groups or Usenet newsgroups without contributing any.

Mailing Lists—(Lists, Discussion Lists, Discussion Groups) Discussions carried on by e-mailing messages to an automated re-mailer, which then sends a copy of each message via e-mail to everyone who has subscribed to the list for that particular discussion group. (See Chapter 7.)

MIME (Multipurpose Internet Mail Extensions)—An improvement on the Internet mail system standards that allow binary files to be sent as e-mail through the Internet. Formerly only ASCII files could be sent. This system is not available on all sites yet.

Mosaic—A new program, still under development, that serves as client software for FTP, Gopher, Usenet News, WAIS, and WWW. It provides a graphical user interface. (See Chapter 10.)

Modem (MOdulator/DEModulator)—An electronic device that converts computer signals into audio (sound) signals so that they can be sent over normal phone lines and received by another modem which will convert the sound back into computer signals. Virtually all modems combine the send and receive functions in one circuit. (See Appendix B.)

Moderator—In discussion lists (groups) that are moderated, the moderator watches the postings as they come in to be sure, for example, that they relate to the topics and goals of the list and that the language and nature of the messages are suitable for public posting. The types and extent of moderating varies widely, from merely restating the goals and limits to, occasionally, editing incoming messages. (See Chapter 7.)

Netiquette (network + etiquette)—Customs and socially accepted behavior for using networks.

Network—A group of computers connected in any way that allows data to be sent between these computers.

Newbie—Anyone new to the Internet. Due to the rapid growth of the Internet, most people on the Internet are newbies, and therefore this is not considered a particularly negative term.

NIC (Network Information Center)—A site designated to provide useful information services to network users.

Node—A computer that is directly connected to a network—whether used to transfer and route data or to provide end-user services.

NSFnet (National Science Foundation + net)—The system of high-speed data transfer links and nodes that form the backbone of the Internet in the United States. (See Chapter 1.)

Offline—Anything that happens when your computer is not connected to another computer. For instance, you may use a program that downloads many messages and files quickly and then allows you to read them *offline* in order to save on connect charges and long distance phone charges.

Online—Any activity carried out while your computer is connected to another computer or network.

Plan File (.plan)—A file, in your home directory on your Internet access provider's computer, to which you write to tell anything you want about yourself or your business or any other subject. A copy of it can be obtained by anyone who uses the finger program to check your e-mail account.

Post—To send an e-mail message to one of the public discussion groups.

Postmaster—The person at each site who is responsible for handling e-mail problems at that site. Send e-mail to the postmaster at a site if you are having some difficulties getting a message through or need other information about the site. E-mail messages to this person are addressed to **postmaster@***site name*; for example, **postmaster@kite.binford.com**.

Prompt—What is displayed when a computer system is waiting for some sort of input from you.

Protocol—A formal, standardized set of operating rules governing the format, timing, error control, or other aspects of data transmissions and other activities on a network.

README file (READ.ME)—A commonly used filename in program documentation and in directories at FTP sites to direct the newcomer to index files or other useful information about the files in that directory.

RFC (Request For Comments)—Documents relating to the Internet system, protocols, proposals, and so on.

Real Time—Usually used to describe situations when two or more people are communicating via their keyboards at the same instant—versus the delayed back-and-forth situations with e-mail.

Shareware—Software available from many locations on the Internet. It is initially free, but the authors expect payment to be sent voluntarily after an initial test period. Quality varies from bad to better than some commercial software. Prices are usually excellent. Some initial versions are limited in function in some way, with an upgrade available if you pay the fee.

SIG (Signature File)—A short message placed at the bottom of an e-mail message or a discussion group posting that identifies the sender and includes items such as phone number, fax number, address, information about the person's occupation or company, and even a philosophical saying or humorous message. (See Chapter 6.)

Smiley—Any of several smiling faces created by various keyboard letters and symbols such as :) and 8-). (See *Communicon* and Chapter 4.)

Snail Mail—An irreverent reference to standard paper-based postal mail, from those on the Internet used to the speed of e-mail.

Sysop (SYStem OPerator)—The individual who does the hands-on work of being sure a computer system, or some portion of it, is operating correctly. Sometimes called "sysgod" in jest.

TCP/IP (Transmission Control Protocol/Internet Protocol)—The agreed-on set of computer communications rules and standards that allows communications between different types of computers and networks that are connected to the Internet.

Telnet—(also called *remote login*)—A system that allows access to remote computers on the Internet. Many of the features of the remote computer can then be used as if your computer were directly connected to it. (See Chapter 8.)

Terminal Emulator—Communications software that can make itself "appear" to another computer as if it were a specific type of terminal. Some common terminals that are emulated are VT100, VT52, and ANSI. (See Appendix A.)

Thread—Within Usenet newsgroups and topical discussion groups, a thread is one of several subdiscussions. For instance, in a forestry discussion group, there may be ongoing discussions of old growth forests, the spotted owl, and forest fires. Each thread is started with an original posting which others follow up using the same subject name preceded by **RE:**. (See Chapter 7.)

TN-3270—Telnet software that provides IBM full screen support.

UNIX—An operating system, widely used on the Internet, developed by AT&T Bell Laboratories, that supports multiuser and multitasking operations.

Uploading—File transfers in the opposite direction from downloading (See *Downloading*; also, Appendix B.)

Usenet Newsgroups (Netnews)—Thousands of discussion groups that use newsreader software and servers (these groups use different software and are organized differently from the listserv e-mail discussion group system). (See Chapter 7.)

User Name—A short name (with no spaces allowed) unique to you on your Internet access provider's system. Sometimes these are assigned and sometimes you can select your own. The user name (or ID), followed by your site address, becomes your e-mail address. For example, if Ben Franklin had an account at **world.std.com** and he chose a user name of **bfranklin**, his e-mail address would be **bfranklin@world.std.com**.

UUCP (Unix to Unix Copy Program)—A protocol used for communication between consenting UNIX systems.

VAX—Hardware produced by the Digital Equipment Corporation in wide use on the Internet. The VMS operating system is used on VAX computers.

Veronica—A client/server system that provides a way to search for a particular word of interest in all Gopher menus at all Gopher sites known to the Veronica server database. (See Chapter 10.)

Virtual Reality—Any of various combinations of user-interface features that permit a user to interact with a computer or system in a manner that more closely mimics how humans normally operate in the real world. It may include use of speech synthesis, speech recognition, three-dimensional graphics, and so on.

VT100—Originally, a type of terminal used by DEC (Digital Equipment Corporation). Now, a widely used Internet standard terminal which is usually emulated by communications software.

WorldWideWeb (WWW)—Created in Switzerland, WWW is client/server software designed to use hypertext and hypermedia. It uses the HTTP (Hypertext Transfer Protocol) to exchange documents and images. The documents must be formatted in HTML (Hypertext Markup Language). Mosaic and Lynx are WWW browsers. (See Chapter 10.)

Z39.50 Protocol—A standard developed by the National Information Standards Organization to aid in searching remote databases such as library catalogs. It provides for a uniform standard within which differing systems can interact.

References

Carmody, Deidre. 1993. "Magazines going on-line with modern-day salons." New York: New York Times News Service.

Chew, John. 1993. *The Inter-Network Mail Guide*. (Available from **ariel.unm.edu**, in the */library/network.guide* subdirectory.)

Frey, D. and R. Adams. *1990. !%@:: A Directory of Electronic Mail Addresses and Networks*. Sebastopol, CA: O'Reilly and Associates.

Kames, Jonathon. *Finding Addresses* (Available via **FTP** to **pit-manager.mit.edu.**)

Kehoe, Brendan P. 1992. *Zen and the Art of the Internet*. 1st ed. (Available for anonymous **FTP** on host **ftp.cs.widener.edu**, directory *pub/zen*, filename **ZEN-1.0.PS** (PostScript file) and other formats.)

Levin, Jayne. 1993. "The Top 150 Commercial Users on Internet." *The Internet Letter* 1, no.1. [Electronic edition.]

National Science Foundation. December 1993. "History.Hosts." **nic.merit.edu** */nsfnet/statistics/history.hosts*.

National Science Foundation. December 1993. "History.Netcount." **nic.merit.edu** */nsfnet/statistics/history.netcount*.

Newsweek, 1994. "Riding the Data Highway." 21 March, pp. 54–55.

Index